INSIGHTS
FROM THE
BLIND

INSIGHTS FROM THE BLIND

Comparative Studies of Blind and Sighted Infants

Selma Fraiberg

with the collaboration of
Louis Fraiberg

A MERIDIAN BOOK
NEW AMERICAN LIBRARY
TIMES MIRROR
NEW YORK AND SCARBOROUGH, ONTARIO

Library of Congress Catalog Card Number: 76-9676

This is an authorized reprint of a hardcover edition published by
Basic Books, Inc.

MERIDIAN TRADEMARK REG. U.S. PAT. OFF. AND FOREIGN COUNTRIES
REGISTERED TRADEMARK—MARCA REGISTRADA
HECHO EN FORGE VILLAGE, MASS., U.S.A.

SIGNET, SIGNET CLASSICS, MENTOR, PLUME and
MERIDIAN BOOKS are published in the United States by
The New American Library, Inc., 1301 Avenue of the Americas,
New York, New York 10019, in Canada by
The New American Library of Canada Limited,
81 Mack Avenue, Scarborough, Ontario M1L 1M8

First Meridian Printing, March, 1979

1 2 3 4 5 6 7 8 9

PRINTED IN THE UNITED STATES OF AMERICA

For my husband

Contents

CONTENTS

CONTENTS

CHAPTER VII

CHAPTER VIII

CONTENTS

CONTENTS

CHAPTER XI

Self-Representation in Language and Play / SELMA FRAIBERG AND EDNA ADELSON

CHAPTER XII

Conclusions / SELMA FRAIBERG

APPENDIX

Methods: Supplementary Information

Tables and Figures

Preface and Acknowledgments

THE WORK which is reported in this volume could not have been achieved without the financial support and scientific leadership which came to us from the National Institute of Child Health and Development. The project, which bore the title "The Early Ego Development of Children Blind from Birth" (Grant No. HD01–444), was mainly supported by NICHD during the period 1966–71. Leon Yarrow, then serving as a Health Sciences Administrator at NICHD, brought his own extraordinary gifts as a researcher to this administrative position, and within a rigorous peer review system, helped to create a climate in which diversity and even audacity in research design were accommodated.

It was our good fortune to do this work during a period of extraordinary ferment and far-reaching discoveries in the psychological study of infancy. To a very large extent these discoveries were made possible through government-sponsored research. As the story began to emerge, early in the sixties, there was a growing consensus among investigators from diverse fields that the human capacities for love and for learning were rooted in the first two years of life, the embryonic period of personality development.

Our own study would examine the effects of a visual deficit upon early ego development and, by inference, the specific functions of vision in the organization of early experience.

The comparative data for sighted infants, especially in the area of human attachments, were emerging through a large number of studies during this period. Our own work became dependent upon the work of other investigators, and our close communication with them. This brought immeasurable benefits to our own study and a joy in working together that cannot be fairly celebrated in the dry lines of an author's "acknowledgments."

Our indebtedness to these colleagues is very large. It is fair to say that this work could not have been accomplished without the continuous scientific exchange and the climate of mutual support and criticism provided by our colleagues in infant research. And, it must be added, that all of us, in turn, were indebted to the governmental agencies which made our work and our scientific collaboration possible.

Nearly all of the leaders in infant psychology (and many of them were our consultants) were supported in their work through one or another of the institutes in the National Institutes of Health. What NIH and its constituent institutes provided for government-supported research was a kind of "laboratory without walls," to paraphrase Malraux. A typically modest research grant included a miniscule budget for "consultants" and a miniscule budget for "travel." A thrifty grant recipient learned how to use the continent's resources in his field with, perhaps, $1,000 per year and the aid of an imaginative travel agent. If each of a dozen grant recipients husbanded his funds, and traded services and lab visitations, he had the nation's experts in any of several related fields available for consultation and argument. It was as good as having the nation's best department or institute on the same campus. In our case this anonymous "institute," in a specialized field of infant development, was spread across the continent but represented, as a group, many authorities in this field who would never, by chance or munificence, have all turned up as residents in the same community.

Our meetings were informal and dealt with "work in progress." When we visited each other it was to exchange information and to borrow each other's expertness. We shared raw data, problems of methodology, puzzles in results, and sometimes, victoriously, a solution to a puzzle. If an important finding emerged from one or another of these investigations we usually knew about it one or two years before publication.

Whether, or in what ways, we ourselves brought fruitful ideas to the work of others I cannot say. But out of these exchanges, in our own lab and in those of others, came the shape and the scope of the work as it is presented in this volume.

The cost to the taxpayer for this "laboratory without walls" was very small. An average grant in those days was $35,000 per year, which bought part of the salaries of a research scientist, two assistant research scientists, a typist, and the previously mentioned budget for consultants and travel. (What might we have done with a larger travel budget!) The returns on this modest investment have been very large. The "basic research" of the sixties in infant development has led to the "applied research" of the seventies, and the new "infant intervention" programs which have begun to proliferate in this decade have made babies the beneficiaries of that research.

Over the years, then, this "laboratory without walls" brought us the wisdom and expertness of a very large number of colleagues. I recall with special gratitude the counsel of Sibylle Escalona who was, in fact, the first consultant to our study in the early years in New Orleans. It was her encouragement, at a time when the complexities of the study of blind infants were overwhelming to David Freedman and me, that gave us the energies to pursue the work. Later, in the Ann Arbor period of the studies, I turned to her for guidance on a number of occasions and marveled at her unfailing ability to get to the core of an issue, to ask exactly the right questions.

Peter Wolff, throughout the early years of the Project, brought encouragement, sound advice, and good arguments. He examined object permanence data with us and brought his own expertness in this area to an examination of criteria transposed to a blind child's perceptual field. It was Peter, too, who introduced me to Thérèse Gouin Décarie and gave us another distinguished consultant who applied her Piagetian background to the formidable task for the blind infant in the constitution of an object world. (Since every blind baby in our study solved the problem, it is a matter of considerable embarrassment that we have had to summon the world's experts to help us figure out how he does it.)

It was Thérèse Décarie who told Piaget about our work and our problems, and Piaget, who appears cheerfully resigned to such problems and positively enjoys being outwitted by the intelligence of infants, came to visit us in 1967. We had invited him to review a sequence of film clips illustrating stages in the development of object permanence in one blind child. We asked if he would serve as judge and argue criteria with us. When Robbie, on film, made his final demonstration (which we judged to be stage 6), Piaget tossed his beret into the air and cheered.

It was Peter Wolff, also, who introduced us to Eric Lenneberg. (As I write this I feel that *nobody* got more mileage out of a low-cost travel budget than Peter Wolff. I think he had a bicycle!) Lenneberg arrived on our campus in 1967 and became a volunteer consultant to us for one year. As a linguist he was immediately intrigued by the problems we were facing in examining our language data. He gave his own time, most generously, most enthusiastically, in teaching our staff and in working with us on design problems. When he moved to Cornell University the following year he maintained close ties to our work and through exchange visits he followed the development of our work over the years. He was our consultant at many turning points in our study. Eric died in June 1975 and it is painful to record this in a section of this book called "acknowledgments." I have not yet acknowledged his death.

René Spitz, who is justly the father or the godfather of research in human attachments, became a friend to me and a consultant to our program at a moment that almost never gives birth to an enduring friendship in science. I was very much a junior colleague; he was a sage close to seventy when I presented our earliest data on smiling in blind infants at a meeting of the American Psychoanalytic Association. The data, with film illustration, did not support Spitz's hypothesis regarding visual stimuli for the smiling response in infants. Blind babies smile in response to the human voice. Spitz, watching the film, took in this new evidence with a cheerful countenance. Like Piaget, he loved to have babies argue with him. He introduced himself to me, wanted to know everything I could tell him about our work, and we began a professional friendship which lasted to the end of his life.

He never left the smiling problem. In 1969 he brought his colleagues Robert Emde and David Metcalf to Ann Arbor for a two-day marathon weekend in which the Denver team and the Ann Arbor team talked and argued, and the Denver team presented a stunning and exhaustive study of the eliciting stimuli for the smiling response which nicely accommodated both Spitz's early findings and our own findings in the study of blind infants (see Chapter V). Spitz, during such team meetings, was indefatigable. He was in his eighties, the rest of us were much younger, yet he out-talked, out-argued everyone. I remember that hours after the first-day sessions were scheduled to close, he was off on a brilliant discourse while a festive dinner in his honor burned slowly to a crisp in my oven. When he noticed that my attention wavered between his discourse and my dinner, he did not hesitate to speak sharply to me.

Later there were team meetings in Denver in which we watched film together for many hours and I presented new material from our language study. Between visits there were letters, exchanges of new papers, more arguments (always graceful), and finally, toward the end of his life, no more letters, and I began the mourning for René some months before his death.

Mary Ainsworth consulted with us throughout the last years of the blind studies, keeping us up-to-date on her most recent findings in her own studies of the course of human attachments in infancy. With each visit our own studies took a leap forward as the data from her work began to narrow the focus of attention on key indicators of attachment. There were visits, exchange of papers, and always the feeling that we might never catch up with the latest word from Mary's lab. When I wrote the final version of the paper on human attachments, I sent up a prayer that Mary would not discover anything new for a year.

Over the years many of our most distinguished colleagues came to visit and to join us in watching blind babies on film. The great danger for us in seeing large numbers of blind babies was that we ourselves might become "blind" to the differences, especially the subtle differences, in the behavior of blind and sighted infants. We needed Sally Provence's expert eyes to discern a fine difference in patterns of reaching, an ambiguous sign or posturing in the hands of a baby. We welcomed the questions of Arthur Parmelee and James Prescott as they observed with us the puzzle of transient motor stereotypies in certain blind infants. It was splendid to have James Bosma visit once or twice a year to ask provocative questions about the mouth and the hand in the early development of blind infants. When Justin Call came to visit he provided a balanced critique of a piece of work in progress that might easily have led to trouble without his counsel. Dan Stern and Ken Robson, both experts in the area of mutual gaze patterns, each with a special interest, brought us to sober reflections on the adaptive problems for blind infants and their parents when visual exchange cannot bind two partners.

Our gratitude to all of these colleagues is immeasurable. We hope that this report of our work will fairly acknowledge their support, their counsel, and their generosity.

Then, how can one acknowledge fairly the work of an extraordinary staff in bringing this study and this book to completion? I am glad that we chose from the start to place central responsibility for data collection and data analysis in the hands of senior, most able investigators. Each of these staff members brought exceptional gifts in observation and interpretation to this study. It was plucky of us, now that I consider it, to insist in our proposal to NICHD that this work, data collection in unknown territory, be trusted only to the most skilled investigators. I remember that this idea did not sit well with at least one of our original site visitors. When the site visitors left, one of them left behind a page of note paper with doodles and a single scribbled line: "Too many chiefs. No Indians." In short, as we understood it, our budget would be considerably relieved by the substitution of low-paid student assistants for the "high-paid" senior investigators. Fortunately, this view did not prevail in the site committee and the "chiefs" were approved as requested. If good and useful things have emerged from this work I must praise "the chiefs," a number of whom are co-authors of chapters in this volume. Edna Adelson, Evelyn Atreya, Ralph Gibson, Marion Ross, Barry Siegel, Marguerite Smith, and Lyle Warner were senior investigators who brought exceptional gifts to the primary investigation. To David A. Freedman, my friend and colleague during the New Orleans phase of this work, my special gratitude for a collaboration which brought rewards to both of us and the discovery of the joys of team research.

Yet we might all have drowned in the vast accumulation of data generated by the senior investigators if we had not had a splendid system for data retrieval, for which Edna Adelson took central responsibility along with an exceptional group of student assistants who worked in teams with senior investigators. We are grateful to Susan Tracy Adelson, Ted Grossbart, Gloria Hool, Karen Hufnagel, Judith Larrick, and Mary Ann Malefakis for indispensable contributions to our work.

The prodigious task of preparing this manuscript was undertaken by Beverly Knickerbocker, Adele Wilson, and Anita VanderHaagen of our staff, who somehow have managed to combine meticulous attention to editorial detail with good humor, infinite patience, and devotion to the work. We are all grateful to Linda Herwerth for her fastidious reading of galleys and the preparation of the index for this book. Lily Ladin, administrative assistant for our program, performed her customary miracles in organizing work schedules to accommodate this heavy task and in supervising many details which required her editorial judgment.

With all this, it must be said that this volume would never have reached fruition without the collaboration of my husband, Louis. By 1975, 4 years after the completion of the original research, there was not yet a book. (One of the melancholy facts of research direction is that before 1 program has reached the "write-up" stage, a new study is under way, and new commitments have been made.) In 1975 we had a group of papers which constituted the core of a volume, but other facets of the work were not yet in written form. The papers themselves fairly constituted a report to our sponsors and represented our commitment to NICHD but did not, as a group of papers, cover all major aspects of the original investigation. Nor did they flow into one another to tell the story of the research as it unfolded. New chapters needed to be written. Old and new material needed to be integrated. It seemed to be an impossible task and I was ready to forsake it.

It was at this point that my oldest collaborator, Louis Fraiberg, reread the old papers, read drafts of new papers, and told me that there *was* a book, that he thought the work was important, and offered to work along with me to produce a coherent manuscript. In the summer of 1975 we turned our dining room table into an editorial desk and began the collaboration. Louis, who exercises a stern blue pencil, gave shape and continuity to the writing. I finished the writing of new chapters and transitional material and turned them over to Louis for criticism. It was, as always, a most amiable collaboration and, for me, the work became alive again. The book was largely completed by the end of the summer. As it appears now, the book is the result of this collaboration. One change in organization was suggested by Midge Decter of Basic Books (another form of Chapter I) which we all agreed benefited the structure. In other ways, too, we are indebted to Midge Decter for her personal devotion to the task of bringing this book to publication and for suggestions which were unfailingly in the service of clarity and exposition.

INSIGHTS FROM THE BLIND

Chapter I

SELMA FRAIBERG

Introduction

THE STORY of this research begins, very simply, as a clinical problem in a social agency. In 1960, Dr. David Freedman and the author were consultants to the Family Service Society of New Orleans when the agency was asked to provide a guidance service for 27 blind children between the ages of three and fourteen years. Neither we nor any other member of the staff had ever worked with blind children, and we were in no way prepared for their impact upon us.

Of the 27 children, at least 7 presented a clinical picture that closely resembled autism in the sighted. There were stereotyped hand behaviors, rocking, swaying, mutism or echolalic speech. These were children who were content to sit for hours, sucking on a clothespin or a pot lid, rocking, detached, vacant, virtually unresponsive to the mother or to any other human being. The most striking feature of these cases was their uniformity. We had the uncanny feeling that we were seeing the same case over and over again. In reading the records we had to provide ourselves with mnemonic cues to distinguish one from the other. ("Martin is the one who likes to suck on clothespins; Martha is the one who chews rubber jar rings; Jane is the head banger; Chrissey butts her bottom against the wall.")

Of the remaining 20 children, nearly all showed one or an-

3

other form of stereotyped motility and idiosyncratic mannerisms. But they differed from the first group in having attained
some level of ego functioning, a differentiation of "self" and
"other," of "I" and "you": language which served at least elementary communication. In contrast with the first group, these children had human ties, but the bonds were precarious, and it was
not unusual to see children in the late school years who were
reduced to helplessness during the absence of a parent or teacher.
Several of these children at school age were clearly unable to master Braille. Their hands, which, it is said, are "the eyes of the
blind," could not discriminate among objects or forms and
seemed to bring them little information about the world outside
of their bodies.

We were to learn that these 27 children were fairly representative of the congenitally blind child population. The 7 children
who appeared autistic fairly represented the incidence of autism
in the blind population. The 20 children, with varying degrees of
competence and impairment of ego functioning, many with autistic patterns, constituted the "normal" range for blind children.

Dr. Freedman, who is both a neurologist and a psychoanalyst,
reviewed the medical findings, which included electroen-
cephalograms on several cases, and personally examined certain
children. For most of them there was no evidence of neurological
impairment. This did not, of course, rule out the possibility of
damage due to unknown causes, but in the absence of positive
signs we were free to consider other possibilities.

We reviewed the birth histories of each of the children and
found no correlation between birth weight, length of time in oxygen (in the case of the premature baby), and the clinical picture
of autism.

The question of possible brain damage is still debated in the literature of both the sighted and the blind autistic child. It is entirely possible that the clinical picture of autism can be produced
by either central impairment or gross impoverishment in the
stimulus nutriments for early sensorimotor organization. A child

Introduction

who cannot register experience because of central impairment and a child who cannot register experience because his world is empty may produce the same clinical picture which we call autism.

In the 1950s the high incidence of ego deviations in blind children and the prevalence of autistic patterns in the blind child population as a whole, began to attract the interest of a few clinicians in pediatrics and psychology. (It was around the same time that Kanner's 1949 studies in early infantile autism aroused the interest of psychologists and psychiatrists on behalf of sighted children who could now be discriminated as a group of afflicted children with common characteristics.)

The clinical picture of arrested development in the blind, for our New Orleans group, is one that we were to find repeatedly in the literature that we examined. Even as our 7 autistic blind children could barely be discriminated from each other, so the descriptions of other clinicians added numbers of bizarre young children to the slowly growing literature. Between Parmelee's cases (1955), those of Keeler (1958), Norris (1957), and our own there was such a striking uniformity that we were left once more with the feeling that we were reading the same case over and over again.

This clinical picture remained essentially unexamined until the 1950s. Speculations regarding possible brain damage were offered, but the available evidence did not give strong support for a neurological etiology in a large number of these cases. The situation remained ambiguous. Until the 1950s the large number of retrolental fibroplasia cases in the blind child population had further obscured matters and, in the eyes of many clinicians, weighted the possibilities in favor of a neurological etiology. Retrolental fibroplasia, the oxygen-related blindness of the premature baby, was one of the most frequent causes of blindness in infancy before it was identified in the late forties. In Norris's Chicago census (1957), retrolental fibroplasia was the cause of blindness in 71% of the blind child population.

It was not until the publication of studies by Norris, Spaulding, and Brodie (1957) and Keeler (1958) that a comparison of the children with retrolental fibroplasia and children blind from other causes was made. The new evidence required a clinical reassessment of the blind child with gross ego deviations. *The clinical picture of deviant ego development was not associated with any specific etiology for blindness.*

The Norris report, which involved 295 blind preschool children, is one of the most extensive studies to date. The sample included 209 children (71%) with the diagnosis of retrolental fibroplasia; the remaining 86 cases (29%) included children blind from other causes. Testing was conducted at intervals throughout the first six and a half years of the child's life. Tests included the Cattell, adapted for use with the blind child in this study, and the Interim Hayes-Binet Intelligence Scale for the Blind. It was found that the performance of the children in the retrolental fibroplasia group was well within the range for blind children in general with a distribution pattern that did not distinguish this group from the group of children blind from other causes.

Keeler's work in Toronto (1958) brought additional insights to the problem of etiology in the deviant blind group. His investigation began with 5 preschool blind children who presented a clinical picture that struck him as remarkably similar to that of "infantile autism." The description of these children, as given by him, is practically identical with that which we saw in our New Orleans group. The cause of blindness in all 5 of Keeler's cases was retrolental fibroplasia. From the total of 102 cases registered in Ontario he subsequently selected a sample of 35 cases of children with retrolental fibroplasia and found that the histories and behavior patterns of all 35 were in many ways similar to those he had seen in the 5 intensive cases referred to his hospital. However, none of the second group of children showed ego deviations to the degree seen in the intensive group, and the 10 children in the sample who were in school were up to grade in spite of their disturbances of personality.

Introduction

In order to examine more closely the factors at work in the ego disturbances found among the retrolental fibroplasia cases, Keeler decided to study two other categories of blind children: one group blinded at birth and another group blinded postnatally, in infancy or early childhood. The first group consisted of 18 children who were congenitally blinded by such conditions as cataracts, familial macular degeneration, buphthalmos, endophthalmitis, etc. It is important to note that in all these cases the amount of vision was much greater than that present in the children with retrolental fibroplasia, but none of them had more than 20/200 vision in the better eye. In this group the developmental patterns more closely approximated those of sighted children: there were not the developmental delays in motor achievements, feeding, and toilet training. Among these children with some degree of vision, Keeler did not find autistic patterns and abnormalities in motility to the same degree that he saw them in the retrolental fibroplasia group.

In the second group, which consisted of 17 children blinded postnatally, abnormalities in development and behavior were least conspicuous. The majority of the children in this group became blinded during the first and second years of life, and in many cases mobility, acquisition of language, and feeding and toilet habits had been established before blindness occurred.

Keeler's analysis of the developmental histories and behavior patterns of the blind children in each of these 3 groups focuses clinical attention on these points: the gross abnormalities encountered in certain blind children appear to be associated with *total or nearly total blindness from birth and a history of inadequate emotional stimulation in the early months of life*. If the incidence of abnormal ego development is conspicuously high in the retrolental fibroplasia group, we are obliged to include in this assessment the fact that it was, at that time, the largest single category of blindness in which total or nearly total blindness from birth occurred. Each of Keeler's children who showed gross abnormalities and developmental arrest also had a history of inadequate emotional stimulation in infancy. The number of children in Keeler's retrolental fibroplasia group who were in fact functioning adequately appears to confirm the findings in the Norris study and also shows clearly that blindness from birth is not in itself a predisposing factor to deviant development. Both studies bring attention, finally, to the factor of emotional stimulation and incentives for development in an infant blind from birth.

Our cases at the Family Service Society gave additional support to the findings of both Norris and Keeler as reported here. We may add, however, that the severe ego deviations which Keeler reported only in his retrolental fibroplasia cases appeared in our agency cases outside of this group as well. As retrolental fibroplasia cases became rare, we found in both the New Orleans study and the Ann Arbor consultation program that autism in the blind child was not associated with any specific ophthalmological disease.

None of these studies excludes the possibility that brain damage of unknown origins exists in these deviant blind children. While the ambiguity remains, it should be noted: (1) that stimulus deprivation in early development is known to be one etiology for autism in both the sighted and the blind. Spitz's studies of extreme deprivation in institutionalized infants and Harlow's studies of monkeys reared in isolation show that the autistic syndrome can be produced through extreme deprivation of sense experience; (2) when blindness, which constitutes a central form of stimulus deprivation, is united with deprivation in tactile, kinesthetic, and auditory experience (through insufficiences of mothering) a state of extreme deprivation may exist which threatens ego development; (3) in a number of cases known to us and to others, autism with a presumed etiology in early and pervasive sense deprivation in blind young children has been successfully treated through enlarging and enriching the experience of the blind child with his mother. In the brilliant case report of Omwake and Solnit (1961) an educational and psychotherapeutic approach brought about normal ego functioning in a blind child who, at three years of age, resembled in every way the clinical picture of developmental arrest we have described here. In our own guidance program at the Child Development Project we have brought about normal functioning in blind children under three years of age who were autistic at the time of referral.

The ambiguities regarding etiology of early infantile autism are by no means settled at the time of this writing in 1973. Brain damage of unknown cause may be the determinant for a number of these cases. Extreme deprivation of experience has been identified as the cause in a number of cases reported. It is reasonable to presume that whether a child is deprived of experience through central impairment of the systems for registering and integrating stimuli or through extreme deprivation of the stimulus nutriments for sensorimotor organization, the result may be the same—a child who does not know "me" and "other," "I" or "you."

It is, of course, not blindness alone that closes the world for the child but insufficiency in the stimuli for tactile-kinesthetic-auditory functioning in the early years of life. A number of children who became known to me in our Ann Arbor program presented a picture of autism in the first or second years which was demonstrably related to sense impoverishment. In our work with these babies and their mothers we were able to bring the child to adequacy in functioning—and even to a very high level of functioning—by helping the mother provide the essential nutriments for sensorimotor experience.

Clinical Observations

As clinicians, Dr. Freedman and I began by asking ourselves certain questions. First of all, we were impressed by the picture of developmental arrest in the autistic blind child, of personalities frozen on the level of mouth-centeredness and non-differentiation. There was no "I" or "you," but there was also no "me" or "other"—no sense of a body self and "something out there."

All of this was of a piece with the most distinguishing characteristic of these children—the absence of human connections. The mother was barely distinguished from other persons; her comings and goings went unnoticed. There were no cries to summon her, no sounds of greeting when she appeared, no signs of distress when she left. We know, of course, that in the absence of a human partner the baby cannot acquire a sense of self and other, of "me" and "you." But should blindness be an impediment to the establishment of human attachments? How about other blind children, those who had demonstrable human ties?

The sighted child in the first year makes increasingly selective and highly differentiated responses to his mother. So far as we know from developmental studies, the preferential smile, the discrimination of mother and stranger, and indeed the whole sequence of differential human responses are predicated upon visual recognitory experiences. In the absence of vision how does the blind baby differentiate, recognize, become bound through love? There must be an adaptive substitution for vision. The mother of a blind baby must find some ways of helping the baby find the route. (How? And if she does not? And if the baby does not find the route? Would the blind baby then live in a near void in which persons and things have no meaning to him?)

We observed that in all of these children perception was largely centered in the mouth. The cliché "the hands are the eyes of the blind" had become a terrible irony in the case of these children. They had blind hands, too. The hands did not reach out to attain objects or to get information about them. Most strikingly, the hands had remained in a kind of morbid alliance with the mouth. They could bring objects to the mouth to be sucked. But, when the hands were not serving the mouth in some way, they were typically held at shoulder height with stereotyped inutile movements of the fingers.

In addition, these children had virtually no independent mobility. Even walking with support was a late achievement: in one case, at the age of nine!

In the literature these children are classified as "the blind mentally retarded." If we are interested only in developmental measurement, this is indisputable. But to the psychoanalytic investigator these blind mentally retarded children presented some apparently inexplicable problems. If the systems for receiving nonvisual stimuli were intact (and for our group this was demonstrable in the neurological examination) how could we explain this extraordinary picture of developmental arrest, this freezing of personality on the eight-to-twelve month level with virtually no gains, no small increments of learning thereafter?

INFERENCES FROM THE CLINICAL PICTURE

As clinicians we observed a number of behavior signs in the clinical pictures of these children that led our thinking along certain paths.

It is immediately apparent that the body schemas which normally lead to adaptive hand behavior had failed to integrate in these children. Normally, vision insures that at five months the thing seen can be grasped and attained. In the absence of vision, other sense modalities must be coordinated with grasping. How is the adaptive substitution found by the blind infant? (And if it isn't found? Then do you have inutile hands that can only serve to bring things to the mouth?)

Next, our attention was drawn to the delay in locomotion. Were all motor achievements delayed in the case of these deviant blind children? No. A puzzle appeared in the developmental histories. Rolling over, sitting with support, and sitting independently were not markedly delayed. But creeping, walking with support, and of course, walking independently were either markedly delayed or never achieved. If the histories were reliable, neuromuscular adequacy was demonstrated in the postural achievements during the first six months. Why the impasse in creeping and later locomotion? (And if you do not creep and you have no mobility in the second and third years, and if you are blind and your hands are blind, too, what is left in sensorimotor experience that can be used to learn about the world outside of the body?)

As you can see, our first questions were addressed to the unique adaptive problems of a child totally blind from birth. In the case of the autistic blind child the sensory deficit and unknown factors in early experience had produced a picture that suggested adaptive failure. But what about the 20 other children in our sample who had found the adaptive routes with varying degrees of success?

As a group, the remaining 20 children demonstrated human attachments, with some variability in the quality of these ties or the capacity in later childhood to function independently. I cannot give you the range in adaptive hand abilities because in those days we did not yet know how to "read" hand behavior in blind children. But for most of these children, too, the achievement of independent mobility was very late by sighted-child standards: between two and three years for independent walking. Typically, too, there was no mention of creeping in the developmental histories. But strangely enough, in this "normal" group of blind children, nearly all the children demonstrated one or another kind of stereotyped motility—rocking, swaying, hand waving, eye rubbing, or idiosyncratic movements. These behaviors have long been known to workers with the blind and called "blindisms." With the exception of eye rubbing, all of these behaviors can be found in the sighted autistic child. But these children were not autistic. What did this mean?

If we now looked at the entire group of 27 children it appeared that certain characteristics such as the delay in locomotion and the stereotyped motility were found in both groups with qualitative and quantitative differences. The range for the achievement of independent mobility was not nearly as great for the "normal" group as for the autistic group. The stereotyped motility constituted a large part of the repertory of the deviant group and a small part of the repertory of the "normal" group.

Introduction

At this point our observations and questions provided some kind of framework for our thinking. We were reasonably sure that what we saw in the range of personalities available to us in this group of 27 children was a range of adaptive behaviors to the problem of blindness during the first eighteen months of life. The picture of developmental arrest in the autistic blind child showed failure to find the adaptive routes on the six-to-eighteen month level. We inferred this from the clinical picture of an undifferentiated self-not-self, from the arrest in locomotor achievements and language, and from the absence of coordinated hand behavior to an external stimulus. *We reasoned that for every developmental failure in the blind autistic child there should be a correlate in the development of all blind babies in the form of a unique adaptive problem posed by blindness. The difference between the autistic blind child and the child in the "normal" group should appear in developmental studies in which one group found the adaptive solutions and the other group met a developmental impasse.*

A Need for Observation of a Blind Infant

Our own group of 27 children could not help us in searching for clues. They had come to us with poor developmental histories from a variety of agencies that had no clinical interest in the problems we were concerned with. The differences between the autistic blind children and the "normal" group in the first year of life could not be discerned from the retrospective histories. In both groups the babies were described as "quiet babies," content to lie in their cribs for the best part of the 24-hour day. In both groups the mothers were described as "depressed." In both groups there were the delays in gross motor achievements during the last quarter of the first year.

We turned to the literature in search of longitudinal studies of blind infants which could provide us with detailed information on the blind babies' development. To our surprise, we learned that no detailed longitudinal studies of blind babies existed! We found Norris (1957) which described the developmental achievements of 209 blind children as measured by a modified Cattell scale. We found 5 useful case histories in this volume which gave some picture of the developmental achievements of a selected group. But our problems were different from those investigated by the Norris group when they undertook their study. We needed to know in fine detail how the blind baby finds the adaptive routes and how ego formation takes place in the absence of vision.

If a research begins at any one point I suppose ours begins here. We waited for the first new baby to be referred to our Family Service Society program. The baby turned out to be Toni, a five-month-old girl, blind from birth because of ophthalmia neonatorum. We ascertained that Toni was otherwise intact and healthy. The agency obtained the mother's interest and consent, and we arranged to set up regular monthly observation sessions and to record Toni's development on film.

Chapter II

SELMA FRAIBERG

Toni *

WHAT can we learn from one baby?

When David Freedman and I set out to visit Toni we brought with us a number of hypotheses. We had hypotheses regarding blindness as an impediment to the establishment of human attachments. We had a hypothesis regarding the adaptive substitution of sound for vision. And there were others which are fortunately obliterated by time. In the next 18 months Toni threw out each of our hypotheses one by one, like so many boring toys over the rail of a crib.

We were quite fortunate in our first baby, since she had been selected with no other criteria than her blindness and her age. Toni was a healthy, robust little girl, the youngest of 6 children. Her mother was an experienced mother. In spite of her feelings of guilt and fears for the future of her blind child, she was a woman whose motherliness responded to need, and this baby who needed her in special ways evoked deep tenderness in her.

Toni tossed out one of our hypotheses on the very first visit. She was five months old, making pleasant noises in her crib as we talked with her mother. When her mother went over to her and called her name, Toni's face broke into a gorgeous smile, and she

* All names of children and families in this book are fictitious.

made agreeable responsive noises. I called her name and waited. There was no smile. Dr. Freedman called her name. There was no smile. Mother called her name and once again there appeared the joyful smile and cooing sounds. Her mother said, a little apologetically, "She won't smile for anyone. Not even her sisters and brothers. Only me. She's been smiling when I talk to her since she was three months."

Now in 1961 it was written in all our books (including one of my own) that it is the *visual* stimulus of the human face that elicits smiling in the baby at three months. Toni's smile had just shattered a theory, which shows you what one baby can do. Seven years later I could have given you a long list of blind babies who smiled in response to mother's or father's voice. But that doesn't really matter. If only one blind baby smiles in response to a mother's voice, it demonstrates that there is something wrong with our theory.

In our notes of this session we recorded a number of observations showing the selective response of Toni to her mother, paralleling in all significant ways that of a sighted child at five months. Three months later, at eight months, Toni demonstrated another achievement in the scale of human attachments. Soon after she heard our voices, strange voices, she became sober, almost frozen in her posture. Later, when I held Toni briefly to test her reactions to a stranger, she began to cry, squirmed in my arms, and strained away from my body. It was a classic demonstration of "stranger anxiety." But—in 1961—we all knew that stranger anxiety appears at eight months on the basis of the *visual* discrimination of mother's face and stranger's face.

Very well. We conceded that under favorable conditions blindness need not be an impediment to the establishment of human attachments. But we still had a lot of other hypotheses tucked away.

One of these had to do with the adaptive substitution of sound for vision. We all knew that around five months of age the sighted child can reach and attain an object on sight. In the case of the blind child we expected that a coordination of sound and grasping would take place at approximately the same time. But at five months of age, at six months, and—astonishingly—even at nine months, Toni made no gesture of reach toward any of the sound objects we presented to her. We sneaked around with jangling keys, rattles, squeaky toys, always in a range where Toni could easily reach them. She looked alert and attentive, but she made no gesture of reach. It did not matter whether we used her own familiar toys or Dr. Freedman's car keys; there was not a gesture of reach. Was the baby deaf? Certainly not. As soon as she heard the sound of the camera motor, for example, she would startle or wince. She could discriminate voices. She could imitate sounds at seven months. What was it then?

At ten months Toni demonstrated for the first time her ability to reach and attain an object on sound cue alone! (Thereafter she became expert in grabbing objects sounded within arm's range.) As we drove back from Toni's house that day we were stunned by the implications of this observation. Toni had given her first demonstration of a direct reach for a sound object at ten months. (The sighted baby coordinates vision and grasping at five months.) But how did Toni solve the problem? We knew perfectly well that no developmental achievement appears overnight. A coordinated action of hand and external stimulus is the result of complex sensorimotor learning. There were antecedents which must have been present for months, unrecognized by us. Now we were obsessed by the problem and its implications. Since memory could not serve us, we went back over hundreds of feet of film, frame by frame, to try to reconstruct the sequence. But the story was not there. And we knew why. Film and film processing are expensive. Since we were financing this research out of pocket we had to be thrifty in our use of film. We had devoted only a small amount of footage to each of the areas we were sampling, and we had thought that our sampling was adequate. In order to pick up our lapse we would have needed generous and unprejudiced samples. The story of Toni's coordinated reach-on-sound cue was lost to us, and we already knew that this story would prove to be a vital clue in the study of the blind baby's development.

To return now to Toni and to go back a bit in the story: At eight months Toni had excellent control of her trunk and was indisputably moving toward an upright posture. She could support her weight on hands and knees, she could elevate herself to a standing position, and she could let herself down easily. There was no question, knowing babies, that Toni was getting ready to creep. As we were leaving Toni's house at the end of the eight-month visit, I said to the mother, "I'll bet when we come back next month Toni will really be into everything!" These were foolish words and I came to regret them.

At nine months Toni was not creeping. Nor at ten months or twelve months. This is what we saw: Toni, with demonstrated postural readiness for creeping, was unable to propel herself forward. On the floor in prone position she executed a kind of radial crawl, navigating in a circle.

Why couldn't Toni propel herself forward? Clearly there needed to be an external stimulus for the initiation of the creeping pattern. What happens in the case of the sighted child? The sighted child at nine months, let us say, is supporting himself ably on hands and knees. He sees an out-of-range object. He reaches for the object. And what we see now is a reach and a collapse, a reach and a collapse, each time moving forward until the object is attained. Within a few days the motor pattern begins to smooth out and becomes a coordinated action of hands and legs in what we call "creeping."

Why didn't Toni creep? Clearly because no external stimulus was present to initiate the creeping pattern. But why shouldn't a sound object provide the lure? We were back to the same problem.

Even years later, I can still remember the stunning impact of that discovery. Toni had brought a brand new insight into the understanding of locomotor development in sighted children.

Toni

We, all of us, had never had occasion to question the assumption that locomotion in infancy follows maturational patterns that are laid down in a biological sequence. Toni demonstrated that motor maturation follows its biological pattern, but in the absence of an external stimulus for reaching, the creeping pattern will not emerge. We reminded ourselves that in the retrospective histories of all blind children it is common to find that creeping was never achieved, and, in fact, there is a marked delay in the achievement of all locomotor skills from this point on, with independent walking a very late achievement in the second or third years.

Between eight and ten months we began to see something in Toni that roused our own anxieties. At times during the observational session we would see Toni stretch out on the floor, prone on the rug, and for long periods of time lie quite still, smiling softly to herself. The passive pleasure in immobility was chilling to watch. Her mother, watching this with us, looked strained and anxious. "She does that all the time," she told us. She was an experienced mother, you remember, and she knew as well as we did that no healthy baby at nine months will lie on the floor for long periods of time, smiling softly to herself. And when did Toni assume this posture? At any time, we observed, when external sources of stimulation were not available to her, i.e., if no one was talking to her, playing with her, or feeding her. In such moments of non-stimulation she would fall back on this form of self-stimulation in which the ventral surface of her body was in contact with the rug.

Did this mean that the mother was neglecting her? We thought not. During the same period, pleasure in mother's voice and pleasure in being held by mother were clearly seen whenever mother resumed contact with her. But in a normal busy household, where 5 other children must also make their claims upon a mother, there were inevitably periods when Toni was not being played with, talked to, held in mother's arms. It happens to sighted children too. What does a sighted child do at nine months when he is "by himself"? He occupies himself with toys, or if he is creeping, he goes on excursions to visit the underside of the dining room table or the top side of the living room couch, or the inside of the kitchen cupboard. And if he has no toy handy, and if he can't creep, he will occupy himself by looking—just plain looking around. Visual experience creates its own appetite for repetition; the hunger to see and the functional pleasure of vision are among the great entertainments of a baby after the first days of life. Vision keeps the baby "in touch" with his mother and with the world of things, giving continuity to experience. The sighted child at nine months does not have to be continually held by his mother or talked to by his mother in order to be "in touch" with her.

But when Toni could not touch her mother or hear her mother's voice she was robbed of her mother and of a large measure of the sensory experience that linked her to the world outside of her body. In this insubstantial, impermanent world, her own body and body sensations became at times the only certainty, the only continuous source of sensory experience in the otherwise discontinuous experience of darkness. And because proprioceptive experience provides the chief means for "keeping in touch" in the near-void of blindness and the only means for experiencing continuity of self feelings, Toni stretched out on the floor, face down upon the rug. In this posture, which afforded maximal contact between the body surface and the rug, she might obtain feelings of comfort, safety, pleasurable tactile sensations, and a sense of body awareness. We are reminded, too, that the ventral surface of the baby's body is normally stimulated in the posture of being held against the mother's body and that pleasure, intimacy, comfort, and safety are united for a lifetime of love in this posture—the embrace.

What we saw in Toni, face down, nuzzling a rug, was a form of stimulus hunger. Where vision would have insured abundant sources of stimuli and the visual alternatives to contact hunger for the mother, blindness caused this child in periods of external non-stimulation to fall back upon the poverty of body sensations. Like a starving organism that will finally ingest anything where there is not enough food, the stimulus hunger of this child led her to ingest the meager proprioceptive experience of body contact with a rug.

Later, in the University of Michigan study, I was to see variations of this posture in blind children. But when we first saw this in Toni we found it chilling. We had not foreseen such a development in an otherwise healthy child. And remember, too, that during this period, at nine months, we were also sobered by the fact that Toni was unable to locomote in spite of the fact that she had maturational readiness for creeping. In other respects, too, Toni seemed to have reached a developmental impasse. Although she was still lively and responsive to her mother and her sisters and brother, there was almost no interest in toys, and at nine months she was not reaching for objects. Her mother, we observed, seemed anxious and discouraged. For the first time we saw a number of instances in which mother was manifestly out of rapport with her baby.

When we returned at ten months, the entire picture had changed. Toni's mother, entirely on her own, had purchased a walker, and within a short time Toni had become expert in getting around in it.* She was still unable to creep, but the walker provided mobility, and Toni was cruising around the house with tremendous energy and making discoveries and rediscoveries at every port. "Did she still want to lie down on the rug?" we asked, concealing our own anxiety. Oh, no, the mother assured us. In fact, she absolutely refused to get into the prone position. Mother took Toni out of her walker and gave us a demonstration. The moment Toni was placed on the floor in the prone position, she yelled in protest and uprighted herself. This was now the posture of immobility—and Toni had found mobility. The moment she was put back in her walker, she stopped crying and took off like a hot-rodder.

* This is not, however, our recommendation for facilitating mobility in blind infants. There are better ways described in Chapter IX.

We never saw this passive prone posture again in Toni. Within 3 months, at thirteen months of age, she began walking with support—and now also creeping (!). Toni was "into everything," exploring the cupboards and the drawers and getting into mischief. At thirteen months she had a small and useful vocabulary, she was using her hands for fine discriminations, and she was now expert in reaching and attaining objects on sound cue. From this point on, Toni's development progressed without any major impediments. (Only one pathological behavior appeared in the second year, and I will describe this later.)

But now, what about the stereotyped prone behavior which had so alarmed us at eight and nine months? It is clear from the sequence that once Toni acquired mobility she could not even be persuaded to get back into the prone position on the floor. Mobility provided functional motor pleasure, of course, but mobility also put her in touch with a world beyond her body and a world that she could act upon; mobility gave her for the first time a sense of autonomy.

Here, we thought, we had found another clue to the ego deviations encountered among blind children. If we understand that the blind child lives in a near-void for much of his waking day, he can make few discoveries about the world around him until he becomes mobile. And if mobility itself is delayed until well into the second year, he will live for a perilously long time in this near-void in which the presence of the mother or other persons or ministrations to his own body become the only experiences which give meaning to existence. In these periods, when neither sound nor touch, feeding, bath, nor play occur, there is nothing except his own body. Now we began to understand how some blind babies may never find the adaptive routes and remain frozen in the state of body-centeredness, passivity, immobility, and ultimately, non-differentiation.

I mentioned that one pathological trait was observed in Toni beginning in the second year. Let me briefly describe it. When Toni became anxious, when she was separated even briefly from

her mother or when a strange person or a strange situation signaled danger to her, she would fall into a stuporous sleep. We observed this ourselves. It was as if a light were switched off. As far
as we can reconstruct the onset of this symptom, it was first
manifest in connection with a brief separation from her mother.
She retained this symptom as late as the fourth year when we obtained reports on her. In all other respects she was a healthy, active little girl, able to ride a trike, play ball, join in children's
games. Her speech was good; eating and sleeping were entirely
satisfactory. There was only this. We asked ourselves when we
would find an otherwise healthy sighted child who defended
against danger by falling into a pathological sleep. Never, of
course. But then, one should ask, what defenses against danger
does a blind child possess?

Chapter III

SELMA FRAIBERG AND
DAVID A. FREEDMAN, M.D.

Peter*

NINE-YEAR-OLD PETER, who will be described in this chapter, was treated by us concurrently with our observation of Toni. Selma Fraiberg was the child's therapist; David Freedman was the mother's analyst. Toni had taught us that the route to successful adaptation is a perilous one for a blind baby; Peter was to teach us how blindness can lead to adaptive failure.

Peter was one of the 7 children in the Family Service Society program described in our Introduction who presented a clinical picture of developmental arrest with characteristics that resembled those of early infantile autism in the sighted population. Peter was one of a large number of premature babies whose blindness was caused, in the period before 1950, by excessive concentrations of oxygen in the life-saving isolette.

Dr. Freedman's neurological examination of Peter and the EEG administered shed no light on the clinical picture of autism we saw in Peter. There was occipital spiking in the EEG. This is consistent with the observations of Levinson (1951) who has shown that abnormalities in the occipital leads occur in a wide va-

* This chapter was presented in another version by the authors as a section of a longer paper entitled "Studies in the Ego Development of the Congenitally Blind Child," *Psychoanalytic Study of the Child*, Vol. XIX (1964), pp. 113–169.

riety of children with ocular difficulties, Chang (1952) who has also shown that spike-like responses are likely to occur in the occipital leads of animals deprived of vision, and Gibbs, Fois and Gibbs (1955) who made similar observations in the EEGs of children suffering from retrolental fibroplasia. It is apparent that these local abnormalities are not related to the autistic syndrome.

Peter was eight years, ten months old when his treatment was begun. Some months after the work with him was under way, his mother began her own analysis, which then made possible a more detailed study of the complexities of the mother-child relationship and illuminated portions of the child's history that had earlier been obscure.

Peter was the youngest child of his family. His mother was thirty-five and his father forty at the time of his birth. Peter was a surviving member of a set of identical twins who were born prematurely. His birth weight was 2 pounds, 2 ounces. Immediately after delivery he was placed in an incubator with an oxygen-rich atmosphere. When he was approximately six months of age the parents became concerned about his lack of responsiveness and his apparent indifference to his surroundings. At this time the child was examined and a diagnosis of retrolental fibroplasia was made.

Both parents were intelligent and well educated and had demonstrated their capacities for parenthood in the rearing of 2 older daughters, then in adolescence, who presented no unusual problems, performed well in school, and were attractive and responsive youngsters.

The mother became depressed immediately after learning that Peter was blind. She remembered the early years of Peter's life as a kind of bad dream. When her suffering became too great for her she simply withdrew from her blind child. Peter was in the care of servants a good deal of the time; there was a succession of maids, so numerous that their names could hardly be recalled by the mother when we later needed to verify one or another of the allusions which Peter made to them in his treatment.

We had very little information, therefore, regarding Peter's early development. We were told that his locomotor development was slow during his first year, but his mother could not give us dates, or even approximate dates, for any of the achievements. We know, however, that he never crept, that walking with support was achieved sometime between the ages of two and two and a half, and that even at the age of three, when he entered a nursery school for the blind, he did not walk independently but moved from place to place by hanging onto objects.

When Peter was eight, his parents grasped at a new hope for their apparently uneducable child and arranged for him to be sent to an eastern community where a new residential program for disturbed blind children was being set up. Since there were initial difficulties in establishing the new facility, Peter lived in a foster home for several months and was finally transferred to the institution, where he remained for approximately 5 months. The institution closed its program unexpectedly at the end of this period, and Peter was returned to his home. We have been unable to obtain any reports from the clinical staff of this institution, and the little we know we can only piece together from the child's communications to his therapist and from the mother's observations of Peter when she visited him.

As Peter grew to know his therapist and progressed in his ability to communicate, he gave us vignettes of this year. He reenacted nighttime scenes in which he made the noises of crying and imitated the voice of one or another of the nurses in this institution: "Sh'h! What's the matter?" "Stop that!" "Stop that crying. You're not a baby!" "You'll wake up all the boys!" And on other occasions he would mimic an angry adult voice, "Sit there! Just sit there until I come back!" (referring to the toilet), and "You made a mess!" The degree to which he had regressed during this period also came out in unexpected ways. A disgusted voice is imitated: "What! Eating your stool!" And when he was first seen approximately a month after he returned from the institution, he was emaciated and in such a poor nutritional state that it seemed certain that he had been refusing food for some time, for there was no question that in this institution the children were adequately fed. Occasionally one caught a hint from Peter's verbal memories that his nutrition had become of great concern to the staff at the institution, for he would repeat in alien voices, "Eat your custard now! Now, come on—just a little bit, just a little bit more!" Variations on this theme were common in his "reports."

Initial Observations *

When I first visited Peter at his home I saw him on the front lawn with his nurse, entwining himself around her body. He was tall for his age, extremely thin, pale, with an absent self-absorbed look about his face. His arms and legs seemed to flop like a rag doll's. He walked uncertainly with support, and several times his nurse picked him up in her arms and carried him from place to place.

Later we moved to the garden. Peter paid no attention to me or to my voice and sat or lay on the picnic table absently mouthing a rubber toy. Occasionally he made an irrelevant statement. Once he sang, in perfect pitch, "Pussy cat, pussy cat, where have you been?" His mother told me that he spent hours at his record player.

After a while he came close to me and fingered me. Then, without any change of facial expression and without any show of feeling, he began to dig his fingernails into the skin of my arm, very hard, causing me to wince with pain. From this point on, it was nearly impossible to divert Peter from digging his nails into me or, alternately, pinching me with great intensity. It is impossible to describe this experience. I cannot call it sadistic in him. It was as if he did not know this was painful to me, and I really felt

* The case narrative is reported in the first person by the therapist (SF) in the form of her case notes.

that on the primitive undifferentiated level on which Peter functioned he was not able to identify with the feelings of another person. This digging into me had the quality of trying to get into me, to burrow himself into me, and the pinching had the quality of just holding onto me for dear life.

I observed that when Peter lost an object he was mouthing, he showed no reaction to loss and did not search for it. Repeated observations in this session and in others confirmed this point. Very clearly this child had no concept of an object that existed independently of his perception of it.

While his mother was with us, I observed that his reaction to her was in no discernible way different from his reaction to me, to the nurse, or to the dog. At no time, both then and for many weeks after I began to work with him, did he ask a direct question, express a need through gesture or language, or answer a question put to him. His mother told me that until very recently he did not call her "mama," but referred to her as "Too-hoo." She explained that this word derived from her own greeting to him when she entered the house.

Peter always referred to himself in the third person. The word "I," his mother told me, had entered his vocabulary before he had gone to the institution last year, but when I was able to observe him directly I felt that "I" was not employed for self-reference and was mechanically interpolated into speech as if he had been given lessons in "I" and "you."

There were no toys to which Peter had any attachment. When he showed transitory interest in objects, he brought them to his mouth, sucked on them, and chewed them. He did not explore them with his hands; he did not manipulate them. Prehension was poor and the fingers were rigidly extended. The only well-coordinated movements observed were those employed in bringing an object to the mouth.

Peter's mother reported that he could feed himself adequately, and I was able to confirm this through direct observation. He still preferred soft foods, had great difficulty in masticating, and usually spit out the masticated food rather than swallow it.

In speech samples which I obtained in later sessions there were typically much echolalia and toneless repetition of stereotyped phrases.

When my early efforts to work with Peter and his mother began to bring favorable results, I suggested to the parents, with all necessary caution, that we might attempt a treatment program, that we should have reservations regarding its outcome, but that I thought I could promise some improvement in functioning. The parents were able to accept a treatment program on this basis. Both parents said honestly that they did not even know whether he was educable to any extent, but if only he could come alive, be responsive, be a happier child, be a member of the family, they would consider the treatment well worthwhile.

I shall briefly describe the treatment approach. Peter was visited at his home 5 times a week. From the beginning, I discovered that there were great advantages in having his mother present during my visits with Peter. Not only did it constantly afford me a picture of mother and child together, but the mother could gain insight into Peter's behavior. As Peter began to communicate more and more to me, the mother could share the knowledge and the insights and make use of them in her handling of him.

Peter was in no sense "analyzable," of course. What I attempted to do was to apply analytic insights in a kind of education and therapy for a particular child.

The report that follows is a summary of observations over a 2½-year period.

The Mother-Child Relationship

The earliest educational work with the mother was, of course, focused on promoting ties between her and the child who barely discriminated her from other human beings in his environment. Mrs. M. was encouraged to take over a major part of the child's care and she was helped to understand how need satisfaction and continuity of care were the indispensable first steps in establishing human ties. Gradually, in the early months of treatment, Peter's attachment to his mother became evident. He showed joy when she appeared and awareness of separation. He began to use the word "mama" consistently for the first time.

Concurrent with the work in building the mother-child ties was the education of the mother to the unique needs of a blind child in acquiring knowledge of his world. Ironically, much of this information was not new to the mother, who had read widely in the literature of education of the blind; but until the treatment of Peter was begun and her own analysis was under way, she had been unable to apply this knowledge.

Whereas the blind child is almost entirely dependent upon mobility for discovering a world of objects, Peter had been very largely restricted to his home. As opportunities for free movement and exploration of his environment were opened up to him, and as the range of his experience expanded, his exploration and manipulation of objects led to naming of them, and there followed a rapid expansion of his vocabulary.

The mother's own reaction to the child's evolving ties to her was ambivalent. On the one hand, she was gratified by the signs of progress; on the other hand, the demands of the child who had awakened to a human relationship were at times depleting her energies. She confessed to irritation and anger and a longing to have someone else take over. Mrs. M. had not yet begun her own analysis, and in my educational role I could not easily explore the dimensions of this conflict.

Many months later, when Peter's feeding had become the topic for discussion, I inquired about details and learned that Peter usually ate alone or in the company of a servant. When I encouraged Mrs. M. to join Peter for at least one meal a day and report the results to me, she burst into tears and said, "You don't know what you're asking of me!" He was repulsive at mealtimes, she said. He threw food, spit out food, smeared it. But behind the complaints about the child's repulsive eating habits was a profound conflict which was illuminated later in the mother's analysis. This analytic material and her own communication to me revealed that she had avoided the feeding of Peter in infancy and that her own pain had expressed itself, among other ways, in an inability to feed him. The pattern of turning over the feeding of the child to servants was a very early one. Yet it is important to note that even before the diagnosis of blindness was made, this baby, like all infants totally blind from birth, had appeared to the mother as curiously unresponsive. He was quiet and content to lie in his crib for hours. *"He never seemed to need me!"* the mother told us, and because this was a woman whose capacities for love were largely called forth by expressed needs of a partner, this baby who did not seem to need her could elicit no response.

With some working through of this material in her analysis, Mrs. M. was able to find solutions. She found, to her surprise, that when she began to join Peter at mealtimes, the repulsive food habits declined in a very short period, and the child's own ties to his mother were strengthened by the association of mother with eating pleasures.

Another motive in the mother's avoidance of contact with her child appeared early in treatment. In the period that preceded the mother's own analysis, I saw how she typically employed reaction formations against anger and rage, both in relation to her child and to me. With encouragement she was able to express more and more of her feelings toward Peter. She was able to see how, when her anger toward Peter became dangerous to her, she avoided contact with him. When her guilt about, and fear of, her feelings became evident to her, she accepted my recommendation of analytic treatment for herself.

The mother's analysis made it possible to conduct my educational work with greater freedom and flexibility. Mrs. M. continued to work closely with me and to be present during Peter's sessions, but it was no longer necessary for me to deal with aspects of her own conflicts that impeded the child's treatment.

With analytic help the mother demonstrated unusual capacities to support the child's treatment.

The Mouth and the Hand

Peter's mouth, it appeared, had remained the center of his primitive personality organization. All objects were brought to the mouth; it was almost never empty. Perception largely centered in the mouth. There was almost no handling or exploration with the hands. We know that this is not typical for normal blind children, and yet it is important to note that for many blind persons the mouth functions as a discriminating sensory organ throughout life. (Villay [1930] described how, even as an adult, he relied upon his mouth, and particularly his tongue, to make the finest perceptual distinctions.) In Peter the mouth had also remained the center of erotic and aggressive impulses, and when I first knew him it did not even appear that these were differentiated. When he made contact he mouthed: often the moment after, he bit, and this biting had the quality not of intentional aggression but of incorporation.

Very early in Peter's treatment I began to understand the behavior of the hand in the clutching and clawing that I described earlier. Peter could at first make contact with me only by clawing me, burrowing his fingers into the skin of my arm and neck. When at such times I moved away from him and maintained contact with him merely through my voice, he would immediately revert to apathy or to autistic mannerisms (rocking, swaying, etc.). But on one such occasion as I withdrew in pain, he stopped his clawing of me, withdrew his fingernails from my arm, then bit me on the head. When I recovered, I was again struck by the fact that there was no sadism in this act—again it had the quality of taking me in so that I could not go away. Then, recalling the sequence of the frustrated digging into me with his fingernails and the biting that immediately followed, I understood the fuller meaning of the hand behavior. The hand behaved like a mouth, the fingernails like teeth, and the pinching activity was like biting also. The oral-incorporative aspects of mouthing and biting had been transferred to the hand.

When I understood the oral-incorporative significance of this clutching and clawing, I was able to make a useful interpretation to Peter. The next time he seized me and clawed me in this way, I did not immediately extricate myself, but said, "You don't have to be afraid. I won't go away." And with this he released his "death grip" on me. In the same session, when he began to claw his mother I repeated the interpretation, "You don't have to be afraid. Mother will not go away," and he released his mother. From this time on we were able to bring about a marked diminution of the clutching and clawing with these words. His mother was deeply impressed. It was "like magic," she said; but most important of all, she had achieved insight into a piece of behavior that she had always interpreted as aggressive and now began to understand as a kind of inarticulate terror. (Later, when this same hand behavior acquired the significance of intentional aggression, other ways of handling it had to be employed.)

In this connection it is worth mentioning that this biting, clawing, pinching behavior is commonly observed among preschool blind children, and it is retained by the blind children with severe ego deviations. It is as if grasping has not freed itself of the oral mode and the hand has not achieved autonomy from the mouth.

For Peter the progress from mouth to hand was slow and laborious. The mouth retained its primacy as a perceptual organ for most of the first two years of my work with him. Even after he progressed in grasping he was slow to acquire pleasure in manual exploration of objects. For the most part it appeared that an object was desirable or not desirable to the degree that it stimulated the oral cavity in some preferred fashion. When I tried to encourage tactile discrimination by bringing him various textiles and textures for him to handle, he brought them to his mouth and discarded them when the texture or taste was not pleasing. When Mrs. M. and I covered bean bags with a variety of materials—velvet, satin, corduroy—he did not discriminate among them on the basis of their qualities. When we introduced him to a toy flute, hoping that mouth satisfaction, sound, and manual prepriocep- tive experience might make this an attractive object to him, he produced one note and tossed it away. He did the same thing on subsequent attempts.

However, there were small and encouraging achievements along the way. There were periods during which he evidently en- joyed fitting together pots and lids, or jars and covers. He began to enjoy filling and dumping a milk bottle with clothespins, and successfully inhibited the impulse to bring the clothespins to his mouth.

A big step was achieved at the beginning of the third year of treatment. He became interested in seashells and brought a number of them home from the beach. He played with them for long periods, tracing their whorls with his fingers and gradually discriminating among them. In a box of several dozen there were a few that he preferred and he quickly sorted them with his finger- tips until he found these, using his mouth only minimally for dis- crimination. His mother and I encouraged this newly found in- terest and collected shells for him.

Then, almost as soon as Mrs. M. and I became aware of this new progress in use of the hands, we noticed something else. The clawing and pinching had disappeared altogether! Prior to this period there had been much intentionally aggressive scratching and pinching—a later sequel to the undifferentiated clawing we had seen earlier. The hand, which had largely functioned as an auxiliary mouth, now appeared to be freeing itself of the oral mode.

There is nothing in my observations that tells us exactly how this was achieved and why it occurred at this particular time. In the meantime, there was a new behavior toward inanimate ob- jects in general. Objects that had once served only self-stimula- tion now began to acquire qualities for themselves. An old wooden bowl that Peter used to suck on and earlier had used to bang his head with, now, for the first time, became a vessel, and he spent long periods filling it with shells or other small objects.

During this period I had the feeling that something new was taking place in Peter's personality. And then, at the end of a 6-week period, the new behavior was lost, the shells and the bowl were again brought to the mouth to be sucked, the pinching and scratching returned, and the promise of these new developments faded. (This regression will be discussed later along with other data from the same period.)

A number of provocative questions derive from these observations of a personality that has remained mouth-centered, as in the case of Peter and other deviant children. Following a suggestion given to us by Dr. Joseph Michaels at an early stage in this study, we began to consider the implications for ego development when an organ that serves primary need satisfaction also serves as a primary organ of perception. The prolonged mouth-centered perception of the blind infant and young child may impede the development of "conflict-free" perception. In the development of the sighted infant the primary autonomy of vision becomes one of the guarantees of conflict-free perception. In the normal development of blind infants and young children, the hand takes over as the leading organ of perception and achieves autonomy from the mouth.

We are accustomed to speak of the hands as the "eyes" of the blind. Until we studied the infant Toni, we did not understand that the achievement of hand autonomy in a blind infant is a feat of extraordinary virtuosity. *In this healthy, normally developing infant, we saw that perception remained mouth-centered until well into the second year, and the hand did not achieve primacy as a perceptual organ until the last half of the second year.* *

Where vision mediates the evolution of hand autonomy in the

* Later, in the Ann Arbor study, when we learned about the impediments in adaptive hand behavior, we were able to translate these findings into an educational program that facilitated hand autonomy from the mouth in the course of the first year. See Chapters VI and XI.

sighted child, the absence of vision obstructed this crucial progress in the healthy blind infant, and hand autonomy was achieved finally through an elaborate detour. From the history of Peter and other deviant blind children we began to understand that in less than favorable environmental circumstances the progress from mouth to hand may not be achieved at all and the personality may remain arrested on the level of mouth-centeredness and nondifferentiation.

Object Concept

We have already described Peter's inability to search for lost objects or even to attempt to recover them after he lost contact through mouth or hand. At the same time, he could orient himself to a certain degree in his own room, could find his bed, and could make his way from his bed to his record player. When I observed him in the family kitchen at a mealtime it was clear that he was not well oriented there, and his behavior in the downstairs rooms suggested that he had explored them very little. His own room, it is important to know, isolated him to a very large extent from even the ordinary household noises. This was a large house, and his room was so situated that very little sound carried from the first floor to the second. A circular staircase broke up sound so successfully than on occasions when I had to call his mother or nurse for assistance, my own voice could not be heard.

Peter had shown in many ways that he had no concept of the existence of an object after he lost contact with it; in the same way he showed that he had no concept of the existence of human objects independently of his perception of them. He did not call for his mother, he did not search for his mother. He showed his concern over the disappearance of persons through repeated questions, "Where is Aunt Cora?" "Where is Roger?" "Where is Jonathan?" It did not even matter that some of these people had had only the most casual relationship with him. He would ask one question most urgently, "Laura, Laura! Where is Laura?" Laura was a cousin of his mother's who had died during the time when Peter was in the institution. He of course did not know what "dead" meant, but his mother had told him that Laura could not come back.

The "where is . . ." questions need clarification. "Where is Aunt Cora?" for example, did not mean that Aunt Cora must be "someplace," i.e., that she had an existence for Peter when he was not in contact with her. This could be tested by means of Peter's behavior toward inanimate objects during the same period. When Peter dropped his bowl or his block there was no attempt at recovery or even a gesture of recovery. He would say in a flat voice, "Where is my bowl?" and his mother or I would retrieve it. If we did not pick it up for him, he would shift his attention. "Where is . . . ," then, was a magic formula to bring back the object. The "where is . . ." construction was also the magic formula in peek-a-boo games and hiding games that Mrs. M. and I played with Peter, an incantation that "caused" someone to return. Following Piaget (1954), we should probably take the failure to search for human or inanimate objects after loss of contact as a fair sign that Peter had not acquired a concept of the independence of objects from his perception. At a later stage in treatment, which will be described, Peter demonstrated active search, and with this achievement his behavior toward people and things altered in significant ways.

For many weeks at the beginning of my work with Peter I played hide-and-seek games with him and taught him to find me through tracing my voice. These games gave him enormous pleasure and we played them repetitively hour after hour after hour. After a while he began to formalize the games, sending me away with a push, saying "Good-by!" then finding me and spontaneously hugging me in a greeting. I had also encouraged his mother to play these games with him, but during the early months of treatment she had very little luck in engaging him in such games. I soon understood why. Once when I asked her to join in a game during one of our sessions, Peter himself refused to go on. I saw through his behavior that it was too dangerous for him to play "going away and returning" with mother herself. As a neutral object I could serve the game purpose very well; his mother could not.

On one occasion I employed an innovation in these games in order to test his ability to follow cues in locating objects. I began the game with the ritual, "Good-by, Peter!" and then walked to a corner of the room clicking my heels on the wood floor to give him an opportunity to track my movements. Then I waited in my corner, but did not give him the signal of my voice as I usually did. He started in search of me, was obviously not oriented, walked right past me, went through the door of the bathroom that communicated between his room and his parents' room, passed on into his parents' room, and then there was silence. He did not return. After a little while his mother and I went in search of him. We found him lying on his mother's bed, his shoulders heaving convulsively and a look of mute terror on his face. He could not cry in those days; he could only go through a kind of motor parody of grief. I tried to put his feelings into words and I tried to explain to him what had happened and that I had not been lost at all. But he refused to have anything to do with me for the rest of that hour and he would not play the hide-and-seek games with me for a very long time.

For many months Mrs. M. and I found every means available to us to teach Peter the substantiality and permanence of objects through games and other devices. We taught him to find the cookie jar in the kitchen and get his own cookies. We taught him to find the cracker cupboard. He discovered the joys of the pots and pans cupboards, and then, of course, there came a rapid expansion of searches into everything. From the initial discovery of objects that could always be found in the same place he moved on to the discovery that the same object could be found in a different place and was still the object he had known before. And yet it was nearly a year of work before Peter demonstrated real gains in this area. By then he was searching actively for objects and if he did not find them in the expected place, he would search for them in another place. When he wanted his mother he went in search of her.

There was an interesting corollary in speech development at the same time. We recall that in the beginning Peter did not call for his mother and, as a matter of fact, he did not even cry to summon her. Since his mother did not have a substantial existence for him, speech did not possess one of its vital functions—to summon the lost object, to bring it back. But later, when Peter clearly demonstrated his ability to search for objects and recover them and when the concept became stabilized, the change was reflected in speech. He began calling his mother, summoning her to his side, or even calling her while she was in the same room in order to locate her. At this time his incessant calling of mother nearly exhausted her. Mrs. M. also provided us with an interesting observation. On the one hand, she understood very well that this was a wonderful achievement for Peter; on the other hand, she found herself disturbed. For now, she told Dr. Freedman and me, when he was able to express his needs for her in words, she felt herself bound to him in a new way and one that was not altogether satisfying. "When he couldn't express his need for me before, I didn't feel quite so guilty about going out and leaving him, and now that he puts it into words, I feel torn each time I go away." While the ambivalence of the mother needs no comment here, we were struck by the fact that for the first time something like a genuine human relationship was developing between the child and his mother.

These observations regarding the emergence of an object concept raise a number of questions. As Piaget (1954) demonstrated, during the period nine to eighteen months the sighted child makes a series of experiments which lead him to discover that an object exists independently of his perception of it. The sighted infant demonstrates an evolving concept of the object through his behavior toward a screened object, a failure to search for the object under nine months of age, followed by recovery of the object in successively complex situations in which the displacements of the object are traced by means of visual reconstructions. Somewhere between fifteen and eighteen months, the sighted infant demonstrates through his search for screened objects that he has a concept of the object that had achieved independence of his perception of it; when he conducts his searches he demonstrates that he knows the object is "someplace." This is, of course, one of the crucial developments in the process of differentiation of self and outer world.

When we consider the role of vision in constructing an object's displacements in space, the parallel achievement in the case of a blind infant must be regarded as an adaptive feat. In the first stage of building the object concept the blind infant must trace the object's displacements by means of perceptual cues that are highly inadequate substitutes for vision. Audition, for example, can substitute in tracking only certain classes of objects—those that have sound-making properties. Tactile experience cannot tell the infant where the object is located when he has lost contact with it. The blind infant, then, has a fragmentary and discontinuous experience with objects during the period of tracking and probably can evolve a concept of the independence of objects from his own perceptions only after his own locomotion provides him with spatial references and repetitive experiences with object finding.

In all this it is undoubtedly the human object that provides maximum experience for the blind infant's building of an object concept. Where no single sense modality can substitute for vision as a distance receptor and an organizer of perceptual wholes, the mother and other highly invested human objects carry the main burden of "teaching" the blind infant about the permanence of objects and, through their own persons, offer the possibilities of synthesizing and uniting these impressions. Where cathexis of the human object and nonvisual sensory data have established a stable object representation for the blind infant, the goings and comings of the mother, the tracking of the mother through auditory cues, and later the search for the mother by means of the child's own mobility will all lead the blind child to the concept of a mother who exists even when he has lost contact with her. In the early stages of the evolution of this concept it is unlikely that inanimate objects can serve the blind child's learning in the same way, although the sighted child's learning during the same period is achieved through countless experiments in which both human and inanimate objects are employed. The totally blind infant has a restricted range of interest in inanimate objects, as we saw in the blind infant, Toni, and infants known to us in the Family Service Society project. Within this range (which may in the first year include the bottle, the pacifier, a rattle, or bells) only the noise-making objects are useful in tracking the movements of an object.

It is, then, probably the mother who becomes the center of this learning for the totally blind child, and while a parallel development can be constructed for the sighted infant, the functional advantages of vision over other sense modalities and the infinitely larger experience with objects provide the sighted child with rich and diverse data for constructing a world of objects; the mother is not the exclusive teacher. Since the blind child's learning must emanate from the experience with mother, insufficiencies in mothering or deficiencies in the mother-infant ties can cut off all possibilities for learning in this sphere.

The arrested ego development of Peter and other deviant blind children shows, almost uniformly, the failure to acquire an object concept. While this is only one of a number of interrelated problems having to do with differentiation and individuation, the adaptive failure in this area suggests that the absence of vision creates a developmental hazard. The mother's resources must be heavily exploited to compensate for the impoverished fund of information available to a blind infant, and when the mother can provide such compensation, a normal sequence in ego formation takes place. In those cases where developmental arrest occurs we also find a tragic failure on the part of the mother to get her blind baby's signals and to serve as the unifier of perceptual experiences. In this way the double handicap of blindness and insufficiencies in the experience with mother may for many blind children cut off the developmental path that leads to the achievement of an object concept.

Mobility

The importance of mobility, and particularly the achievements of independent locomotion, have been stressed by Norris, Spaulding, and Brodie (1957), Burlingham (1961), and other writers and students of the blind child's development. Until the blind infant is free to explore his world, he has very limited possibilities for learning about it. Peter, we were told, never crept at all. (Many blind babies do not.) In this respect his mother blamed her own ignorance, since she did not put him on the floor and did not give him opportunities for creeping. This is certainly a valid point; but as we observed in the blind infant Toni, in the absence of a visual stimulus there is not a strong incentive for the child to creep. And, as mentioned earlier, the blind child achieves independent walking much later than the sighted child.

Peter was still supporting himself by touching walls and other objects when I first met him. He had had very limited opportunities for exploration of his own house. It was a house furnished with antiques, a house of china lamps and crystal and silver ornaments, and clearly, from the furnishings of the downstairs rooms, it was not expected that a still clumsy blind child would enter them. His mother, who had so much anxiety about his retardation and who tried to employ her own experience as a teacher in educating Peter to handle toys and to manipulate them, had not understood that a crucial experience in learning had been omitted. He needed mobility and the opportunity to explore.

When Peter's mother fully understood this, she was able to

bring about many changes in his life. She and I encouraged independent walking, simple climbing, swimming, playing ball. Within a very short time he was walking independently, and his motor skills improved rapidly. During this period we saw a great improvement in Peter's overall physical appearance. He gained weight, he acquired muscle in his pipe-stem arms and legs, and his skin lost its pallor. He was encouraged to explore the house, and although his mother had thought that he never had shown interest in exploring, once these opportunities were opened up to him he was very soon "into everything"—cupboard, drawers, and all the rooms of the house.

It was at this time that Peter's language began to make tremendous leaps. As he discovered objects, handled them, discriminated and named them, his vocabulary enlarged very quickly. He was actively encouraged, at the same time, to express his needs and wishes in words, and his mother learned to be not so quick in anticipating his gestures and tactfully to postpone gratifications until he expressed his wants in words. While these were good achievements, it is important to note that a good deal of his speech was echolalic and did not, properly speaking, serve communication. Also, for a very long time, his speech had no affective quality.

Aggression and Motility

As I mentioned earlier, the biting, pinching, and scratching which I had observed at the very beginning of treatment reappeared later in connection with intentional aggression. It was impressive to realize that until the second year of treatment Peter had not used his hands for hitting, or his feet for kicking, in directed aggression. Aggression was expressed either through the mouth or by means of the hand following the oral model. At the same time Peter was reluctant to masticate or use his teeth for biting food.

I observed fairly early in treatment that Peter did a lot of throwing of objects, particularly of his blocks, but this throwing was aimless and without energy and reminded me of the way a child throws food or toys in the last quarter of the first year. It seemed as if Peter could do only two things with objects: either put them in his mouth or throw them away. At that time, because I was still groping in my educational and therapeutic approaches, I would, after a certain point, interfere with this aimless throwing of objects. For example, when we were "making cookies" with play dough and Peter began to throw it, I would repeatedly remind him that play dough was for making things, for playing games with me and Mommy, and that when he wanted to throw things he could throw balls. If he was in good rapport with me on these occasions he would accept the prohibition, but almost immediately, I saw, he would revert to passivity and lethargy and begin his swaying or rocking, or nonsense chants.

I began to understand that this throwing was necessary to him. I then changed my tactics and permitted, even encouraged, the throwing without knowing where this would lead. During these throwing sessions he was undoubtedly in better contact with me and his mother and there were evident signs of release in his personality. Yet my conscience as a child analyst troubled me very much during this period as I watched play dough, blocks, and plastic toys go flying through the air in an apparently meaningless barrage. Never before in my therapeutic career had I given permission for such aimless throwing or had the feeling that it was justified for therapeutic purposes. While all of this was going on I would sometimes remind myself that normal infants go through such a phase in the last quarter of the first year, but I had never observed this closely or reflected upon its significance in development.

As I watched Peter in many such sessions I saw that gradually the throwing itself became energized and lost its aimless quality. He was throwing hard, and showed evident satisfaction when the object made contact with the floor or the walls. He began to make noises and to accompany his throwing with little cries and sounds that had an aggressive quality. As the throwing grew more aggressive, his mother and I, in self-defense and as part of Peter's education, began to provide him with good substitutes for the blocks and other toys for throwing. His mother made about a half dozen bean bags which had enough weight and made a sufficiently satisfactory noise on contact so that they gave satisfaction to Peter. Gradually we now began to limit the throwing to bean bags and balls, and Peter was able to accept the substitution in a way that earlier he could not.

From my recorded observations and notes, I saw very clearly another connection that seemed to be significant. As Peter became more active in throwing, and as throwing became more energetic and more aggressive in quality, the biting, pinching, and scratching diminished markedly.

Circumstances provided me with several good tests of the relationship between the different modes of aggression. On one occasion, for example, I arrived to find Mrs. M. bitten and scratched, and she reported that she had had a very bad weekend with Peter. In order to get a picture of the weekend, I asked to what extent Peter had also been throwing. Mrs. M. became embarrassed by my question and said a little defensively that she had decided to put a stop to it this weekend. She knew I had recommended that he be given permission to throw, but it all seemed so pointless and so chaotic. (Naturally, I could sympathize with her in all this.) I then suggested that there was probably a connection between his attacks on her and the deprivation of throwing and asked her if she could bear with us for a while. She agreed. When throwing was permitted again, the attacks on the mother ceased.

Somewhat later, however, Peter himself gave up the throwing, without any external prohibition as far as we could judge. He reverted once again to biting and scratching, and at the same time his mother reported a severe eating restriction. He was "eating next to nothing except milk and soft foods." There had been progress in masticating for a while, but now this was lost entirely. The content of our sessions gave me a few clues. He talked incessantly about Laura and other absent persons. "Where is Laura?" "Where is Bryan?" "Where is Aunt Cora?" At the same time I saw how he tried to inhibit his biting and scratching and observed a mouth tic exactly representing the urge to bite and the inhibition of biting. Along with the tic, Peter would begin swaying, rocking, or bouncing, or uttering gibberish.

The repetitive content of this period strongly suggested that he thought that he could cause people to go away in analogy with eating. Once he even put it quite exactly, "Laura is dead. Laura is all gone." ("All gone," of course, was a phrase he used when he had eaten all of his food.) I decided to put my understanding of the eating inhibition in the form of an interpretation. I told Peter that when he bites his celery or apple he makes it go away inside of him and it is all gone. "But Mommy is not food, Daddy is not food. I am not food. Laura is not food. You cannot eat a mommy or daddy or me. You can't make me all gone." He listened intently to me. After this session his mother reported that he had a hearty lunch, accepted an apple, which he had not done for a very long time, and enjoyed his dinner that evening. The eating inhibition returned several times in the weeks that followed. Each time I made a similar interpretation. Each time the eating inhibition disappeared. Along with this he once again returned to throwing and showed much less biting, scratching, and pinching.

Later he demonstrated a similar fear that his own aggression could destroy objects. He had broken a couple of his favorite phonograph records. In the old days we had replaced these. Now he had made enough progress to begin to learn that breaking is an end to things and that they cannot be magically brought back. He was saddened with this knowledge, of course, but then we noticed that he became very anxious when he accidentally broke something. At such times he would revert to apathy and solitude, and we would hear his melancholy chant, "The record is all gone!" "Mommy's vase is all gone!" It was very clear that once again he needed help in understanding that while his aggression could destroy phonograph records and certain other inanimate objects, his aggression would not make "Mommy all gone" or other people "all gone." I had to repeat this interpretation to him many times before he appeared to grasp it.

We think we can now understand, or begin to understand, the relationship between the aimless throwing of the early period and the differentiation of the aggression described here. In the sequence from oral-centered and undifferentiated aggression in the early behavior to directed and energetic throwing in the later behavior, the aimless throwing forms a bridge. This must represent part of the process of separating the skeletal muscles from the mouth. We would need to make close observations on normal infant development in the last quarter of the first year to carry our thinking further; but if our interpretation of Peter's behavior has any validity, the transfer of function from the mouth to the skeletal muscles constitutes an essential progress in the differentiation of aggression, and the aimless throwing by infants must signify that the skeletal muscles are beginning to take over. We must remember, however, that in the sighted child, progress in locomotion normally is made during the same period—a period in which so many events occur that this transitional state in normal development might ordinarily be obscured. In the blind infant there is commonly a maturational readiness for crawling and a failure, in the absence of vision, to achieve locomotion. The fate of aggression during this crucial period merits careful study. This may be another vulnerable period in the development of the blind child, and the particular fate of aggression may be another of the predisposing factors to deviant ego development.

Is the delay in motor development, specifically in locomotion, a key to the fate of aggression in the deviant children? At the point where the skeletal muscles should take over and serve discharge as well as integration of new patterns, a failure in motor function takes place. The achievement in the deviant child may be delayed for another two years or longer. During this period, if we follow the history of Peter and other deviant blind children, libidinal and aggressive impulses remain undifferentiated and centered in the mouth; perception also remains centered in the mouth. By the time locomotion is achieved, a state of oral-centered adaptation may also have been achieved, and locomotion can no longer lock in with progressive tendencies in ego development that were in a state of readiness during an earlier stage.

Body Image

When I first met Peter he was unable to identify parts of his own body when asked such questions as "Where is your nose?" "Where is your ear?" He had so little awareness of internal sensations that he gave neither sign nor signal when he was about to urinate and defecate, and of course could not be trained to use the toilet. He showed little interest in his penis. As we should expect, there was no awareness of sexual differences. As our work progressed, it was evident that some crude image of his own body began to emerge. He was able, at the end of the first year of treatment, to identify parts of his own body (nose, ear, finger, etc.) and to find the corresponding parts on his mother and me. He was able to ask to go to the toilet for urination and defecation.

The discovery of sexual differences took place in an extraordinary way around the eighteenth month of treatment. He had walked into the bathroom as his mother was emerging from the bath. According to the mother's report, he began to explore her body with his hands. The mother chose to use this occasion to enlighten Peter on sexual differences. She allowed him to explore her breasts and the genital area and told him that she had breasts but she did not have a penis. The mother said that Peter showed no reaction at the time.

She was much pained when I raised questions about these means of enlightening her child in sexual differences. How else, she wanted to know, could a blind child learn about body differences? There were no good answers to this question, but I recommended verbal explanation along lines that we were following in Peter's treatment sessions.

Following the anatomy lesson in the bathroom, I began to see Peter's reactions very clearly in my sessions with him. I saw him make reaching gestures for his mother's breasts, giggling with excitement when he made contact. On two occasions he reached boldly into her blouse, and his mother explained to me, with some embarrassment, that he had recently discovered that she wore "falsies" in her bras and had even succeeded in removing them in one swift gesture. He called them "little hats" and searched them out in her bureau, bearing them off as trophies.

During the same period Peter began to suffer from constipation. He would withhold for days in evident discomfort. When he sat on the toilet he was visibly frightened, but could not put his fears into words. At the same time his mother reported that he had been wandering around the house for several days searching for "something," but he could not say what he was looking for, and in fact did not seem to know. In a session during this period I saw Peter jumping wildly on his bed and saw him move his hand furtively to his penis. His mother then told me privately that the night before Peter had been snuggling close to her at bedtime and had suddenly taken her hand and put it on his penis. She had withdrawn her hand and said, "But you may put your own hand there." Today, as I watched Peter, he was evidently preoccupied with his penis and more than once I saw his hand move to his penis and move away. When I made a neutral comment to Peter on his wish to touch his penis—as a way of opening up the topic for discussion— he suddenly switched to "The hat! I want the little hat!" His mother asked whether it would help if she brought in one of the "falsies" and I agreed. When Peter was given "the little hat" he became completely preoccupied with it, brought it to his mouth, and explored it manually.

Clearly, the anatomy lesson had added to Peter's confusion. He behaved toward "the little hats" as if they were breasts and could be removed. And there was the strong suggestion in his switch from penis to little hats that he believed that a penis could be removed in similar fashion. Since his exploration of his mother's body in the bathroom had already confirmed for him that she did not have a penis, he could only conclude that a penis, too, was portable and removable. And when we add to this his most prominent symptom at this time, the retention of his stool, it seemed most probable that fear of loss of a body part was operating in all these spheres.

In this session Peter and I talked a little about "the little hats." I told him that the little hats were something that mommy wore inside her clothes. The little hats were not breasts. Mommy had breasts and all ladies had breasts. They belonged to a mommy and stayed right on her. He listened to me without comment. At the end of the session his hand moved to his penis once again and then he said enigmatically, "The ski is all gone." I asked him what a "ski" was and he did not answer. But in Peter's magic language I knew that he sometimes substituted one word for another when he needed to disguise a painful thought or memory.

For several weeks Peter's concerns with penis-no penis, loss, and breaking became repetitive themes. He began a chant in his hours with me. "Where's your penis, Where's your penis, Where's your penis?" I used the opportunity to clarify his mother's earlier statements in the bathroom and told him that boys and girls and men and women were made differently. Peter was a boy, made just like Daddy. Margaret (older sister) was a girl, just like Mommy. After a while a new chant made an appearance, "I am a she. I am a he. I am a he. I am a she."

Stool retention continued off and on during this period, but there was no opportunity to make a meaningful connection between the fear of loss of his stool and fears regarding his own penis. Then in one session I arrived to find Peter disturbed and ambivalent toward me. He first reached out for my hand and stroked it softly, then began to bite it. Suddenly, most urgently, he asked, "Where is Laura? Where is Laura?" (the dead cousin). And scarcely waiting for an answer he began a recital of the names of absent or long-forgotten people. Then again in an urgent voice, he began to inquire about lost and broken phonograph records. "Where is Hokey Pokey? Where is Genie?" "Where are they, Peter?" "Broken. All gone. Broken." I said, "Records can be broken. But people can't be broken." As I said this Peter's hand went swiftly to his penis. I said, "Peter can't be broken. A penis can't be broken." He seemed not to take this in.

But now for many sessions the theme of "broken" appeared as a refrain. In the session following the one reported above, Peter began by uttering the single word "tooth" and showed me the place where he had lost a tooth several weeks ago. We talked about the tooth, and how another would grow. I spent a great deal of time in this session telling him how a nose could not go away, a finger could not go away, etc. They belonged to Peter. "Laura?" he said plaintively. "Where is Laura?" (Laura, of course, belonged to the category of objects which go away and cannot be restored.) Once more we talked about Laura. At the end of the hour he said, again with some urgency, "Where is the penis?" and made a tentative reaching gesture toward me. Again I told him that I knew he had found that Mommy and ladies do not have a penis and that it was very hard for him to figure out. Again I gave the explanations, and again I said explicitly that nobody could make a penis "all gone"; Peter's penis would always stay with him.

For many weeks the anxiety about "broken" and "all gone" was dealt with in ways very similar to those I have described. I was present on one occasion, during a period of stool retention, when Peter asked to go to the toilet and I could see the anxiety on his face. I used the occasion to make a connection with his fear of losing his penis and again gave reassurances. His mother reported that soon after I left that day he asked to go to the toilet again and had a bowel movement. There were to be a number of occasions thereafter when I was able to handle the stool-retention problem through such interpretations. However, I should mention that this problem was very complex; a number of other motives were uncovered before the problem finally cleared up.

The inadequacies of Peter's speech were serious handicaps to an investigation of his blind-child's version of castration anxiety. It was impossible, of course, to get details of his fantasies or to get him to elaborate his cryptic comments. I employed an approach which is very different from child analysis. I had to use "educational" techniques to deal with his body concerns, to promote, if possible, the integration of each piece of knowledge into a stable image.

There were other observations of anxiety in connection with the penis. Though the meaning of these observations remains obscure, I believe they should be reported. On several occasions both his mother and I saw that Peter was manifestly anxious when he had an erection. Erections typically occurred while he was straining for a bowel movement or when he was about to void. The moment the erection appeared, he became frozen and immobilized. At these times he would never touch his penis, nor did he do so when erections appeared spontaneously on other occasions. It seemed to me that he then avoided touching his penis.

He refused to hold his penis under any circumstances when he was voiding. For long periods during the 2½ years that I knew Peter he avoided handling it. In the early days of treatment I discerned some remembered prohibitions—the "Uh! Uh! Uh!" which Peter chanted in an alien warning voice when he chanced to touch his penis. When this and similar material was discussed with Peter, he would take a more relaxed attitude toward touching his penis, but before long the avoidance was manifest again. After many months of observations I was unable to come up with a better explanation than that offered by his manifest anxiety in connection with erections. Was the experience of erection and detumescence an equivalent of loss or "castration," the "disappearance" of the penis? Was the loss of sensation that accompanies detumescence a disturbance to this deviant child for whom strong sensations were an affirmation of self? I do not know. Occasionally, when I talked with Peter about how sometimes his penis got big and sometimes quite small, I had the impression from his response that I was on the right track, but I never received any positive confirmation from him or further material that permitted investigation. Perhaps the only justification for including this in the record is the possibility that such a detail may be useful to another investigator.

Grief, Pain

When I now describe and bring together data relating to the affective disturbance in Peter, it is with some uncertainty and incompleteness of observations.

When I first became acquainted with Peter, he was incapable of expressing grief. If he reacted at all to loss or danger of loss, it was through the convulsive heaving of shoulders and distortion of face which I described earlier in the hide-and-seek game. We do not think that such behavior is typical of deviant blind children.

The measures by which Peter warded off grief, however, were similar to those that he employed in warding off any strong undesirable or unpleasurable stimulus, external or internal as judged by the observer. His reaction to pain may be considered a model. (And here, incidentally, we do have parallels with other deviant blind children and autistic children in general.) Initially, Peter showed no reaction to pain. When he injured himself, even badly, he did not cry out, did not complain, but typically reverted to autistic mannerisms. Once when he burned himself severely his mother, who was with him in the kitchen, had had no way of telling that he had done so and discovered it only later on. Once when he had the flu we inferred that he had severe stomach pains and internal distress from the way he waved his hands in a gesture of warding off an external bothersome stimulus. More typical, however, was his attempt to ward off the perception of the painful stimulus—a device he adopted with regard to pain and a variety of other stimuli originating within or without.

I have already reported that he would ward off an aggressive impulse by means of repetitive speech or nonsense words. He employed identical mechanisms in the warding off of grief. His mother and I would sometimes see him with shoulders heaving and the tic-like grimacing of the mouth. We would encourage him to cry, tell him it was all right to cry, that all boys cried sometimes. And sometimes we would see the muscles of his face reacting to our words, giving us the impression that he was on the verge of tears, but suddenly he would come forth with a repetitious phrase like, "I want a triangle cracker, I want a triangle cracker, I want a triangle cracker" and would repeat this sometimes for as long as 15 minutes.

We cannot attribute to this primitive personality anything like repression. In my notes I employed the provisional term "blocking of affect," but finally discarded this, too, as not being descriptive. My observations of Peter suggested that his ego at that time was incapable of forming countercathexis. What I saw could best be described as simple shifts-of-attention cathexis, a withdrawal of cathexis from a painful perception and an indiscriminate shift to another perception. The repetition of such a phrase as "I want a triangle cracker" showed that the original impulse was still active while the goal had shifted. When the impulse had exhausted itself the repetitious phrase would cease. I could bring about a complete repetition of the whole sequence if, after Peter became quiet, I should say, "I still think that you want to cry." What I have described here, then, is a very primitive mechanism for warding off a disturbing stimulus. Such shifts in cathexis are not, properly speaking, "displacements," for in displacement the original impulse would break through since only the goal is changed. What we see in Peter is something close to what we mean in laymen's language by the term "distractions." It is what the patient does in the dentist chair when he counts the squares on the ceiling to take his mind off the drilling.

Very early in treatment, my efforts to help Peter express his grief were rewarded by several episodes in which grief broke through. This was during a period in which Peter expressed his fear that he was bad and would be sent away (to the institution). Then, following a real but brief separation from his parents when they took a holiday over a weekend, these favorable signs disappeared and it was actually many months before he could again express grief with genuine emotion. When grief emerged once again it took the form of a series of emotional storms all in connection with his fear that his mother would go away and be "all gone." One of these episodes appeared during one of my sessions with him; the others took place with his parents at times of leave-taking.

In this chapter, I shall not go into the details but only comment on a significant change which occurred in Peter when he once more acquired the ability to express grief. For the first time he began to react to physical pain. There were several episodes in which he cried after an injury. He even acquired the word "hurts" and was able to say on several occasions when he was constipated and could not expel his stool, "It hurts! It hurts!"

Differentiation, Separateness

While in the 2½ years of treatment a slow progress toward separateness and a sense of identity could be observed, the boundaries between "me" and "other" remained unstable and were easily blurred or temporarily lost. As late as the third year of treatment, Peter would occasionally lapse into states of confusion between his body and his mother's body. For example, when he and his mother were swimming in a pool, she said, "Peter, come here and pour some water on my feet." Peter came over and carefully poured water over his own feet.

The use of "I," which appeared to have stability at the end of the first year of treatment, became a kind of barometer for the whole period I knew Peter. "I" could disappear from his vocabulary for days or even weeks, and self-reference in the third person would come back. After a while, "I" would emerge once again, stay with us for weeks, and mysteriously disappear once again. At such times I studied my notes for cues regarding the conditions under which "I" became lost or reemerged. At first I thought I saw patterns related to separation. Following the parents' short holidays there was nearly always some regression accompanied by loss of "I." But after I had accumulated more observations, I saw that the loss of "I" occurred just as frequently when no separation had taken place. At the end of the second year of treatment I could trace another pattern that I had missed throughout. "I" disappeared just as frequently immediately following a period of relatively good integration and functioning, often accompanied by healthy strides in the direction of independence!

I saw this most clearly toward the end of the second year of treatment. We had made good progress in reducing the anxieties in connection with separation and mother. Bowel and bladder control were good, and Peter was now dry at night for the first time in his life. He was often in good contact with me and could now even put into words some of the things he was afraid of. "What are you afraid of, Peter?" "I'm afraid of Mommy" (i.e., I'm afraid *about* Mommy"). "What woke you up last night, Peter?" "I had a dream." "Tell me a story about the dream." "The garage was all gone." (On the dream day the garage had been torn down in order to enlarge the garden.)

Peter now had a new awareness of states of waking and sleeping. At the same time he showed reluctance to go to sleep. Often Peter was wakeful until 12:00 or 1:00 in the morning, making frequent requests for food or soft drinks or playing with his phonograph. In part, the reluctance to go to sleep may have been the warding off of a disturbing dream. Moreover, since being awake now brought pleasure and satisfactions to Peter, the wish to prolong contact with his family must have been another motive.

But there was also something else. Peter had a favorite shell which he now took to bed with him; when he awakened at night and could not find it, he was greatly disturbed until it was restored to him. The shell, like the transitional objects of children in their second year, appeared to symbolize the absent mother and also affirmed his own identity, a substantial something that could be clutched in the hand when the insubstantial self feelings dissolved in sleep. From this and a number of small details I inferred that one of the motives in the reluctance to go to sleep was the fear of loss of identity. I suggested that at such times his mother tell him stories about how Peter goes to sleep but doesn't lose Peter. He's always there. And when he wakes up he is still Peter, and he will find Mommy and Daddy and everyone waiting for him. These little stories seemed to help him go to sleep.

With all these small signs of an emerging sense of identity, the use of "I" appeared to have more stability for a time. Then new anxieties appeared. Suddenly in the midst of play in the garden, with mother and me present, he would stop, go indoors, and climb the stairs to his room. When we followed him we could see his tremendous relief at entering his own room. Typically he would then go to his bed, cover himself up, ask for his favorite shell, and lie there in complete self-absorption. In a very rapid development, he now became reluctant to leave his room and would have been content to stay there all day if we had not encouraged him to come down for meals or go for walks. This behavior was not connected with fear of loss of mother, because at these times his mother was usually present and he knew it. It seemed rather to be associated with an urgent need to establish the connections with a base, the room which affirmed his own unstable core of identity. And during this period "I" was lost again, his contact with his mother and me was poor, and there was regression in eating and toilet habits. But after a period of weeks the anxieties diminished and he climbed back to a level of integration that was fairly close to the one preceding the regression.

It was during this period that I began to see the pattern I had missed. There was no apparent external reason for the regression. It struck me that each time Peter had achieved a new level of integration around "I" and separateness, there were fresh anxieties and regressions which I was helpless to prevent. It was as if the achievement of separateness, of aloneness, was in itself a state of danger that promoted regression to the tension-free state of non-differentiation.

Termination

Peter's treatment was terminated after 2½ years, when he was eleven years old. While his overall functioning was greatly improved, the limits of therapeutic possibility seemed to have been reached. Now, too, an early puberty was adding its own complications to the picture of this unstable personality organization. Growth of pubic hair and changes in the size of the genitals had been noticeable already at the age of ten. As puberty advanced we saw increased excitement and indiscriminate discharge through gross body activities, such as jumping on his bed with wild hilarity and a sustained erection until he reached exhaustion. This behavior was not, strictly speaking, new, but now appeared more frequently and with a marked increase in excitement. Although the family had already made extraordinary sacrifices in accommodating itself to Peter's unique demands, we could foresee the difficulties ahead for both. I therefore began to prepare the parents for the possibility of institutional care for Peter and to help them accept the fact that we had gone as far as we could in treatment in the home.

Peter

Summary

The clinical picture of Peter and that of other blind children with arrested ego development shows certain resemblances to the picture of autism in sighted children, but there are significant differences as well. We are struck by the fact that these deviant blind children show a picture of uniform developmental arrest. The mouth has remained the center of this primitive personality; perception is largely mouth-centered; and those qualities that we call "aggressive" and "erotic" remain mouth-centered and appear to be undifferentiated. Tactile perception is minimal; in fact, the hand appears to have no independence from the mouth. These characteristics of the blind deviant child have no parallel among sighted autistic children.

The unique characteristics of the blind deviant group and the uniformities encountered in the clinical picture must be linked to the common defect in the group—blindness from birth. We must assume that during critical phases of ego formation the blind infant is faced with unique problems of adaptation which have led, in these cases, to adaptive failure.

Each of these deviant blind children had a mother who felt estranged from her blind baby, who could not establish a "dialogue" (Spitz's [1963] term), and who became in this way one of the tragic determinants in the child's adaptive incapacity. But we must give equal attention in studies such as these to the adaptive problems presented by blindness itself. When we consider our present knowledge of the role of vision in ego formation, the substitutions and circuitous routes required of the blind infant must be regarded as adaptive feats.

The observations of Peter and other deviant blind children open up two lines of inquiry: (1) blindness as a communications barrier between mother and infant with extraordinary demands upon mother's own adaptive capacity; (2) blindness as an impediment during critical phases of ego formation with extraordinary demands upon an infant's adaptive capacity. (The two problems are, of course, interdependent.)

(1)   Many of the mothers of the deviant blind children, like Peter's mother, were adequate or more than adequate mothers in rearing their other children. While we may suppose that in each of these mothers the blind baby struck old wounds in personality, we need to be attentive to blindness itself as a barrier in the establishment of the mother-child dialogue. Before the diagnosis of blindness was made (usually around five or six months among the retrolental fibroplasia cases) the mother was already aware that this baby did not respond in expected ways. He was strangely uninterested in his surroundings; the unseeing eyes made the face seem blank and remote. When the mother sought contact with him through her eyes the child's eyes did not meet hers—which feels curiously like a rebuff if you do not know that the baby is blind. The appearance of the mother's face did not cause the baby to smile. All those ways in which the eyes unite human partners were denied to this mother and baby.

It seems reasonable to suppose that when these early signals between mother and child failed, the dialogue between them became halting and uncertain. A mother might still carry on a tactile and auditory dialogue with the baby whose eyes never met hers, and some mothers succeeded in this even before the diagnosis of blindness was made. (In those cases where the diagnosis of blindness was made soon after birth, as in the case of the infant, Toni, the mother could more easily exploit the nonvisual repertory that was open to her.) But many of the mothers of the deviant blind children seemed unable to find some bridge of communication, and the estrangement of mother and child began in the early months. When the diagnosis of blindness was made, depression and a sense of hopelessness completed the estrangement for some mothers.

While it is true that the mothering of the deviant blind babies was deficient, the successful mothering of a totally blind infant requires extraordinary qualities indeed. And while the developing ego of the sighted infant is insured when the mother is unexceptional or even less than adequate, the blind infant's ego development is imperiled when his mother does not have adaptive capacities which are exceptional.

Omwake and Solnit (1961), in discussing the case of Ann, point out that "the absence of a visual representation of the mother may seriously impair the capacity to form a useful memory of the mother if the mother is unable to provide other modes of libidinally cathected perceptual experiences, especially touching, to compensate for the absence of the visual experiences."

While the histories of Peter and other deviant blind children show marked deficiencies in the earliest ties with mother, other deviant blind children achieve a demonstrable human tie by the seventh or eighth month which is then followed by a developmental impasse during the crucial nine-to-eighteen-month period. Typically, the child regresses, reverts to passive postures, exhibits autistic behavior, and remains frozen on the level of mouth-centeredness and nondifferentiation. Clearly there are a number of points in the process of ego formation where blindness creates hazards.

(2) The specific ways in which blindness may impede the process of ego formation can be inferred from the characteristics of the blind children with arrested development.

Perception remained mouth-centered. The hand appeared to have no autonomy from the mouth, and tactile discrimination was minimal. The mouth, as a strongly endowed instinctual zone, is ill-adapted for the achievement of conflict-free perception. The adaptive substitution of the hand as a primary organ of perception is an indispensable step in the development of the blind child. However, our study of the development of Toni, a healthy blind infant, shows that hand autonomy evolved very slowly during the first two years and that the hand did not achieve primacy over the mouth as a perceptual organ until twenty months of age. Clearly, since vision mediates adaptive hand behavior in the sighted infant, the adaptive use of the hand as a primary organ of perception requires the blind infant to make an elaborate detour, even under the most favorable circumstances. Under less favorable circumstances, as in the case of Peter and other deviant blind children, there may be no incentives for this complex adaptive task. Perception remains mouth-centered, and this adaptive failure has a morbid significance for the future of these children. When the mouth remains the primary organ of perception the distinctions between "inner" and "outer," "self" and "not self" will not emerge. Perceptual experience is restricted to a narrow range of objects—those that stimulate the mouth in some preferred way. The qualities of objects cannot be known. The failure to achieve hand autonomy was one of the crucial factors responsible for maintaining these personalities on the level of nondifferentiation.

Those qualities that we call "erotic" or "aggressive" remained mouth-centered and were in fact not differentiated. The biting and oral-incorporative behavior of the mouth in relation to human and nonhuman "objects" had, as its corollary, a hand behavior in which scratching, clawing, and pinching were employed in a frenzied seizing and holding of human objects. In the case of Peter, we saw that this behavior was not intentionally aggressive; the hand had not freed itself of the oral mode, and oral-incorporative characteristics of the mouth had been transferred to the hand.

There was a striking failure to employ the skeletal muscles for the discharge of aggression. Dorothy Burlingham (1961) reported that nondeviant blind children show an inhibition in the expression of aggression, but we cannot suggest parallels here because of the great difference in ego organization between the children studied by her and the deviant blind children. That which is clearly "inhibition" in Burlingham's group actually appears to be a developmental failure in our New Orleans group. In the case of Peter, for example, we saw inhibitions in expression of aggression only after he had made considerable progress and after aggression had become linked to specific intentions.

Peter affords an extraordinary insight into the process of differentiation of aggression which may have implications for gen-

Peter

eral studies of early ego development. The work with Peter demonstrated that as opportunities for motor discharge were provided (throwing, large muscle activity), the biting-pinching-scratching behavior receded, and patterns that were recognizably "aggressive" emerged from the undifferentiated behavior of the mouth and hand which had previously not been intentionally aggressive.

A significant delay in the achievement of independent locomotion was reported in nearly all of our deviant blind cases. Many of these children did not crawl at all and most of them did not achieve independent walking until the age of three, four, or later. We have mentioned that for all blind children independent walking is a late achievement by the standards of the sighted child. In our study of the blind infant, Toni, we found that the delay in creeping was closely linked with the absence of an external stimulus usually provided by vision. Nonvisual stimuli did not provide the same incentives for reaching and, by extension, crawling. The healthy blind infant with good adaptive capacity and very good mothering found the route to these later motor achievements by means of a detour which we have described.

Our deviant blind children were immobile during the first three or four years of life. There may be a close connection between the failure to discharge aggression through the skeletal musculature and the inactivation of the apparatus during a crucial period in development. When independent locomotion was finally achieved, a critical period in ego formation and drive differentiation was lost, and it may no longer have been possible for the components of this process to lock in and produce new patterns.

The delayed locomotion may be another factor in maintaining the personality on the level of nondifferentiation. Until the blind child achieves independence in locomotion, he cannot fully experience separateness. Nor can he, in the absence of vision, construct a world of objects until he has made physical contact by means of his independent locomotion.

The failure to acquire an object concept was demonstrable in the case of Peter and other deviant blind children. The concept of an object that exists independently of the field of perception is achieved among sighted children by means of a visual construction of its displacements in space. In our earlier discussion we described the unique adaptive problems presented to the blind child in making such a construction on the basis of nonvisual information. This is another of the adaptive feats beyond the capacity of the deviant blind child and another of the factors that maintained the personality on the level of nondifferentiation.

Chapter IV

SELMA FRAIBERG

The Ann Arbor Study: The Questions and the Methods

IN 1963 I moved from New Orleans and came to the University of Michigan. David Freedman also moved shortly afterwards to Baylor University. Since then, each of us, following his and her own special interests, has continued research in the area of sensory deficits.

In Ann Arbor, I received support and funds from my department to continue the studies in the development of blind infants. Two years later we received a grant from the National Institutes of Child Health and Development to expand these studies. From this point on we were in a position to study the development of blind babies on a larger scale.

The questions that had brought us to the studies of Toni and Peter generated still more questions and made it apparent that further investigations were necessary. These were carried out at the University of Michigan between 1963 and 1973. As answers emerged from the Ann Arbor studies, the earliest hope of the New Orleans studies was fulfilled: when we identified the blind infant's unique adaptive problems in the sensorimotor period, we were able to translate our research findings into a program of education and rehabilitation for infants and young children blind from birth.

Essentially, these questions were at the center of a vast territory which was under intensive exploration in psychoanalysis and other psychologies. The concept "ego" in psychoanalysis embraces not only the sense of self and the executive and cognitive functions of personality but also the regulation of drives and appetites and the capacity to form enduring human ties. In the most concise terms, the ego is the agency of adaptation.

In any consideration of the ego's adaptive functions we assume intactness of biological systems and a human environment that provides at least minimal conditions for adaptive functioning in the human infant. The systems that serve perception, motility and vocalization play a primary role in the earliest adaptive behavior of the infant (Hartmann 1939). Long before we can speak of an ego in the sense of personality organization we can speak of adaptation on a sensorimotor level. As an ego, properly speaking, emerges from an undifferentiated state these systems remain central in its organization, and in a certain sense, as Hartmann points out, they constitute at birth the rudiments of the ego.

On the environmental side we have compelling evidence that certain minimal conditions in nurture must be provided during the early formative period of ego development in order to insure adaptive capacity in the infant and to bring about ego organization. From the studies of infants reared in institutions and pathological homes we have learned that the deprivation of human partners and human love will result in marked impairment of adaptive capacity and the self-regulatory functions of the ego. In cases of the most extreme deprivations there will be developmental arrest and actual deterioration of functioning regardless of the constitutional adequacy of these children at birth.

The study of infants with sensory or motor deficits can tell us another part of the story. In the case of the blind infant we are enabled to study the process of early ego development when one of the systems that serves the organization of experience is absent. The study of the consequences of this deficit should also tell us, of course, about the function of vision in the development of intact infants.

Questions from the New Orleans Study

Toni and Peter had, in effect, provided a contrast study in the adaptive problems posed by blindness from birth.

Toni had found the adaptive route, but we now understood that this was a perilous route for a blind infant even under the most favorable circumstances. Even with a very good and experienced mother (and in addition our help to the mother) we had seen that blindness was an impediment to crucial areas of ego formation. The adaptive substitution of the ear for the eye was slow to emerge. The coordination of ear and hand appeared only late in the first year. Locomotion was markedly delayed. Moments of solitude caused this otherwise healthy blind baby to withdraw into self-stimulating behaviors. The sense of "something out there," which gives the earliest experience of the self and other, and later the constitution of a self and an object world, was slow to emerge in the blind infant. Blindness reduced Toni to helplessness before danger, as we saw in the instances of pathological sleep. Yet, having found the route, the intact systems were consolidated in the second and third years of life, and we had good reason to believe that the ego organization which emerged had stability along with the promise of future stability.

From the retrospective history of Peter and from the clinical picture when we first saw him at nine years, we could construct a developmental story during the first eighteen months that resembled Toni's in certain respects.

For both children, blindness had been an impediment to the

coordination of ear and hand, in reaching for and attaining an object "out there." But Toni found the adaptive solution at ten months of age; Peter, when I first knew him, did not yet search for a sound object that was dropped or was removed from his hand. For both children, there had been protracted delays in locomotion, in creeping and walking. But Toni found mobility and was walking independently at eighteen months; Peter was not yet walking independently at nine years. For both children, there were self-stimulating behaviors in the first year, which testified, we thought, to the poverty of exogenous stimuli in the world of the blind infant. But Toni, when she found mobility and was lured by exteroceptive experience, relinquished her stereotyped postures; Peter had an extensive repertoire of such postures at nine years. Both children, finally, faced the unique problems for a blind child of constructing a world of objects in which he himself is an object. For Toni there were solutions. At the time of this writing (1973) Toni is eleven years old, a healthy, active child, performing adequately in school and presenting no extraordinary problems. There is no evidence of deviant ego development. For Peter, the constitution of a self and an object world were never accomplished with certainty.

At one point in the New Orleans study many interested colleagues offered their own explanations. Clearly, some of our colleagues said, one child, Toni, was healthy and, except for blindness, otherwise intact. The other child, Peter, must have suffered irretrievable brain damage. It was difficult to argue against this explanation. Yet, Dr. Freedman's own neurological examination and study of Peter did not link Peter's autism with neurological impairment. Since there was already mounting evidence from the study of sighted children that severe and pervasive sensory deprivation in infancy was *one* etiology for autism, we chose to keep open the alternative hypothesis: that the prevalence of autism in children blind from birth may, in certain cases, be related to primary and secondary forms of sensory deprivation in which blindness has a reciprocal effect upon other systems and upon the human partners who are themselves a primary source of sense experience.

More than 10 years later, I am very glad that we kept the hypothesis open. We have known blind babies and young children in the Child Development Project guidance program who were clearly autistic and who were brought to normal functioning through our program.

Other colleagues who examined the cases of Toni and Peter with us considered that the differences in developmental outcome must be attributed to differences in mothering of the two infants. Toni's mother was "a very good mother," "very intuitive." Peter's mother, these colleagues argued, appeared to be "not intuitive," had been depressed after Peter's birth, and had given over much of his care to others. Yet this explanation did not admit many ambiguities which appeared to us as the co-therapists for mother and child.

First of all, Peter's mother had reared two older children, bright, vivacious youngsters who showed no sign of personality disturbance. Her intuitive capacities were certainly adequate or superior in the mothering of these sighted children. What had happened to this intuitive capacity when the blind baby was born? It would be easy to say that depression and guilt or revulsion at blindness had stifled this intuition, but was there something else? I had already discovered something in myself during the work with Toni. I was not the mother of a blind baby, I did not suffer with depression or revulsion against blindness, but my "intuitiveness" seemed considerably diminished when I was with the blind baby. I felt strangely cut off at times. I was not sure what Toni "wanted." What had happened to my intuitiveness? What, in fact, was "intuition"? It was a problem that I was to explore later. (It is examined at some length in Chapter V.)

The complexities of human object relations in early ego development were given new dimensions for us through the study of these two children. The dialogic aspects of the mother-child relationship were being studied in a number of investigations of sighted children during the early sixties. To a very large extent this was a dialogue in which visual signals between partners were exchanged. When the signs are obliterated through the blindness of the baby, what happens to the discourse between child and mother? Between mother and child? In what ways might blindness become an impediment to the development of human attachments? And if the pathways to human attachments are not found, as in Peter's case, the essential conditions for ego formation will be lacking.

There were important theoretical issues involved as well. Since everything we knew about human object relations at that period was predicated upon the existence of intact biological systems, and vision was preeminently the organizer of experience, the study of blind infants could inform us very largely about the function of other sense modalities in the development of human attachments.

Toni, whose human attachments followed a course that closely paralleled that of sighted children, provoked the most difficult questions of all. Under the most favorable circumstances, with a devoted and experienced mother, there were developmental roadblocks throughout the first two years which spoke eloquently for the visual deficit. If we examine the roadblocks and the detours, we see that adaptive hand behavior and locomotion were most severely affected.

The implications of these questions for a study of ego development were very large. Until I began to study the blind child, I had not seriously reflected upon the functions of adaptive hand behavior and locomotion in the constitution of the ego. These were the "givens" in personality, unfolding silently, I thought, in a biologically ordained sequence. But clearly, the blind children were telling us that in the absence of vision the motor patterns for reaching and attaining an object, and for creeping and walking, are impeded, and until an external stimulus provides a lure, the motor pattern does not emerge. And since the blind child's hand and his ear and his own mobility must give him the sense of self and other, of "I" and an objective world, the impediments to the coordination of ear and motor systems become impediments to the constitution of an ego.

It was not blindness alone that imperiled the child, I began to see, but the effects of a visual deficit upon all other modalities which must serve adaptation. Vision normally serves the coordination of all systems; it is the central agency in sensorimotor adaptation, the synthesizer of all experience. Toni and other healthy blind children had informed us that under favorable circumstances, the intact systems can be united to bring about a coherent sensorimotor organization and a coherent ego, but the adaptive route followed an order and a timetable which differed markedly from that of the sighted child.

Toni was one child; her story had much to tell us. But we could not know whether the idiosyncrasies in Toni's developmental history were her own or whether they were common to the population of infants blind from birth. To fairly examine the unique adaptive problems of the blind infant we would need a number of children, blind from birth but otherwise intact, with a wide spread in socioeconomic background and a range of family styles in child rearing. All this became possible when the study was continued at the University of Michigan in 1963.

The Questions and Problems of Research Design

The research plan which I will describe later in this chapter emerged from the questions themselves.

CRITERIA FOR SELECTION OF BABIES

In order to insure the integrity of the study as an examination of the effects of blindness on ego development, we would need a carefully selected group of infants blind from birth, babies who were intact in all other systems and who were admitted to the program as early as possible in the first year of life. Regular and frequent medical examinations would inform us of any change in the child's status which would affect his inclusion in the research sample. (For children who were found to be ineligible for the research sample we felt that we must be able to offer clinical services, so that no baby and his family would suffer in the event that the child did not meet our research criteria.)

THE AREAS OF STUDY

(1) In what ways does the blindness of an infant affect, (a) the dialogic aspects of the infant-mother relationship, (b) the sequential development of human attachments in the infant which leads to focused relationships?

(2) How does blindness affect the course of adaptive hand behavior leading to the coordination of ear and hand for intentional reach and grasping and leading to primacy of the hand as a perceptual organ?

(3) How does blindness affect the sequential unfolding of postural and locomotor achievements in the sensorimotor period?

(4) In what ways does blindness affect the acquisition of language?

(5) How does the blind child acquire the sense of a "self" and an object world; how does he construct a world of objects which have "permanence" in Piaget's term; i.e., objects which exist independently of his perception of them?

METHODOLOGICAL CONSIDERATIONS

The questions which were stated at the outset raised some formidable problems in the design of the research.

We can already see that the problems we had isolated for study have reciprocal and interlocking relationships throughout the course of development. Human attachments, the differentiation of a self and an outer world, prehension, gross motor development, and language cannot be isolated as separate studies unless we first know the relationships which exist among these developmental schemas. In the case of the sighted baby we know a fair amount, which means that if we isolate areas for study we are working within a known framework. But if we are beginning the investigation of a previously uncharted territory, such as the psychological development of a blind infant, we cannot assume from the start that the relationships among these sectors of development will be the same if vision is not available to the developing child. This means that we are practically obliged to conduct a systematic primary study of every sector of development in the blind infant in order to find the relationships which exist among them.

The problem of design was further complicated by the fact that in 1963 a number of problems which were at the center of our investigation had not yet been examined in the sighted infant population, or were just beginning to appear in the literature. In the crucial area of human attachments, empirical data for normal infants were just emerging from the studies of Spitz, Bowlby, Benjamin, Ainsworth, Schaffer, Wolff and Décarie. Normative data for the emergence of such indicators as differential smiling, stranger reaction, and separation and reunion behaviors were incomplete or did not exist. Where the strength of our study would be, in the *comparison* of the developmental characteristics of blind infants and intact infants, we did not yet have comparative data.

Similarly, in the area of motor development and language, the existing scales (Cattell, Gesell) had long raised questions regarding reliability and standardization, and the Bayley scale, which is now accepted as the standard infant scale, was not published until 1969.

In the area of object permanence we did not yet have standard scales based upon a Piagetian sequence. (Décarie's scale appeared in 1965, the Uzgiris and Hunt scale in 1974, and the Escalona-Corman Albert Einstein Sensorimotor Scales in 1970.)

What we did know in 1963 was that there was work in progress in all of these areas and, if our data collection procedures for the blind infant studies provided a fine net, through detailed and exact description and film documentation, we might acquire the comparative data within a decade. This is what actually occurred, and it would have been easy to predict since a number of us engaged in parallel or contiguous research were in close touch with each other, visiting, sharing preliminary findings, exchanging early drafts of reports and papers.

Then, too, we were not only interested in the eventual comparison of our blind infants and sighted children on a number of dimensions; we wanted to know how the blind baby (and his parents) found the adaptive solutions. This could only be derived from longitudinal study, with closely spaced observational sessions, a method of continuous recording which embraced everything that transpired in the observational sessions, and periodic film documentation.

If we reexamine the central questions in this study we can see that each of them requires its own investigatory method, yet is linked to every other question by the biological coherence underlying a sensorimotor organization and by the reciprocity that is established from birth between the baby and his physiology and the baby and his human environment. I will attempt in the next pages briefly to describe the problems and the methods which were, in a sense, dictated by the problems themselves.

Question (1): In what ways does the blindness of an infant affect the dialogic aspects of the infant-mother relationship and the sequential development of human attachments in the infant which leads to focused relationships?

In the area of human attachments, where the most complicated design problems lay, there was clearly no economical procedure which would lead to the answers we were seeking. Rating scales, for example, which would give us quickly some of the correlates between maternal behavior and infant adaptation would not give us the complex interactional elements which were of primary interest to us.

Hartmann (1939) speaks of "the autonomous functions of the ego" and the "guarantees" for adaptiveness in "an average expectable environment." But if a baby is born with a sensory or motor deficit, the "average expectable environment" has some built-in hazards. The minus on the side of "state of adaptedness" will require plusses on the side of a mother who will have to substitute for the deficit and take over the role of facilitating adaptation where the intact equipment would have virtually guaranteed it. This requires a mother with a high degree of adaptive capacity herself, and while mother love is certainly a great facilitator in responding to an infant's needs, the birth of a defective child can test love cruelly. Even if love passes the test there is no guarantee that love alone will open up all the pathways of development that are imperiled by the defect.

Toni's mother would be rated as "superior": "a very good mother," we would say. When Toni reached nine months and lay for long periods on the floor nuzzling a rug, or when she was condemned for months to the futile navigation of a circle, did the "good mother" become a "poor mother" because her baby's defective equipment led her to an impasse? No, clearly the problem was more complex. Since no one had yet studied the complexities of a mother's relationship to her blind infant we needed to begin at the beginning.

The second part of the question, which is really an examination of the process by which the blind baby attains focused human attachments, posed extraordinary problems for us. For the sighted baby the study of human attachments had by the 1960s advanced to the point where we had identified some of the key indicators and milestones in human attachment (differential and preferential smiling, discrimination of mother and stranger, stranger avoidance)—a small inventory compared to the one we have available in the 1970s—but each of these preferential behaviors was manifest in the sighted child through progressively differentiated visual behaviors. It would be hazardous to assume that the blind baby followed the same course through simple substitutions of other modalities. We could not assume that either the items or the sequence of indicators would be the same for the blind baby as for the sighted baby.

Method: The blind baby and his mother would need to teach *us* how they formed their bonds.

We would need to observe and record in a detailed descriptive narrative everything that could be observed by senior investigators in the communications between the mother and her blind infant. We would need to employ film documentation at regular and frequent intervals to examine the subtle, fleeting registrations and exchanges which our eyes might not discern unaided. We would need to devise a method which would give us uniformity in data collection for comparison within the group. We would need to devise a system of coding for retrieval of all relevant items from protocols and films.

Analysis of protocols and films in team meetings should lead us finally to see how the blind baby's signals were read (or not read) by the mother, what information the baby used when he discriminated his mother from others, and how he expressed preference and valuation of his mother and others. We would expect to learn how the mother provided experiences for the baby that substituted for visual experience, how the mother helped her baby find the adaptive solutions when blindness created roadblocks in development. When we ourselves provided information or educational guidance for mother and baby, our record must describe the intervention exactly, so that intervention as a variable could be assessed.

Our findings are discussed in Chapters V and VI.

Question (2): How does blindness affect the course of adaptive hand behavior leading to the coordination of ear and hand for intentional reach and grasping and leading to the primacy of the hand as a perceptual organ?

We already know that Toni did not demonstrate directional reach for an object on sound cue until ten months of age. We cannot generalize this finding from one case to the blind infant population, but one case can tell us that the substitution of sound for vision is not "guaranteed" in the same way that vision guarantees that the thing "out there" can be attained through reaching and grasping at five months.

If we are only interested in the characteristics of prehension in the blind child there are a number of valid approaches to the problem. We can, for example, conduct a testing program for all blind infants in the state of Michigan at quarterly intervals in the first year. We would then obtain information on the characteristics of prehension in blind infants in each quarter of the first year and the age range for all blind infants in the attainment of an object on sound cue. This would be a very interesting and useful study in itself. But it could not give us the answers to the questions we were seeking.

In our study of ego formation in the blind infant we wanted to know how the hand serves ego development. If there is an extraordinary problem in the adaptive substitution of sound for vision, this will have effects not only in prehension, but in contiguous and/or reciprocal lines of development. For all babies, the hand becomes one of the executive organs of the emerging ego, the bridge between the body self and the external world, the organ that serves intentionality and permits the baby to act upon his world. In the case of the blind baby, the hand must serve all these functions and must also serve as a primary perceptual organ. We needed to know the adaptive process as well as the adaptive solution.

In designing this aspect of the research I was helped by a clinical hunch, a hunch derived from my observations of Peter. When I first knew Peter I was struck by the fact that when he dropped an object from his hands or lost an object he did not search for it. He did not even make a gesture of reach. From these and hundreds of other observations it was very very clear that when he lost contact with an object it "ceased to exist."

Watching Peter, I was struck by the fact that this must be an extraordinary problem for the blind infant. In the absence of vision the baby must learn to track objects on sound alone. How does the blind baby learn that when he does not hear a person or hear a sound object it still exists? How does he build a world of permanent objects? And if he fails in this learning, if he cannot acquire the concept of objects which exist independently of himself and his perception, there will be no differentiation between self and object world; he will be, clinically speaking, autistic—meaning that all phenomena are experienced as part of the body self.

My hunch was that Toni's inability to reach for and attain an object on sound cue until ten months of age might be related to a conceptual problem for a blind infant. In the absence of vision it was possible, I reasoned, that the sound of an object at tactile remove would not connote substantiality or "graspability" until an elementary concept of "permanence" (Piaget stage 4) had emerged.

Method: At twice-monthly intervals we presented problems of retrieval and search to our blind babies. The procedures were very simple. In the first year, for example, we presented sound toys and soundless toys, the child's own toys and interesting toys of our own. We allowed the child to hold them and play with them and then gently removed them from his grasp and placed them within easy reach. We worked out procedures that would tell us clearly how the baby reacted when the toy was experimentally silenced or moved from one place to another, what sensory information he used to discriminate objects and identify them. We also followed the evolution of grasping, mutual fingering, transfer, the coordinate use of hands, unilateral reaching, and thumb-finger opposition. We provided only enough structure in the testing to assure us that we could identify the variables at work.

We recorded all of the testing on 16mm film. We then studied the film on a variable-speed projector at approximately one-third speed, or sometimes frame by frame. While viewing the film at one-third speed with the senior staff present, one of the investigators dictated a narrative record covering every gesture, every motion in fine detail. If there was any disagreement on what was seen we played the sequence over again until we had reached consensus or, if there was no consensus, that fact was recorded. We then had both a film record and a corresponding written document. The film protocol could now be used flexibly for coding and for sorting patterns. The film itself was available for checks and rechecks. (Our results are described in Chapters VII and VIII.)

Question (3): How does blindness affect the sequential unfolding of postural and locomotor achievements in the sensorimotor period?

As an independent study, the area of gross motor development might have occupied us fully as a staff for the next decade. But Toni had already shown us that the adaptive problems in locomotion were inextricably interwoven with all other aspects of development. If we had selected motor development as a single area of study, we would have obtained a map of the developmental route which could be compared with that of sighted children, and we would then have identified through variance the site of an adaptive problem for the blind child and might hypothesize that delays in the blind group at sites (a) (b) (c) and (d) represented the effects of blindness. Our tables would appear as they do in Chapter IX, but we would not know precisely *how* blindness affected the motor adaptive task, and we would not know how the adaptive impasse affected contiguous lines of development. And these were the problems at the center of our study of ego development. In the end, as we will see, the clues to the blind child's delay in locomotion did not emerge from the gross motor study, but from the prehension study! (The interlocking components are described in Chapters VII, VIII, and IX.)

In designing the gross motor study we needed a plan which would place all observations within a context in which reciprocity between motor development and other areas of development could be examined, and we needed fidelity in observation which would permit us to study the subtle as well as the readily observable differences between the course of locomotor development in blind children and sighted children.

Method: For contextual study, observations of gross motor achievements were recorded in the descriptive narrative of each visit. In this way, the possible relationship of a locomotor achievement or a locomotor impasse in development could be examined in relationship to mother-child interaction, adaptive hand behavior, object concept, and language.

For exactness in recording motor patterns, we employed film and film analysis. Some of the patterns were so novel and unexpected that even trained eyes could not assimilate them. At twice-monthly intervals (as in the prehension study) we recorded on 16mm film samples of the baby's gross motor achievements. The film record was studied on a variable-speed projector, following the same methods as those described in the prehension study, using reduced speed and the dictation of a descriptive narrative. The protocol became a flexible instrument for classification and coding, but the film record itself was examined again and again to pick up the subtle differences in the blind child's adaptive program. Finally, in data evaluation, the scoring of a performance, following sighted-child criteria, was derived entirely on the basis of the film record, and credit was given only through staff consensus.

Question (4): In what ways does blindness affect the acquisition of language?

Our language questions embraced a very large territory. We were interested not only in the vocal language, from the earliest utterances through the acquisition of words, but in the vocabulary of signs and signals available to a child without vision. Moreover, since the dialogic aspects of language were certain to be of central interest in this study, each language item needed to be recorded in context with descriptive detail.

None of us was trained in linguistic study. (In 1969 the work in this area was given tremendous impetus by our association with Eric Lenneberg.) The study of language acquisition in the sensorimotor period was, in any case, one of the still underdeveloped areas of linguistics when we began the design of this study.

The standard developmental tests available in 1963, Cattell and Gesell, included language items which provided a coarse screening; e.g., imitates sounds, first words, two-word combinations, etc., but these scales did not satisfy rigorous criteria for standard-ization, and scoring of the language items permitted parent re-ports. Nevertheless, they afforded some objective basis for com-parison of our blind children with a sighted-child population. The Bayley scales were published in 1969 and provided us with reliable measures for our comparative assessment.

Method: For contextual and dialogic aspects of language devel-opment (vocal and non-vocal signs and signals, receptive lan-guage, imitation, words, simple sentences, increasing complexity in vocabulary and syntax) we recorded verbatim all observed signs and utterances as they appeared, and incorporated these in the narrative record of the observational session. When a portion of the observational session was filmed (we used silent film), the observer recorded the child's utterances and the vocal com-munications of mother or other partners, with cues to the film sequence. (An audio recorder which we used for a brief period only gave us vocalizations and dialogues without context, and we fell back upon the written protocol as the better source, for us, of qualitative analysis of language development.)

For data evaluation, every item in the language sector was im-bedded in a context that could tell us which factors elicited or mo-tivated a motor sign or an utterance. As words appeared as referents, the recording allowed us to identify the sources of in-formation available to the blind child in naming a person or ob-ject. As complexity in syntax appeared, the verbatim recording and its context permitted a close analysis of forms and possible variance of forms.

It proved to be a workable method, but I have one regret in re-trospect. We could have obtained quantitative measures through the simple device of time notations and a frequency count. I had not anticipated that there might be differences in quantity of vocalizations between the blind infant and the sighted infant. These showed up impressionistically (and by consensus of our own and independent observers) but could not be supported through objective measures.

For comparison with sighted-child norms, the verbatim records gave us data for matching with sighted-child criteria. By the time we began data evaluation, the Bayley scales were available to us and our bank of data for each child provided items for comparison and matching. (Our findings are reported in Chapters X and XI.)

Question (5): How does the blind child acquire a sense of "self" and object world: how does he construct a world of objects which have permanence, in Piaget's terms, objects which exist independently of his perception of them?

In the design stage I had not anticipated the problems in this area. Following Piaget's methods I wanted the blind baby to teach *us* how he constructed a world of objects. Piaget had employed barriers to vision (screened toys) to observe the ways in which the sighted child learns to account for the existence of an object that has left his field of perception. The child's search for the hidden object in Piaget's study revealed stages in the development of an object concept which culminated at approximately eighteen months in a sustained search for a toy that had undergone successive displacements behind screens. In recovering the toy from its last invisible displacement the child demonstrated a capacity for deduction; i.e., "*it* must be hidden *here*" and, of course, a capacity in mental representation which evokes the image of the toy and its successive displacements even when the child cannot perceive it.

We already knew that adequate and healthy blind children of school age could demonstrate in naturalistic circumstance that they had attained a concept of the permanence of objects. But how, in the absence of vision, does the infant *construct* a world of objects? This must be a central problem for the blind child in the sensorimotor period.

Toni had not demonstrated object permanence (stage 6) in any of our observations up to the age of two and a half. That is, we had no observations, even when Toni was freely mobile, that she conducted a sustained search for a person or a toy when voice or sound did not provide cues for tracking. I could only explain this in one of two ways. Either our observations were not fairly made (the circumstance of the one-hour visit might not have given a large enough time-frame to catch the spontaneous demonstrations) or Toni was indeed delayed in the achievement of object permanence by at least 12 months according to sighted-child standards. The second possibility seemed unreasonable to me. Therefore I was inclined toward the first position, that our observational procedures were not fair to Toni.

This brought me to consider experimental procedures for the study of the evolution of the object concept which, I hoped, would provide optimal conditions for the blind child to demonstrate his patterns of search and give us data for a stage-by-stage comparison of our blind infants with sighted infants on a Piagetian scale. This led us down a path which was highly instructive, from the point of view of the research design. The economical approach, as it turned out, was not the most profitable approach.

Method: To give the blind child optimal conditions for the demonstration of search patterns leading to object permanence we chose to include a small amount of testing in one of the twice-monthly observational sessions. (The testing was easily compatible with the prehension testing and became at a certain point an extension upward of the prehension tests described earlier.) Favorite toys or objects were introduced to the baby in games. Both tactile objects and sound objects were employed.

After "reach on sound" was attained by the blind child, typically in the last trimester of the first year, we experimentally introduced tactile barriers and sound "barriers"; i.e., silencing of the toy, and displacing it within a circumscribed space within easy grasp of the child. (The procedures followed those of Piaget, with the necessary modifications for a blind child.) *

---

* Piaget, who visited our program in 1967, reviewed a filmed test sequence with us and was satisfied that the tasks provided fair equivalence to those employed for sighted children in testing object permanence. Piaget was also in accord with our scoring of Robbie's stage 6 performance at twenty-seven months—a delay, by sighted-child norms, of approximately 12 months.

But the administration of these tests for a blind baby was a formidable and sobering task. For the sighted baby it is the "game" aspect of the testing which leads him to search for the toy that has left his field of perception. The blind child, typically, would pursue the "game" with initial interest and spirit, then show flagging attention when the first trial did not lead to success.

For some blind children, the barrier tests which were presented after the attainment of "reach on sound" (approximately nine months of age) were frustrating. Since we did not wish to strain the baby's tolerance, we chose to discontinue testing at any point where we read the signs of discomfort or frustration, always taking care to restore the "lost" toy to the baby. Ralph Gibson, who did much of the early testing in our program, showed great ingenuity in sustaining the baby's interest, and our most complete protocols resulted from his testing. But, for the majority of our babies, formal testing introduced problems for the baby and tester which led us, finally, to discontinue testing of object permanence as a regular procedure.

The data on object permanence can be retrieved from *naturalistic* observation for all of the babies in our series. For our purposes the spontaneous demonstration of permanence and evocative memory will serve as well as the demonstration elicited through testing. But at the time of this writing we see years of work ahead for the systematic evaluation of these data and finding solutions to the scoring problems that are presented in granting equivalence to a blind and a sighted child's performance.

In the area of *person permanence*, the constitution of the mother as object (Bell 1970), data from naturalistic observations are reported in Chapter V. For *toy permanence*, the constitution of the toy as object (Bell 1970), the prehension studies give us baseline information on stages 3–4 and are discussed in Chapters VI and VII.

NEED FOR A UNIFYING STRUCTURE

From this sketch of the problems and the methods, we can see that each of the areas of the study had its own methodological requirements, yet the questions and the areas themselves were interlocking and indivisible in a study of ego development and adaptation in blind infants. The observational procedures and recording must accommodate the areas studied as well as the reciprocal relations among the areas. For data evaluation we must be able to retrieve items in a longitudinal sequence; we must be able to compare each child with others in the group; we must be able to compare our sample with sighted children on a large number of dimensions.

The central objectives of the study, a study of ego development and adaptation in blind infants, make their own requirements. Developmental process can only be studied longitudinally. The problems, in this unexplored area, must be examined in naturalistic circumstance. The ideal setting for this is the home. The observational schedule must have visits spaced to insure coverage of all items of behavior and the developmental transitions that provide the key to adaptive process. (We chose twice-monthly visits.)

The demands of this study made it imperative that primary responsibility for observation and recording be given *only to senior investigators*. The most serious drawback to using beginners or trainees in psychological observation is one that I can remember with pain but with charity for myself. When I was a beginner in psychological study, I could only see what I was trained to see. When something emerged in my work that did not fit the pattern, my tendency was to screen it out or to try to make it fit. In designing this research I remembered myself very well. There was danger enough, for all of us, in drawing inferences from the behavior of children whose perceptual field was different from our own. If we added to this the danger of "making things fit," our investigation would be imperiled from the start.

If good and useful things emerged from this study, then, it was not solely because we developed a workable research plan on paper. The results depended not on this alone, of course, but on the trained eyes of the observers as well.

The recording methods which were employed derived from clinical recording practices. (It was the method we had used as recorders in the Toni study in New Orleans.) Narrative recording is essential for clinical inference. The flow of events and shifting contexts permit the clinician to see the internal relationships among factors which may be diffused throughout a single observational session. The value given to a single observed event will depend upon antecedent and consequent occurrences. The narrative gives temporal contiguity for qualitative analysis of the data. The narrative will also give, through descriptive detail, items of behavior which can be classified, reduced, and employed for comparisons within the sample and with comparison groups.

The narrative lends itself well to systematic data collection and evaluation of data. It is possible, in naturalistic study, to obtain hundreds of items in a single observational session which are essential for individual and comparative developmental study without imposing a formal structure upon the observational session.

In order to insure uniformity in data collection we devised a schedule which included hundreds of developmental and interactional items in open categories, to be observed and recorded in descriptive detail. (No on-the-spot judgments or ratings needed to be made.) The observers memorized the code schedule, which is not as difficult as it sounds, since in a single observational study only 25 to 50 items might be relevant to a baby's developmental stage. We never brought a code schedule to a visit. With experience, an observer could cover nearly all the relevant items in the course of the one-hour observational session with a minimum of interference with the flow of events.

The narrative record was coded for easy retrieval of items and the record itself became a flexible instrument for longitudinal or cross-section treatment of data.

Film Documentation: We would need generous and unprejudiced film samples of all behaviors in the main areas of study. As investigators in strange territory we needed the absolute fidelity of the film record to check our own observations and reach a consensus of judgment regarding the behaviors recorded. We would need a frame-by-frame analysis of the film record to trace the unique course of motor development in the blind infant. We would need to devise a retrieval system for data recorded on film.*

The Children in the Primary Research Group

Our findings are derived from the studies of 10 babies blind from birth.† Table 1 summarizes the characteristics of this group.

Blind babies who satisfy our restrictive criteria are rare. Even with the resources of a major medical center, our referrals for study averaged only two babies per year. Over the 10-year period a total of 19 children were provisionally brought into the study after initial screening by ophthalmologists, pediatricians, and our staff. Admission to the study, then, was based upon presumed intactness of other systems and evidence at the time of screening that the child was either totally blind or had only minimal light perception. The preliminary screening could not rule out the possibility that damage to other systems would show up in later study or, in the case of the newborn, that some degree of useful vision might be manifest in the course of development.

Our sample of 10 represents the children who satisifed the re-

---

* Further description of our methods is included in the Appendix.

† We have no census information on the incidence of blind births in Michigan, or in the counties that we covered in our referral network. Our state is by no means alone in its failure to obtain compulsory or obligatory registration of cases by physicians. When blindness is identified at birth the circumstances favor registration by the attending physician or nurses. But in the largest number of cases blindness is identified some weeks or months after birth, and central reporting may not follow. At the time of this writing both state and national agencies are at work in developing efficient methods of registration, but there is no way in which we can place our 10-year cumulative sample within a larger population designated as "blind from birth" or within a subgroup of unknown number—"blind from birth, no other handicaps."

TABLE 1
Characteristics of Blind Infant Group
(Child Development Project)

CRITERIA:

Total blindness from birth or only minimal light perception.
No other known handicaps or neurological damage.
Less than one-year-old.
Within fifty miles of our office.

DESCRIPTION:

Sex	5 boys, 5 girls
Age at referral	1 to 11 months (1 to 8 months with correction for prematurity in 3 cases.)
Age last seen	2 to 6 years
Ordinal position in family	only (5), first of 2 (1), first of 3 (1), second of 2 (1), fifth of 5 (1), sixth of 6 (1).
Diagnosis	hypoplasia of optic nerve (3), retrolental fibroplasia (3)—(3 months premature birth), infantile glaucoma (2), ophthalmia neonatorum (1), resorption of vitreous humor (1).
Light perception	2 boys, 2 girls
Social class by father's occupation [a]	managerial (1), college student (2), skilled (2), semi-skilled (3), unskilled (2)

[a] Edwards' Occupational Index

strictive criteria of our investigation *after* extended study.* Eight of the 19 children who were provisionally brought into the sample did not meet the criteria after further study. One child, otherwise eligible, moved to another state within 6 months of the beginning of our study. Of the 8 children who did not meet the criteria, 2 showed evidence of useful vision during the first year of study and 6 showed evidence of central nervous system damage which was confirmed through medical examination.

These children, who were ineligible for the research program, were eligible for our guidance program, and it was possible to continue services without causing pain to families or risk to children who did not qualify for the research sample.

* The group of 10 includes Toni of the New Orleans study.

The Ann Arbor Study

The child's age at time of entry into the study is reflected in the table which shows a range from one month to eleven months (or eight months with correction for prematurity). Ideally, we would have wanted all children to come into the study as soon after birth as possible. In fact, the diagnosis of blindness or suspected blindness was not made in several cases until the middle of the first year. Usually it was the mother, who thought "something was wrong," who initiated an anxious inquiry to a physician or to a hospital. By the time the inquiry led to examination at University Hospital (which serves the entire state) or another hospital in the family's community, or by one of the few pediatric ophthalmologists in major cities, some weeks or months might have transpired before the diagnosis of blindness was made.

We became a resource for psychological study and screening for our own department of ophthalmology and for a number of hospitals and private physicians within a 50-mile radius of Ann Arbor. In our own hospital we were "on call" to the ophthalmology department. Immediately after the diagnosis of blindness was made, the physician, nurse, or social worker could call on us, and a staff member of the Project would arrange a visit to the family and the baby on the same day or within 24 hours.

This means that in nearly every case we met our families soon after the dreaded news had been given. We were there to share the grief of parents, to respond to their questions and their fears, and to offer our experience and our help.

Our parents understood our special interest in blind babies. We told them that we wanted to learn how blind babies grow and develop in order to help all blind babies to have the best possible chance for a good and happy future. We would like to visit them and the baby at home, twice a month. We understood some of the problems which a blind baby faced and we were learning more and more in our work. *We would share our understanding and our experience with our families in all ways that might be useful to them.*

This offer was gratefully received by nearly every family that we approached. We began and sustained the study through a sharing of experience. Only one family withdrew from the study after the child was two and a half years of age because of dissatisfaction with our program. No fees to families were needed for cooperation in the research. (Once in the early stages of the research, we had set aside some funds for payment to families. They were never used. The most impoverished families in our study would have felt insulted by the offer.) Our interest and our caring, the sharing of our professional experience were all that our families wanted from us.

Our consultation-guidance program introduced other variables which may be considered along with those characteristics of our sample already cited. At the outset we knew that developmental guidance provided for all babies in the study would affect our findings. The reasonable presumption was that guidance would have positive effects upon development. However, there was no question in our minds or in the minds of our review committees at NICHD (The National Institute of Child Health and Development) that to withhold information or help from these stricken families in the name of "objectivity" would be inhumane. If our guidance program favorably influenced the development of these children we should be able to say, "Under the most favorable circumstances that we could provide for the development of 10 children blind from birth this is what we saw. . . ." And, in fact, as we shall see in the chapters that follow, we did facilitate development, but no amount of educational intervention obscured the unique adaptive problems posed by blindness—those problems which were at the center of this investigation.

Finally, then, this study is based upon a unique sample and we cannot generalize our findings to the larger blind population. In the typical blind-child population we will have children with a range of useful vision who are still legally classified as "blind," and we will have a high incidence of multiple handicaps and neurological impairment. The babies in our sample are advantaged in a blind-child population by the intactness of other systems and are disadvantaged as a group by having no pattern vision.

In summary, we can say that the observations reported in this volume are derived from a group of healthy, otherwise intact blind infants; their families represent a good range of socioeconomic conditions, and the development of these babies has been facilitated through our intervention.

Chapter V

SELMA FRAIBERG

The Sign System *

IN THIS CHAPTER I shall bring together our observations about the elements of communication between baby and mother that must be derived from a nonvisual "vocabulary" of signs and signals.

There will be certain understandable problems as we introduce our findings in this area. A mother who has just delivered a blind baby, or who has just learned that her baby is blind, must cope with immeasurable grief and despondency. When we describe the extraordinary problems of a blind baby and his mother in finding a sign vocabulary, how can we know what belongs to the obliteration of a visual sign system and what belongs to psychological pain as a deterrent to the mother's reading of signs? The self-observations of the researcher and observations of visitors to the Project may offer some measure of the meaning of blindness to an adult for whom blindness is not a personal tragedy.

* An earlier version of this chapter appeared as Selma Fraiberg, "Blind Infants and Their Mothers: An Examination of the Sign System," in Michael Lewis and Leonard A. Rosemblum (eds.), *The Effect of the Infant on its Caregiver*, New York: John Wiley and Sons (1974), pp. 215-232.

The Sign System

Self-Observations

I begin with certain observations of myself. I began the developmental study of blind infants in 1960. Gradually I became aware of many differences in my behavior toward blind infants when I watched myself with sighted infants. Many of these reactions are still with me and catch me by surprise. Yet I think I am reasonably without prejudice toward the blind and, as far as I can judge, my feelings have not been an impediment to my work.

The first self-discoveries came to me in New Orleans during the time that Dr. David Freedman and I had begun our study of Toni. We had been visiting Toni for 6 months when we were asked by a social agency to evaluate another blind baby, Lennie, then nine months old. We arranged for a home visit.

Somebody had made a mistake. Lennie was not blind. We found a neglected baby lying in a filthy crib. If we exerted ourselves in testing, we could elicit brief regard of our faces and tracking. It was the absence of sustained fixation that had led someone to believe that Lennie was blind when he was three months of age. Since that time he had been reared as a blind child and as the unwanted fourteenth child in an impoverished family.

After concluding our testing and having a long discussion with the mother, I began to write up notes for a social agency referral. As I put the observations in sequence I made notations on the conditions that elicited visual regard. I was describing Lennie's responses to my voice when something struck me as strange: it was my monologue. But I always talk to babies, I told myself. No. I don't always talk to babies. I don't talk to Toni in the same way.

I searched my memory. It was true. I had done very little talking when I was with Toni. This troubled me. Toni was a responsive and endearing child; Lennie depressed me. I enjoyed holding Toni. I had to overcome some feelings of revulsion when I held Lennie. But I talked to Lennie. What was the reward? When I searched my memory again I came up with two pictures. When I talked to Lennie long enough I got brief moments of visual fixation of my face and a meeting of eyes. If I could sustain his fixation long enough, I got a ghost of a smile.

Later, I could make use of this self-observation when I was with Toni. I talked to her more frequently but always I had the sense of something missing, something that should be coming back to me from Toni. There was, of course, no visual fixation of my face.

And something else was missing. Although Toni smiled frequently in response to her mother's voice, she rarely smiled to our voices as observers. Later, in the course of years, I was to learn much more about the stimuli that evoke smiling in the blind infant. The voice, even the voice of the mother, does not automatically evoke smiling in blind infants. I missed that in Toni. I still miss it in blind infants, and my team members share this feeling with me.

Twelve years later there are still surprises for me. A few months ago five-year-old Karen, who is blind, was visiting our office. I saw Karen playing in one of the offices and stopped to talk with her. Her back was turned to me. When she heard me speak to her she stopped her play for a moment and listened. She did not turn around immediately. Then as I continued to talk, Karen slowly turned around and met me full face. I had a moment's shock. The words came into my mind, "She's blind!" But I have known for nearly 5 years that Karen is blind.

Sometimes when we have professional visitors to the Project to look at film or video tape, I steal glances at the visitors' faces as the child is on the screen. With sighted children it is always interesting to see the resonance of mood on the viewer's face. We smile when the baby on film smiles; we are sober when the baby is distressed. We laugh sympathetically when the baby looks indignant at the examiner's sneakiness. We frown in concentration as the baby frowns when a toy disappears. When he drops a toy we even look below the movie screen to help him find it.

But the blind baby on the screen does not elicit these spontaneous moods in the visitor. Typically, the visitor's face remains solemn. This is partly a reaction to blindness itself. But it is also something else. There is a large vocabulary of expressive behavior that one does not see in a blind baby at all. The absence of differentiated signs on the baby's face is mirrored in the face of the observer.

One afternoon, during the last months of our blind research, our staff devoted a session to a discussion of self-observations in relation to blind infants. Our consensus as a team of researchers and clinicians who have worked with blind children for some years is that we never overcame this sense of something vital missing in the social exchange. And yet our rewards from blind children have been very great. All of the staff members have strong attachments to children we have known since the first year of life. With rare exceptions the babies have grown into preschool children who are healthy, active, freely mobile, talkative, and mischievous—surely a group of highly personable and attractive youngsters. Among ourselves we talk about them the way proud parents do. We are never aware that something is missing in our response until a sighted child comes to visit.

When a sighted child comes to visit, there is spontaneous rapport and we trot out our repertoire of antics with babies. We are back in the tribal system where the baby plays his social game and we play ours. If one has worked very largely with blind babies for many years, as we have, the encounter with a sighted baby is absurdly like the experience of meeting a compatriot abroad, after a long stay in a country where the language and customs are alien. The compatriot, who can be a perfect stranger asking for directions, is greeted like a friend, his regional accent and idiom are endearing, and with nothing more in common than a continent, two strangers can embark upon a social exchange in which nearly all the tribal signs are understood and correctly interpreted.

What we miss in the blind baby, apart from the eyes that do not see, is the vocabulary of signs and signals that provides the most elementary and vital sense of discourse long before words have meaning.

In this chapter, I shall describe, through our observations, some of the unique problems of a blind infant and his mother in finding a vocabulary of signs.

The Absence of an Eye Language

I have described some of the reactions of professional observers in social exchanges with the blind babies. The blind eyes that do not engage our eyes, that do not regard our faces, have an effect upon the observer that is never completely overcome. When the eyes do not meet ours in acknowledgment of our presence it feels curiously like a rebuff. Certainly mothers attribute "knowing" and "recognition" to the baby's sustained regard of the face long before he can actually discriminate and recognize faces, and this is only because the engagement of eyes is part of the universal code of the human fraternity—which is read as greeting and acknowledgment of "the other" long before it can have meaning to the infant.

It is a potent sign. Robson (1968) describes the role of eye-to-eye contact in eliciting maternal responses to the infant. In his report, mothers speak of the first feelings of love in response to the infant's fixation of the face, of the sense of the baby "becoming a person." Roskies (1972), in her work with the mothers of thalidomide babies, describes two mothers who were considering institutionalization of their deformed babies soon after birth. The baby's eyes "looking back," the eyes "talking" to the mother, were moments recalled by both mothers as compelling. The decision to keep the baby was remembered by both mothers within the context of this engagement of the eyes.

"How will he know me?" This question, sometimes explicit, sometimes implicit, may come to us from the mother soon after she has learned of her child's blindness. And while we know that under all favorable circumstances the blind baby will come to know his mother and that the course of human attachments will closely parallel that of a sighted child, the imagination of the mother may be strained to encompass a "knowing" without vision. Discrimination, recognition, preference, and valuation are signs that the mother normally reads through visual responses of the infant. And while a mother might acknowledge that there can be recognition, "knowing" through tactile, kinesthetic, and auditory experiences, her registration of this "knowing" is normally interpreted through differentiated facial signs. Eye contact connotes greeting and acknowledgment. Eye contact elicits the smile. Visual discrimination leads to preferential smiling. In the case of the blind infant a large vocabulary of signs is either obliterated or distorted for the mother, as I shall describe in the sections that follow.

Vision affords the sighted child an elementary form of initiative in human partnership long before there can be intention. From the responses of the mother of a baby under two months of age we can say that the baby woos his mother with his eyes. He elicits social exchange through the automatic smile in response to the human face gestalt. At five months of age the sighted child extends or uplifts his arms in the gesture "hold me," "pick me up," which most mothers find irresistible, even an imperative.

But the blind baby has a meager repertoire of behaviors which can initiate social exchange, and beyond the vocal utterances of need and distress he has virtually no sign vocabulary which elicits an automatic response from his mother. Instead the absence of eye contact gives the negative sign of "no interest." The absence of a smile to the presentation of the human face has the negative value of "not friendly." The smile to mother's voice, which is in the repertoire of the blind baby, is not an automatic smile and is not employed to initiate a social exchange. The gesture "hold me," "pick me up" does not appear, even among our most adequate blind babies, until the end of the first year, at which time the voice of the mother can elicit a directional reach, and the reach becomes a meaningful gesture to the mother.

Our records document the extraordinary problems for a mother in reading the non-visual sign language of the blind baby. Only 2 mothers among our group of 10 found their way unaided by us. Both were extraordinary mothers and both had had large experience with babies. Other mothers in our group, including those who had older children, showed us at the time of our first meeting that they found their blind babies perplexing and "unresponsive," that it was hard to know what the baby "wanted." No criticism is implied here. A sighted baby does not need an extraordinary mother in order to make the vital human connections and to find the developmental routes in infancy. We provided much help to all of the parents of our blind infants. As we ourselves became experienced in understanding the non-visual vocabulary of the blind baby and the developmental roadblocks, we were able to become the translators for both the blind baby and his perplexed parents. When the mother learned the language, the rewards to both baby and parents were very large.

The Smile Language

Our observations on smiling in blind infants are reported in an earlier paper (Fraiberg 1971) and in Chapter VI. For clarity and continuity, some material from these reports is included in the following summary.

We have observed a blind baby responding with a smile to his father's and mother's voices as early as the fourth week. For sighted babies at the same age it has been reported by Peter Wolff (1963) that there is a selective smile to the sound of mother's voice and by Emde and Koenig (1969) that the familiar voice—as well as a number of other stimuli—can irregularly elicit a smile. The smiling response in blind babies is neither automatic nor regular.

The Sign System

As the number of babies in our sample increased, differences between the characteristics of smiling in blind and sighted infants emerged in a clear pattern.

At two to two and a half months, when the visual stimulus of the human face evokes an automatic smile from the sighted child with a high degree of regularity, there is no equivalence in the blind baby's experience. Thus, though the blind baby's smile becomes more frequent, and the pattern of selective smiling is increasingly demonstrated in favor of the mother, even her voice will not regularly elicit the smile. There is no stimulus in the third month or later that has the equivalence for the human face gestalt in the experience of the sighted child.

For the mother of the blind baby, the selective response smile to her voice signified "knowing" and "preference." Her first fears of "How will he know me?" are diminished by the appearance of the universal sign. When the observers tried experimentally to elicit a smile through their voices, they were only rarely rewarded. We used these failures to help the mother see the smile for her as "special" and the beginning of "knowing" her.

But, as we have noted, the smile is not automatic. In our records and on film we often see the mother coaxing a smile. Sometimes several repetitions of her voice were needed before the smiles appeared. Clearly something was needed that was not automatically given.

Then, in our records of this period, we began to see that the most reliable stimulus for evoking a smile or laughter in the blind baby was gross tactile or kinesthetic stimulation, noticeably greater than that observed among parents of sighted babies. We began to understand that, while the parents' voices alone provided at best irregular results, the bouncing, tickling, and nuzzling games were almost certain stimuli for the smile. The parents' own need for the response smile had led them to these alternative routes to more frequent and satisfying results.

When vision is excluded as a factor in the socialization of the smile, other differences in smiling emerge. Once a familiar voice is heard, the blind child may respond by smiling, but he does not initiate contact by a smile. The smile to initiate, the automatic greeting, is largely mediated through visual signs and is normally reinforced through visual rewards (the return or exchange smile of the partner).

This leads us to the observation that our blind babies do not smile as frequently as sighted babies do. Even when all the criteria for a mutually satisfying mother-child relationship have been met, the smile of the blind infant strikes us as a muted smile. The joyful, even ecstatic, smile that we see in a healthy sighted baby is a comparatively rare occurrence among blind babies. This suggests that the smile on the face of "the other" is a potent reinforcer—even in infancy—of one's own smile.

The effects upon the human partner of a baby who does not greet with a smile, who smiles infrequently and without predictability, are best seen in the judgments that are made about the blind baby's personality by most people—whether clinicians or laymen—who have not had experience with blind babies.

"She looks depressed," says a visitor watching one of our blind babies on film. "No affect! The face is so bland. No expression." The visitor wonders if the mother is giving the baby enough stimulation.

The baby in question is a perfectly adequate blind girl of seventeen months who has given a demonstration on film of her attachment to and preference for mother, of locomotor achievements close to sighted norms, and of a rapt exploration of a new toy with her sensitive fingertips. The amount of "stimulation" provided by the mother must be judged as adequate to produce this kind of investment in persons and things in a blind baby of this age.

Yet, we understand what the visitor is experiencing. He is missing the signs of affectivity, of investment, and of social response which register on the face of a sighted baby and are automatically translated by us. Only when we see a blind baby do we fully appreciate that the largest number of these signs are differentiated through vision.

The Sign System

The Absence of Differentiated Facial Signs

In the range pleasure-displeasure we can read the signs at both ends of the arc for a blind baby. A blind baby who smiles "looks happy." A blind baby who is crying for a delayed dinner "looks unhappy." But between the contrasting states, which everyone can read, there is a tremendous range of modulated affect and attitudes which is normally discerned by human partners through expressive facial signs. By any reasoning, the modulations must exist for blind babies as states of feeling, but we cannot easily read these states by scrutinizing the face.

If we make a brief inventory of expressive facial signs in the sighted child at six months of age, we can immediately see how the child's own eyes lead the way and give us the signs which we read as "affect," "investment," or "attention."

"He looks attentive." (Attention inferred from sustained visual regard.)

"A look of longing." (Can be read through the baby's prolonged visual fixation and visually oriented postures.)

"He looks quizzical." (Visual inspection of an unfamiliar phenomenon.)

"He looks doubtful." (Visual inspection with mixed positive and negative emotion.)

"A coy look." (A visual peek-a-boo game—now you're here; now you're not.)

"She is bored." (Restless or unfocused searching or scanning with the eyes.)

The list can be compounded for the sighted child before he has reached the age of six months. In the third and fourth quarters imitative signs begin to enter the repertoire for the sighted child (Piaget 1962) giving personal style to the face and extending the differentiated vocabulary of facial expression. All this is closed out in blindness.

The blind baby, by contrast, has an impoverished repertoire of facial signs. The blind baby does not "look attentively," "look quizzically," "look doubtfully," "look coyly." He has no object of visual fixation which can elicit these differentiated signs. This leads the uninitiated mother or observer to feel as our visitors do: "He looks depressed," "Nothing interests him."

The absence of signs is misleading. We have no reason to believe that the affective state of longing, for example, does not exist for the healthy blind baby, but the motor expression of longing which is read by us through sustained visual fixation (and visually oriented postures) is not available to him. Since we normally read affective states through expressive facial signs, the absence of the differentiated sign on the blind baby's face is misread as "no affect."

(There are, of course, blind babies who are, properly speaking, depressed, withdrawn, apathetic. But to make the clinically valid diagnosis, we need much more than a reading of the face.)

For the healthy, adequately stimulated blind baby there are registrations of affective states with motor expression. But we have to turn our eyes away from the face to discover them. To do this is so alien to normal human discourse that we might not have discovered the other signs if we had not been looking for something else.

The Hand Language

Our developmental observations included the study of prehension in blind infants. (See Chapter VII.) Very early in our work we saw that adaptive hand behavior followed another route in blind babies. There was no adaptive substitution of the ear for the eye in reaching and attaining an object at five months of age. Our question was "How does the blind baby achieve the coordination of ear and hand which leads him to localize a sound object in space, to reach directionally for the object and attain it?" We were to find that "reach on sound" was not achieved by any baby in our group until the last trimester of the first year. (See Chapters VII and VIII for final reports. See also Fraiberg, Siegel, and Gibson 1966 and Fraiberg 1968.)

As a staff we became "hand watchers." To examine the sequential patterns in adaptive hand behavior we analyzed many thousands of feet of film on a variable-speed projector, viewing at one-third speed. Our prehension film samples were always photographed under circumstances in which the full range of the baby's experience with human partners as well as inanimate objects could be included.

As we watched the baby's hands, we found what we were looking for—and we also found a large number of things that we were not looking for.

We began to see the expressive motor signs in the hands themselves. We began to read "I want" and intentionality through fleeting, barely visible motor signs in the hands. Our staff film reviews took on a curious aspect. If we were examining mother-child reciprocity we looked at the mother's face and the baby's hands. (The baby's face told us very little.) If we were studying investment in a toy or toy preference we looked at the baby's hands. If we were examining emotional reactions to momentary separation from the mother, or toy loss, we looked at the hands. It was—and still is—a bizarre experience for us to read hands instead of faces in order to read meaning into emotional experience. (As a clinician with sighted children I would normally read faces for the signs of emotionality. I would pick up cues from the hands either peripherally or as an alternative when the face was masking emotionality.)

As we ourselves became sensitive to the motor expressions in the hands themselves, we began to read them as signs and responded to them as signs. What we saw we could easily help the mother to see, too, and some of our mothers became as adept as the observers were in reading and translating the baby's hand language.

Since it took us a considerable time as professional observers to "read hands," we should now fairly consider the dilemma of the mother of a blind baby without professional guidance. In the absence of a repertory of expressive facial signs the mother of the blind baby had no differentiated sign vocabulary in which modulated affective states or wants were registered, and from which an appropriate response from the mother was elicited. And since many of the baby's signs could not be "read" by his mother, his own experience in eliciting specific responses to need was largely restricted to elemental need states. "Hunger," "contentment," "fussiness," "rage," and "sleepiness" could be read by the mother, but the full range of affective expression which becomes socialized in the first year could not be exploited until she could read the signs.

Let me give a few examples of the problem:

Toni is seven months old. Her mother (a very experienced mother, remember, with five older children) tells us, "She's not really interested in her toys."

We assemble a group of Toni's crib toys, stuffed animals and dolls, and invite the mother to present them to Toni, one by one. As each of the toys is placed in her hands, Toni's face is immobile. She gives the impression of "staring off into remote space." Naturally, the totally blind child does not orient his face toward the toy in his hands. Since visual inspection is the sign that we read as "interest," and averted eyes and staring are read as the sign of "uninterest," Toni "looks bored."

Now we watch Toni's hands. While her face "looks bored," her fingers scan each of the toys. One stuffed doll is dropped after brief manual scanning. A second doll is scanned, brought to the mouth, tongued, mouthed, removed, scanned again. Now we remove doll number 2 and place doll number 1 in Toni's hand. A quick scanning of fingers and she drops it again. She makes fretful sounds, eyes staring off into space. We return doll number 2 to her hands. She quiets instantly, clutches it, brings it to her mouth, and explores its contours.

In short, there is no message from the face which Toni's

mother can read as "interest" or "preference." But the behavior of the hands showed clear discrimination and sustained exploration of one toy and not another.

Examples such as this multiply throughout our records. The immobile face, the vacant eyes, "no interest"—but the fingers are exploring the tiny crevices of the rattle, the clapper of the bell, the bumps on the soap dish, the bristles of the pastry brush.

The problem is compounded when the mother is called upon to read "wanting" or intention in her blind baby. No mother of a sighted baby at six months is at a loss in reading "I want" from a very large number of visually directed behaviors. At this age the sighted child is very good at getting what he wants within range. He also reaches for things out of range, with eyes fixed determinedly on their target, hands and torso extended, and urgent vocalizations just in case somebody can't read sign language. He has, in fact, a differentiated vocabulary of motor signs in the orientation of the head, and extended arms and hands, which we read instantly as "I want," "gimme," "pick me up," "no, not that," or "oh, please." All of these signs are mediated by vision (e.g., eye and hand) and depend upon visual fixation of the target and a motor expression of want or supplication for a quick reading of intention by the adult partner. If, for example, we should have the implausible situation in which a six-month-old sighted baby produced the motor sign of "gimme" and the eyes did not fixate on a target, we would not be able to read intention.

This means, of course, that even when the blind baby reveals his wants or his intentions through the motor expression of his hands, the sign not only requires fine reading by us or the parents, but there are many wants that cannot be expressed through the hands without orientation and gesture to identify the target. It is only at the close of the first year, when the sound object is localized and the blind baby begins to make a directional reach for the object, that we begin to see the sign of "I want" through the extended hand, and the sign of "pick me up" through extended arms.

The toy drops from his hand, and the blind baby at six months may make no sound of complaint, no gesture of retrieval. The face registers nothing that we can read as disappointment. In the blind baby's world of evanescent objects the manifestations of a toy, its comings and goings, are subjected to a capricious fate. Things materialize out of a void, manifest themselves when grasped, heard, mouthed, smelled, and then are lost, swallowed in a void. The sighted child of this age can follow the trajectory of the falling toy, and the registrations of "I want" on the face and in the hands are sustained through visual contact with the toy that has left his hand.

As we read his face, the blind baby "looks bored" or "not interested" when the toy drops from his hand. But if we watch his hands, another story emerges.

The toy drops to the floor. Robbie "looks bored." But now Robbie's open hand can be seen sweeping across the table surface, then it sweeps back. The "hand watchers" read this instantly as a search. The play table surface is the place where toys are usually found; a toy "belongs to" this space, as it were, it materializes from this space. The exploratory sweep of the hand is the sign of "I want" for the blind baby.

At eight months of age, if we bring Robbie's musical dog within easy reach of his hands and play its familiar music, he will not yet reach for the toy. Does he want it? His face does not register yearning or wanting. But now as the music plays we see his hands in an anticipatory posture of holding, grasping and ungrasping.

At nine months of age we ring our test bell within easy reach of Robbie's hands. The bell is a favorite toy for Robbie. He does not yet reach for it. Does he want it? We watch his hands, and then we see the hands execute a pantomime of bell ringing as he hears the bell "out there."

This leads us to consider the more central problems for the blind baby and his mother in establishing the vital human connections. The alien sign language of the blind baby is not only an impediment to the reading of want and intention in the baby. The baby's sign vocabulary of selective interest, preference, and valuation of his human partners which constitutes the earliest language of love, is distorted for the mother of the blind baby.

Yet once again, if we shift our attention from the face of the blind baby to his hands, we can read an eloquent sign language of seeking, wooing, preference, and recognition which becomes increasingly differentiated during the first six months.

We have observations and film records of 3 of our 10 babies during the first quarter. In the early weeks the behavior of the hands does not yet differentiate, for my eyes, a blind baby from a sighted baby. During feeding, while being held in the mother's arms, we see the blind baby's hands on film, making chance contact with the mother's face or hands, grasping or lightly fingering. In the second month we see the beginnings of active seeking of contact with the mother, the hand, for example, returning to a point of prior contact after interruption. (This behavior corresponds with Piaget's [1952] protocols for Laurent during the same age.) The number of examples of manual-tactile seeking begin to proliferate for 2 of the children between two and five months of age. The hands, not engaged, seek engagement with the mother's hand or her body. The hands linger, lightly finger or grasp, withdraw, return. Sometimes we catch on film a kind of ballet in which the baby's hands seek and find the mother's hand, and the mother's hand sustains or responds to the signal.

I am sure we can see an identical hand language in watching sighted babies and their mothers. But the sighted child, even at two months, is sustaining an eloquent dialogue of eyes, smiles, motor responses, to invite and sustain contact with his mother. To a very large extent the blind baby is dependent upon his hands to woo, to maintain contact, to affirm the presence of the mother. During the period two to six months we can follow the blind baby's adaptive exploitation of the hand in establishing the human connections.

Between five and eight months of age (now reporting on 8

children in the sample) we have examples for all of the children in which the blind baby's hands explore the mother's or father's face, the fingers tracing features with familiarity and giving the viewer a sense that he was anticipating what he would find. The film record gives strong evidence that these exploring hands are discriminating and that the information from the fingers brings recognition as well as non-recognition.

In one example on film, I am holding Toni at age seven months, two days to test her reactions to me as a stranger. She begins to strain away from me and to whimper. Then her hands seek my face, finger my nose and mouth in a quick scanning of this unfamiliar map: she cries louder, clutches my arm in frozen terror. When I return her to her mother's arms, she settles, still crying, then scans and rescans her mother's face with her fingers and finally is comforted.

This tactile language can speak eloquently to the mother who "knows" it. The two mothers who found their way unaided by us in intuiting their blind baby's needs were mothers whose own tactile sensibilities were large and who not only provided abundant tactile experience for their babies but responded with spontaneity to the baby's tactile sign language. Other mothers needed our help both in understanding the blind baby's need for tactile intimacy and manual-tactile experience, and in interpreting the tactile sign language of the blind child.

What we ourselves learned from hand language we brought to the mothers of our blind babies. It was most welcome help. When the baby's expressive signs could be read, the dialogue between mother and baby was facilitated with predictable rewards. The mother who felt out of contact, uncertain, not competent, found her way as a mother who could minister to her child's needs. Even grief could be managed when the baby brought his own rewards in response, in diversity of social exchange, and in becoming an active partner in the love relationship—a partnership that is really only possible when the language of need and intention can be understood.

The Sign System

The Vocal Dialogue

The vocal dialogue which is available to the blind baby and his parents is, finally, the one channel which remains open and available as a relatively undistorted language system between mother and child. Even in this area we will see some qualitative differences (and, we think, some differences in quantity too) but our data do not suggest that blindness is an impediment to the acquisition of language in the first and second years. Here, again, we are speaking of our highly selective and advantaged group of blind infants. Scales available for the larger blind population show marked delays by sighted-child standards.

Within our own sample the expressive vocalizations, the emergence of vowel-consonant syllables, imitative sounds "Mama," "baba," "Dada," and so on, appear within the Bayley ranges for sighted children. Two of our children were using single words "Mama," "Dada," "bopple" (bottle) as correct referents between the ages of eight months and twelve months. In the second year, the majority of our sample attained naming, expression of wants, and simple sentences within the range for sighted children. (See Chapter X.) A linguistic study of one of our children conducted by Eric Lenneberg showed that her language competence at two years of age compared favorably with that of sighted children. (Reported in Fraiberg and Adelson 1973, 1975 and in Chapter XI.)

Yet, throughout the first year, it seemed to us that the spontaneous vocalizations of our blind babies were sparse. In the absence of quantitative measures for sighted children of comparable age, we can only offer our impression and that of a number of independent observers that our babies seemed "very quiet" in comparison with sighted babies, that vocalization for self-entertainment was infrequent and scant (even among the high vocalizers of our group), that vocalizations to greet were rarely recorded, and that the *initiation* of a "dialogue" with mother or other partners was rarely observed. On the other hand, response vocalizations in "dialogue" with the mother are recorded for all the children in our group.

These differences, which we can only support impressionistically, may reflect the poverty of eliciting stimuli in a blind child's world. Where visual stimuli afforded by persons, food, toys, a colorful object, a moving object, can produce a volley of utterances from the sighted child, even under four months of age —and these stimuli are omnipresent from the moment the child opens his eyes—there is no equivalence among the exogenous stimuli in the blind child's world. Sound, voices, tactile-kinesthetic stimulation, are not "at the disposal of" the blind child in the way that visual stimuli are available to the sighted infant from the moment his eyes open. The sound-touch stimuli of the blind child are actually at the disposal of someone outside of the infant self, the human partners whose voice and touch are not constant components of the waking hours. (Only a nonstop talking and touching mother could provide equivalence in quantity of stimuli.)

There may be other factors not explored in our study which have bearing on the seeming poverty of spontaneous vocalizations in our blind babies. We do not know, for example, if the baby's blindness is an impediment for the mother in her vocalizing to the infant. Does the absence of eye contact and of the automatic smile reduce the spontaneity of utterances on the part of the mother (as I reported in my self-observations at the beginning of this chapter)? Is this a reciprocal effect of blindness on discourse between the two partners in which a reduced level of utterances from the mother has correspondence in a reduction of vocalizations in the baby?

During the four-to-eight-month period, our blind-infant observations show that the mother's or father's voice is the prime elicitor of vocalizations. We have a large number of examples of "dialogues" between parent and baby which do not distinguish our blind babies from sighted babies under circumstances in which the adult himself initiates the dialogue.

The Sign System

Vocalizations to initiate contact appear later (in the second year) for our blind children. It is not easy to understand why. In families where the rewards for vocalizations are very large, with much parental "talking to" the baby and echoing of his sounds, we are still struck by the absence of initiative in the baby. We can only guess that vision is a potent elicitor of vocalizations and that what appear as "greeting vocalizations" in sighted babies are stimulated by and reinforced by visual signs (e.g., the human face gestalt). But why, in the circular causality available to the blind infant at six to eight months, doesn't he vocalize with the magical expectation that his sound-making will produce sounds from his partners?

(I realize that in the area of vocalizations and language in the first year I am raising more questions than I can answer.)

When we consider how many social signs have been obliterated by blindness, how resourceful and inventive the mother of the blind baby must be to read her baby's alien sign language, we need no comment from me on the significance of the early vocalizations and the blind baby's discovery of the spoken language in the partnership of mother and baby. With the first words there is, for the first time, a common language.

The Attainment of Human Bonds

From this report we can see that the mother of a blind baby faces extraordinary problems in learning the alien language of her child. Grief and self-recriminations which come with the shock of blindness are compounded by the sense of estrangement from a baby who cannot communicate in the universal code. The perils to the baby are very large. In the general blind population there are a significant number of blind children, otherwise intact, who show grave impairment in their human object relationships. In our consultation service (a separate program not reported in this volume) we see blind children in the second, third, and fourth years who appear to have no investment in persons or things. These are children of families for whom no guidance was available in the crucial sensorimotor period.

Our research sample can tell us more fairly about the capacities for human attachments in blind infants when the nonvisual vocabulary of the infant "speaks to" the mother, and the mother responds and is rewarded by her baby.

For those mothers (the majority) who could not find their way unaided into the alien experience of the blind baby, we shared our own understanding. The benefits to the baby and the mother were demonstrable in all developmental areas.

In the area of human attachments we found close correspondence between the characteristics of our blind group and those of sighted children. These are discussed in detail in the following chapter.

Chapter VI

SELMA FRAIBERG

The Development of Human Attachments *

IN THIS CHAPTER I will describe characteristics of attachment behavior in our group of 10 infants. The data, covering the first two years of life, will include: (a) smiling; (b) discriminating tactile behaviors; (c) stranger avoidance and distress; (d) the constitution of mother as object; and (e) separation and reunion behaviors.

For the sighted child, the developmental course that leads to stable human partnerships in the course of the first 18 months is charted by us through affective signs and by a sequence of increasingly discriminating behaviors toward the partner which speak for preference and valuation. Without exception, as we have seen, these are signs that are mediated through vision. Differential smiling, discrimination of mother and stranger, and separation and reunion behaviors, unite the affective experience of the mother with sensory pictures, and the picture itself is the synthesizer of all sense experience.

In a world without pictures, how does the infant learn to discriminate his mother from other persons, how does he express preference for and valuation of her? How does the visual deficit

* An abbreviated version of this chapter appeared in Fraiberg (1975).

affect reciprocity between the baby and his partners and the reading of signs which must underlie every human partnership?

At eighteen months, 9 of our 10 blind babies demonstrated to their parents and to us that the mother had become the most important person in the world and that the world itself was inexhaustibly fascinating. As creepers and toddlers they set out on excursions around the house, returned to touch base with mother, set out again for another trip, pausing sometimes to say "mama" or "hi," waiting for the reassuring voice to come back. They were wary of strangers, took a dim view of the research team, but put up gamely with our presence and our occasional testing nonsense. Without needing invitation or prompting, they gave embraces to mother and father, or lovingly fingered their faces, and almost never favored our observers with such treatment. The absence of the mother for a few minutes or a few hours produced distress and turning away from the ministrations of substitute care-givers. By all signs these blind babies showed us that they had achieved forms of focused human relationships (Yarrow 1967) which compared favorably with those of sighted children of the same age.

Yet the route that led to love and valuation of human partners was in many ways very different from that of the sighted child. In this chapter, then, I will describe the sequential development of discriminating and preferential behaviors of blind infants toward their human partners and compare these characteristics with those of sighted children during the first two years of life.

DATA SOURCES AND EVALUATION

In examining the course of human attachments in blind babies we recorded and analyzed hundreds of items for each child in a chronological sequence which gave us differential responses to mother, and to other familiar and unfamiliar persons; behaviors showing pleasurable response to and preference for mother; the ability to be comforted by mother; reactions to temporary separation from mother; and tracking and seeking mother (when the baby was mobile). Profiles for each child were constructed, a

selection of indicators was made, and a composite profile was developed for 10 babies.

When our data were sorted and evaluated we saw that there
were differential responses in certain areas which could be examined in relation to sighted-child criteria and sighted-child norms.
There were also a number of indicators of human attachment
which appeared in our blind children and which represented the
blind baby's exploitation of tactile-auditory modes. These may
also be tactile-auditory components of all human attachment that
are normally obscured when vision is available to the baby.

INTERVENTION

In examining the development of human attachments in the
blind infants who were the subjects of this investigation, it is important to note again that a concurrent education and guidance
program was provided for all children in the study. We have
reason to believe that our intervention program promoted the attachment of baby and mother, and the presentation of our central
findings should be read as the development of human attachments
in a group of blind infants who were probably advantaged
through an intervention program.

Our guidance in the area of human attachments can be briefly
summarized: We gave comfort and support and hope to parents
who were without hope and who were still stunned by grief when
we first met them. We became the interpreters of the blind baby's
experience to his parents. His needs for tactile intimacy and for
voice contact were interpreted to his parents and were seen as
central to all learning in the early months. We helped our parents
to read the alien sign vocabulary of the blind baby, to see the
signs of discrimination, preference, and valuation that are often
obscured by the absence of mutual gaze. We understood, through
our own studies, the developmental deviations and lags in prehension and locomotion which we saw in blind infants, and could
share that understanding with the parents along with vital information and guidance which would lead to the child's adaptive

solutions. The baby brought his own rewards as we will see in the pages that follow. Our guidance program is described in two papers—Fraiberg, Smith, and Adelson (1969) and Fraiberg (1971a).

The summary that follows is highly selective and may not do justice to the complexities of the problem for the blind baby and his mother in achieving their bonds. Table 2 summarizes the ranges and medians for milestones in human attachment in our group. These milestones will be explicated in the text. Four papers by the author deal with aspects of human attachment in blind infants—Fraiberg (1968), Fraiberg (1971b), Fraiberg (1971c), and Fraiberg (1975).

TABLE 2
Human Attachment Milestones—C.D.P. Blind Group

ITEM	RANGE	MEDIAN AGE
Smiles to familiar voice [a]	1.0– 3.0	
Manual-tactile discrimination familiar-unfamiliar faces	5.0– 8.0	5.0
Stranger avoidance	7.0–15.0	12.5
Person permanence Stage 4	10.0–16.0	11.5
Separation protest	11.0–21.0	11.5

NOTE:
Ages rounded to nearest half month.
3 cases corrected for 3 months prematurity.
[a] Parent report credited for this item only. All children had achieved this item at time of entrance to study. All other items credited by our direct observation.

Smiling

The course of smiling in the blind infant is of exceptional interest and provides an entree through "known territory" to the "unknown territory" of the blind infant's development. In the sighted child, the differentiation of the smile and the increasing selectivity of the smile for the valued partner gives us a sequence of milestones or indicators of human attachment. (Spitz and Wolff 1946; Ambrose 1961; Polak, Emde, and Spitz 1964; Gewirtz 1965; Emde and Koenig 1969.) From the automatic smile at two months to the selective smile which is well established at six months, the prime elicitor of smiling is the visual configuration of the human face. Indeed, the facial gestalt is biologically overdetermined as a stimulus for attention and smiling in the infant.

For the blind infant, the familiar *voice* is the prime elicitor of the smile. As early as the fourth week we have examples of selective (but irregular) smiling to mother's and father's voice. When we, the observers, tried to elicit the smile through our voices in repeated experiments, we failed. The smile to voice is also reported by Wolff (1963) for sighted children of the same age. Emde and Koenig (1969) report, however, that voice is one of a number of unpatterned auditory, tactile and visual stimuli which elicit the smile as an *irregular* response in the period three weeks to two months.

At two and a half months, however, the smile of the sighted child becomes regular and is relatively automatic to the gestalt of the human face. The blind child smiles more frequently to the voice of mother and other familiar persons, but there is no stimulus except gross tactile stimulation (tickling) which *regularly* elicits the smile.

In the period two and a half months to six months the sighted child's smile becomes preferential for mother, with greater frequency for mother than unfamiliar persons. This preferential smile speaks for an affective-cognitive advance in which the baby can discriminate the familiar face from the unfamiliar face. The blind child, whose smile has been "preferential" from the second month on, continues to smile selectively to mother's voice; the smile to voice is still irregular.

In the period six to eleven months the sighted child reserves his smile, almost exclusively, for mother and familiar persons (Emde and Koenig 1969). But the blind child's smile is not further differentiated from the earlier stage; it is still an irregular smile to the mother's or familiar persons' voices.

Using sighted-child criteria for smiling as an indicator of attachment behavior, the course of smiling in the blind infant would tell us nothing of the development of human attachments. A preferential smile to voice, which does not undergo a course of further differentiation in the first year, leaves us without vital indicators of progression in human attachment. Yet, even though the blind baby's smile does not inform us of complex discriminations or tell us how he gives unity to the disparate aspects of mother—how he "knows" mother, how he comes to value her—we can demonstrate that there are components of sensorimotor experience which are exploited by the blind baby and his mother and which lead him to a stage in human attachments that becomes recognizable to us immediately as an indicator of a level of human attachments.

Between seven and fifteen months of age, the blind baby, like the sighted baby, repudiates strangers, resists their arms and their ministrations, cries in protest, and is comforted only by mother's voice and embrace. The blind baby has kept his appointment, and meets the sighted baby at a certain time and a certain place on a developmental pathway—but he has gotten there by another route.

The tactile reciprocity between the blind baby and his human partners is, of course, only a component of a tactile-auditory-kinesthetic dialogue. The mother and other partners who hold the baby, rock him, feed him, caress him, and play motor games with him, are at the same time partners who talk, who sing, who create movement for the baby as they walk with him, shift postures, offer him rhythmic experiences. Therefore, in speaking of tactile modes it would be more correct to speak of "predominantly tactile modes."

The hands of the blind baby tell a story which begins in the first months. As the story unfolds in the course of the first year we see the progressive adaptation of the hand as an organ for maintaining contact and, later, for fine discriminations. When we consider that in normal development it is vision that facilitates all adaptive hand behavior, the blind child's exploitation of the hand as a perceptual organ is an extraordinary adaptive feat. In our studies we have compelling evidence that this adaptation, which is unique, of course, for blind children, is given impetus and motive through the primary human attachments and tactile intimacy between the baby and his human partners.

Yet the beginning of the story of the blind baby's hands does not distinguish for our eyes the blind child from the sighted child.

In the early weeks of life, we see a form of tactile-seeking in the blind baby which closely parallels that of the sighted baby. In the mother's arms, both the blind baby and the sighted baby in the second month will engage in a brief pursuit of the mother's hand which has been withdrawn from contact, or in other ways attempt to restore a contact that has been momentarily lost. (Our own protocols for 3 children and Piaget's [1952] protocols for Laurent at 0:1:19 show close correspondence.)

But, for the sighted child, manual tactile experience becomes one of several modes which are available "to maintain contact." By the third month, visual regard and tracking are capable of taking over the functions of "making contact" and "sustaining contact" when the child is at tactile and auditory remove from his mother.

The blind child in the third month and for many months to follow can only maintain contact with his mother when she manifests herself to him through tactile experience and through her voice. When his mother does not manifest herself to him through touch or voice, the blind baby is "not in contact" with her.

Yet the condition of physical proximity to the mother can be exploited fully by the blind child, and what we see is a pantomime of hands which begins in the first month as "chance encounter," then moves toward "tactile seeking," and by five months of age grows progressively more discriminating and intentional. For many months before the ear-hand schemas are co-ordinated, the blind child's hands send and receive messages in an archaic language: "Are you there? . . . I am here."

Between five and eight months something new emerges in manual-tactile experience. The blind baby's hands begin to explore the face of the mother, father, and other familiar persons:

> Rob, 0:5:18 (on film)
> Now sitting on father's lap, father nuzzling his face and jiggling him on his lap, Robbie's hands are stretched outright. A sequence of Rob-bie fingering his father's nose and face with great interest follows. Robbie is pinching his father's cheek. Father is talking to him and he strokes father's chin and mouth with his fingers. Now examining with his fingers father's glasses, he grabs hold at one point of the glasses and nearly pulls them off father's nose.

Far less frequently found in our records are examples in which the blind baby explores the observer's face. Our protocols and films give numerous examples from all children in the sample of a sustained, fascinated exploration of facial features of mother, father, siblings, other familiar persons, which gives the sense to the viewer of pleasure in tracing a familiar map and knowing what is to be found. The few examples of manual exploration of the observer's face are qualitatively different; they are brief scannings which appear to give some minimal information. In this behavior the blind child clearly differentiates between the familiar person and the stranger. As an early form of recognition behavior it may be compared fairly with the recognition behaviors which we discern in the sighted child of the same age, in preferential smiling, for example.

The appearance of manual-tactile exploration of faces follows a distribution pattern which is of some interest for comparison. Crediting the first example in the child's protocols of "exploration of the face" we have 5 children at the range five to six months, 2 at seven months, 1 at eight months. (N = 8 for this age period.)

There appears to be some correspondence, then, with forms of discriminatory and recognitory behaviors which appear in the sighted child around the middle of the first year. This was another surprise to us. As the data emerged in first tabulation I found myself disbelieving the evidence, but when I rechecked protocols I was satisfied that the examples were fair. Then I wondered whether our educational program had influenced this distribution pattern and the selective interest in the partner's face. (We had encouraged manual exploration in a number of ways in the early months.) However, when I examined the data for children who had entered the sample between five and eight months (5 children) and those who had been known to us from birth (3 children), the appearance of manual recognitory behavior did not discriminate the 3 "early education" children from the 5 children who had come into the sample with no previous educational advantage. My hypothesis is that the correspondence between visual recognition behavior in the sighted baby and manual-tactile recognition behaviors in the blind baby is a function of brain maturation as well as libidinization of the partner. Both factors must be present, of course, to lead to recognition behavior.

Negative Reactions to the Stranger

On a scale of human attachment, negative reaction to the stranger is regarded as a criterion for the assessment of the positive bonds to the mother and other human partners. (Spitz 1957; Benjamin 1963; Provence and Lipton 1962; Ainsworth 1967; and Yarrow 1967). It speaks for another level of valuation of the mother, in which the positive affect is bound to a partner, in which persons are no longer "interchangeable," and for a new level of cognitive discrimination.

Among sighted children it is the visual discrimination of the stranger's face which elicits avoidance behavior or fear in the child between the ages of seven and fifteen months. (Ranges from

Morgan and Ricciutti 1969.) The experimental situations which have been designed to study the developmental characteristics of stranger reaction require, of course, the presentation of the stranger's face and the reactions of the baby to the visual stimulus of the face.

When I now summarize our findings on the stranger reactions of the blind babies in our sample, I do not wish to strain the comparisons between blind and sighted children. The conditions which elicited negative reactions to the stranger for blind children are not identical with those observed and studied in sighted children; a non-visual percept of the stranger is not a true equivalent of a visual percept.

All that can be said with confidence is that in a longitudinal study of 10 babies blind from birth, negative reactions to the stranger were manifest in naturalistic observation and elicited in experimental approaches by the stranger. The first manifestations of stranger avoidance and fear emerged in the period seven to fifteen months for 9 of the 10 children. This correspondence to the period of onset in sighted children invites inquiry.

For both sighted and blind children, discrimination of familiar persons and strangers is manifest some weeks or months before the onset of stranger avoidance or stranger anxiety. We have already seen in our discussion of "smiling" and "tactile language" that the blind baby shows differential responses to familiar persons and strangers in the period under six months of age. I should also add—and this is an important bridge to the material that follows—that the blind baby, like the sighted baby, in the period under six months reacted with squirming and discomfort to subtle postural differences when held in the stranger's arms. Ainsworth (1967) describes similar reactions in sighted children during the same period. But this is not yet fear of the stranger; rather, as Benjamin (1963) suggests, it is the experience of something different, something strange.

As the data emerge from the descriptive protocols and films there is nothing in our records for any child under seven months that can yet be classified as "a negative reaction" to the stranger. Reactions to the observer's voice and to being held in the observer's arms were recorded at each visit.

Between seven and fifteen months, we find that something new begins to emerge in the blind baby's behavior toward the stranger—struggling, straining away, crying—which, for the majority of the babies in our sample, occurs when the observer holds the baby. These fear and avoidance behaviors appear even though the observer, a twice-monthly visitor, is not, strictly speaking, a stranger. At the same time that these reactions are manifest in relation to the observer, we have parallel reports from the mothers, showing that fear of strangers has emerged with other visitors to the house as well.

To the stranger's voice only (no touching or holding) we have only one observation of fear reaction during this period. (See Karen's protocols below.) A typical reaction to "voice only" is something we have called "quieting" in response to the stranger's voice, that is, cessation of activity or vocalizing (without signs of distress) which may last for several minutes, or even longer. I should state at the outset that we have not scored "quieting" as a negative reaction. However, among our blind children it regularly precedes the developmental period in which manifest stranger avoidance or fear occurs. Among sighted children, Ainsworth (1967) and others describe "quieting" or "staring" in the period that precedes fear of the stranger.

In addition to "voice only" we tested the reaction of the baby to being held in the observer's arms at each of the twice-monthly visits. The observer employed a modulated approach to the baby, speaking to him both before picking him up and during the period of his being held. The cumulative record for each child was then analyzed, and examples of the first manifestations of negative reactions to the stranger were sorted and credited, first by me, then jointly in senior staffing where we debated criteria. The credited "first examples" were made through staff consensus.

The problem of setting criteria and making judgments was dif-

SELMA FRAIBERG

ficult in the case of blind infants. Many of the criteria used in sighted child studies were inapplicable. "Sobering," for example, scored by some investigators as a negative reaction in sighted children, is inapplicable in the case of blind children. There is actually not enough contrast in the facial expressions of blind babies to produce a valid judgment of "sobering." And, since the blind baby's smiles for the stranger are rare, *not* smiling to the stranger has no value in assessment. "Frowning" is not an expressive sign for all of our blind babies, and we have some evidence that when it appears at all, it occurs among those babies who have minimal light perception. But, as an infrequent or atypical sign in our sample, we cannot use "frowning" as a criterion of negative response. In fact, there is a considerable range of expressive facial behavior, normally modulated through visual experience, which is simply not available to the blind child (see Chapter IV), and the observer judgments regarding "negative reactions" must be made through other signs.

We are left, then, with a limited number of signs in our blind children that can fairly be called "negative reactions" and "fear responses" to the stranger. Vocal displeasure—whimpering, crying, screaming—remains the same for the blind child as for the sighted one. Avoidance and motor resistance to the approach of unfamiliar persons, followed by active seeking of the mother, will also appear in blind children and can be fairly judged as a negative reaction.

The following examples represent in each case the first instance in our records of the appearance of negative reactions to the stranger in 9 cases which provided unambiguous evidence.*

Toni, 0:7:2
Soon after the observer (S.F.) picks her up, she freezes, then bursts into tears. She scans the face of the observer with her fingers, registers increasing distress on her face, strains away from the observer's body,

* This report and its protocols supersede Fraiberg (1971). Data here reflect final screening of sample for eligibility criteria and ages of 3 children corrected for prematurity.

The Development of Human Attachments

turns her head and trunk as if seeking to locate her mother by voice. She claws at the examiner's arms. She begins to scream loudly. When she is returned to her mother, she settles, still crying, scans her mother's face with her fingers and is gradually comforted.

Carol, 0:8:22
The observer picks up Carol and holds her. Twice Carol strains away from O's shoulder. When O takes Carol's hand in hers to bring it to O's face, Carol's hand closes in a fist.

Jamie, 0:9:12
E.L. is visiting with the team today. Jamie has never met him before. E.L. picks up the baby and begins to talk to him. As soon as he is picked up, Jamie begins to cry. He is handed to his mother, who diverts him with a game and succeeds in comforting him.

Kathie, 0:10:16 *
The observer speaks to Kathie. She is attentive. Now the observer picks her up. Kathie stiffens, feels the observer's face with her right hand, clutches her shirt with the other hand, whimpers, and is transferred to her mother's arms.

Karen, 0:12:19 *
Mother reached out and took observer E.A.'s coat; she walked to the dining room with the coat and E.A. said "Hi, Karen" very quietly. Karen turned in the direction of the dining room and, crying and whining quietly, crawled after her mother.

Paul, 1:1:5
Later in the morning, when he was standing on the floor, I offered him my hand while talking to him. Once again, he listened but made no move on his own to approach closer. Both with S.F. (second observer) and myself, he turned away from us as soon as he heard his father's voice, and reached toward his father.

Ronnie, 1:3:1
Avoids contact with observer today for the first time. Withdraws from her touch (while in earlier sessions he reached out to her). While he made no overt objection to my picking him up, he would not sit on my lap nor make any attempt to mold in the sitting position, but stiffened and arched back, so that his head hung over my feet.

* Ages corrected for prematurity for these children throughout text and tables.

Joan, 1:3:17
As the observer began to engage Joan in play, he noticed fear and withdrawal for the first time in his regular visits. When he spoke to Joan and touched her, she drew her hand away. Later, too, when he attempted to place her on his lap, Joan withdrew from contact and tried to get away from him. When he offered her objects in a testing situation during this session, she was unwilling to touch and explore any of the items.

Jackie, 1:3:21 *
Jackie is sitting on his mother's lap, not at the moment engaged with mother or the observers. The observer picks him up and brings him to stand, holding his hands. There is not an immediate negative reaction. On film we see an initial smile on his face. But this is followed by constraint and motor signs of discomfort (observer's own notes). Now, on film he turns in the direction of mother, on the couch, correctly orienting himself, and holds out his arms to mother. Mother offers her hand and as soon as Jackie makes contact with the hand he begins to crawl up on his mother's lap. Once on mother's lap he makes chance contact with the observer's hand, fingers it, then turns back toward mother, very actively climbing on mother, and settles in a supine position on her lap. He then engages mother in a favorite game.

This leaves 1 subject out of 10 who has not given evidence of stranger avoidance during the first eighteen months. It may be worth reporting on this child to complete the picture.

Robbie
Robbie provided one example of "quieting" to the observer's voice and no examples of negative reactions to strangers at any time in the second year. During the second year he allowed our own observers and other unfamiliar persons to hold him and to play with him. We have examples in our hospital waiting room and other unfamiliar places in which his indiscriminate friendliness to strangers is recorded. He is also the one child in our group whose attachment to his mother was regarded by us as unstable, without signs of active seeking of the mother for pleasure or comfort.

If we can accept, then, those differences in testing reactions which were required when we needed to translate procedures for testing sighted infants into procedures for blind infants, there is fair equivalence in the characteristics of stranger anxiety in our blind baby sample and those reported for sighted children.

Toward the Constitution of Mother as Object

During the period eight to fifteen months, then, we have identified a number of discriminating and preferential behaviors in our blind infants which speak for the affective investment in the mother. We can fairly speak of "focused relationships" (Yarrow 1972), and we can see correspondence between these signs of attachment in blind infants and sighted infants. Moreover, these affective signs speak clearly for cognitive advances which are seen in the forms of tactile and auditory discrimination that are implicit in preferential behaviors.

But now, if we examine our data closely, we will also see divergence from the patterns of sighted children during the period eight to fifteen months. In the pages that follow I will try to show that these are related to the unique problem the blind infant has in the constitution of objects.

The sighted child at 7.7 months (on the Escalona-Corman scale) has achieved stage 4. He demonstrates through his behavior toward the screened toy that he has an elementary belief in permanence, that an object that disappears from his visual field has an existence when not perceived. The baby's elementary deduction leads him to remove the screen and recover the object. In this achievement we also discern that the baby's memory for the object that has left his visual field is sustained for the brief interval of this simple test (Wolff 1960). From the experimental work of Saint-Pierre (1962) and Bell (1970), we also know that there is close temporal correspondence between the attribution of permanence to persons and to things. Person permanence normally inaugurates the stage. The advance in conceptual development in the sighted child moves apace with the libidinal investment of the

SELMA FRAIBERG

mother. There is, in fact, a remarkable correspondence between the onset of separation protest in the seven-to-twelve-month period and the emerging concept of mother as object (Ainsworth 1967; Yarrow 1972; Fraiberg 1968; 1969).

Now, if we examine our findings on 10 blind infants we will see points of divergence in the characteristics of human attachments which I believe are related to the extraordinary problems for the blind child in the constitution of the mother as object.

When the blind baby at eight months hears his mother's voice at tactile remove from his person, his smile or his vocalizations or his motor excitement will show selective response to her voice but there is no behavior yet that tells us that his mother's voice is united with the very substantial mother whose touch and embrace are familiar to him. If we watch his hands we see that there is not yet an outward reach to her voice, no motor signs in the fingers that speak for touching or grasping. Yet the same baby in his mother's arms must experience her embrace, her distinctive tactile qualities and her voice as a unified experience. The problem, then, for the blind baby is to reconstitute this unified mother of the embrace in another space, at tactile remove, when only one attribute is presented him—her voice.

The sighted child, as early as five months, has a mother with a picture identity; vision has guaranteed that the mother's voice and touch will be united with the picture. The sighted child does not have to reconstitute his mother from her sensory components; the picture gives unity and coherence to all sensory experience of her.

The blind baby at eight months who does not yet reach out to the mother's voice when she is at tactile remove will also show us that he does not yet reach out for a favorite sound toy when he hears it and when it is within easy range of his hands. We have examples from 9 of our 10 children (age range four to eight months) demonstrating that when a cherished toy is sounded close at hand at midline, the blind baby shows alertness and attention, but makes no attempt to reach. It is as if the musical teddy-bear, gently removed from his hands a moment before, is "not the same teddy-bear" when the baby hears the sound alone. The blind baby can-not yet attribute substantiality or a sound-touch identity to the toy through its sound alone. (See Chapter VII; also Fraiberg 1968 and Fraiberg, Siegel, and Gibson 1966.)

For 10 children, the range for achievement of "midline reach for and attainment of the toy on sound cue only" was 6:18 to 11:1; median age 8:27.

Proximity-Seeking Behaviors: The Emergence of the Concept of Mother as Object

Between the ages of ten months and sixteen months our 10 babies demonstrate for the first time proximity-seeking behaviors toward the mother's voice (with mother at tactile remove). This signifies that the mother has acquired a voice-touch identity, that the baby confers substantiality and an elementary form of permanence (Piaget's stage 4) on his mother when only one of her attributes, voice, is given. Our findings are derived entirely from the de-scriptive protocols and films. No experimental procedures were employed because we could not know in the design stage of the study how a blind baby would find the solution to the problem of proximity seeking. The baby was to teach us.

The protocols for each child were systematically examined and submitted to these criteria:

(1) The mother must be at tactile remove from the baby when she is speaking.
(2) The baby must manifest through his behavior a concept of mother as substantial and external to the self.

I credited the following: (a) the baby extends his hands direc-tionally in a reach toward mother upon hearing her voice; (b) if mobile, he creeps directionally toward mother upon hearing her voice; (c) if the word "mama" is now in use as a correct referent, he says "mama."

For (a) I credited 5 children; for (b) 4 children; for (c) 1 child. Crediting the first demonstration in the record, the age range for the attainment of these criteria was from 0:10:5 to 16 months; median age, 11:20.

The concept of mother which is demonstrated in these behaviors has some correspondence with stage 4 for the sighted child; an elementary form of permanence for persons has emerged in which the mother is constituted as an object when only one of her attributes, voice, is given. The extended hands on voice cue, the directional creep toward mother on voice cue, speak for the expectation of a tactile reunion, which is to say that the auditory and tactile schemas for mother are conceptually unified and the previously experienced unified mother of the embrace can be mentally reconstituted as an object in another space.

In this description the reader may experience the same sense of disbelief that I remember in myself earlier in this investigation. To all of us who have worked extensively with sighted children, the gesture of extended hands toward the mother is familiar from the age of five months (Griffiths 1954). Yet it is not until the last quarter of the first year that this gesture appears among our blind children.

I was well advanced in our study when I understood this. It was very simple. The sighted child's extended hands for mother represent exactly his level of prehension. The sighted child at five months reaches for what he sees, grasps what he reaches, and already, through his advance in prehension, has hundreds of lessons every day which unite the tactile, visual, and auditory experiences of both human and inanimate objects. When the sighted child reaches toward his mother he does not need a concept of mother; he only needs to coordinate eye and hand. The blind child must have an elementary concept of permanence of the mother before he can reach directionally toward his mother, or creep directionally toward her. Tragically, this long delay in achieving the coordination of ear and hand for things and for persons has led many observers and examiners of blind infants to label a child as mentally retarded or unaffectionate, whereas we can now see that this achievement gives eloquent testimony of an advance in conceptual development which demands a high level of inference.

There is, then, an expected correspondence between the blind child's achievement of an elementary concept of permanence for persons and for things. However, our findings on "midline reach for the toy on sound cue only" and "proximity-seeking behaviors for the mother" should be interpreted with caution. The ranges cited for "midline reach for the sound toy" are seven to eleven months. For the person data the ranges are ten to sixteen months. Does this mean that the coordination of ear and hand is achieved earlier for toys than for persons? I think not. The discrepancy in age of onset is more likely attributable to the data sources and the criteria employed for scoring.

Firstly, the toy findings are derived mainly from experimental studies, which means of course that we regularly elicited the highest performance available in the child's repertoire. We did not employ experimental procedures for eliciting the baby's proximity-seeking behaviors in response to mother's voice at tactile remove. These data were derived entirely from naturalistic observation. If the behavior was not manifest spontaneously in the observation session, it did not enter the record.

Secondly, the proximity-seeking behaviors toward mother required a higher level of proficiency in localizing sound and the coordination of tactile-auditory schemas than those required in the toy tests, where we tested reach and attainment of the sound toy at midline. To reach *directionally* toward the mother on voice cue corresponds to a higher level of directional reach identified by Edna Adelson in the prehension studies (see Chapter VII). To creep toward mother when her voice is heard requires an advance in mobility which was not required, of course, in the toy experiments. To utter the word "mama" in meaningful use when mother's voice is heard is on a still higher level of concept development. In brief, my examination of the emerging concept of permanence for mother credited the first example in the record which spoke for a spontaneous demonstration of a concept of mother and in naturalistic circumstance these demonstrations tapped a repertoire of behaviors which were not available to the child in the toy experiments.

This long, and possibly exhausting, narrative of the blind child's attribution of permanence to persons and to things finally brings us to a milestone of momentous import. When the blind baby demonstrates to us his proximity-seeking behaviors toward mother he tells us that the concept of mother as an object is emerging. His level of concept development has close correspondence with that of the sighted child at stage 4. The sighted child who is fully equipped with a picture memory when he sets out on this journey toward an object world has long ago passed the milestone. Our maps tell us that he passed stage 4 at 7:7 months (Escalona-Corman scale), and was already equipped at that age with a functioning locomotor capability, that he raced on to stage 5 at 9:4 and was advancing steadily toward stage 6 at the close of the first year (mean age 17.2).

The blind child, in a world without picture memory, has pursued this route in a dark labyrinth. At the close of the first year he has achieved stage 4. He has also just invented his own mobility (late, by sighted-child norms), and he ventures forth into the void to begin the mapping of distant space. In customary language we can speak of these late achievements as the "developmental lags" of blind infants. But if we follow the blind infant as he pursues this treacherous route in the labyrinth, we can see these accomplishments as heroic adaptive feats.

Separation and Reunion

For sighted children, there is now a fair consensus among investigators that separation protest or distress emerges in the third quarter of the first year. Stayton, Ainsworth and Main (1971), in a report of their longitudinal studies, place the median age of onset of separation distress in a "mother leave room" situation at 22 weeks or 5.5 months. Other studies (Schaffer and Emerson 1964; Tennes and Lampl 1964; and Spitz 1965) give us a range of six to eight months in average age of onset. However, criteria and observational procedures differed among these studies.

Allowing for these differences among several studies, the age of onset of separation protest or anxiety appears to have some correspondence with the emergence of a concept of permanence for the mother (approximately stage 4). This means, of course, that both an affective investment in the mother and a cognitive advance enter into the experience of separation distress. There must be at least an elementary concept of mother as an object before her absence is perceived as loss.

In briefest summary, we see that between the ages of six and eight months there is a confluence of events in the development of the sighted child in which affective, motor and cognitive advances unite in the service of human attachments. Valuation of and preference for mother, established under six months of age, are now given poignancy by the cognitive awareness of loss, and the baby protests even the momentary disappearance of his mother. An advance in motor development permits him to follow his mother and maintain contact with her. An advance in conceptual development confers upon the mother some measure of permanence as an object, but it is still an uncertain belief which binds her to a place, and it requires frequent confirmation or verification through vision. During the next 12 months the sighted baby's experiments, plus a tremendous advance in representational intelligence, will permit him to account for his mother's displacements in space and finally to constitute his mother as an object (stage 6).

For the blind children in our group, the first manifestations of separation protest and distress appear in the age range 10:22 to 1:9:24; median age, 11:20. There is, then, about a 6-month difference between our blind children and sighted children in the age of onset of separation protest. The age of onset of separation protest shows some correspondence with the onset of proximity-seeking behaviors described in the previous section and suggests links with a stage 4 level of person permanence.

In the following pages I propose to examine the onset of separation protest in relation to (a) the blind child's awareness of "absence and presence"; (b) his concept of mother as an object; (c) tracking on sound; and (d) locomotion as experience in learning the displaceability of objects.

For comparison with sighted children we will find it useful to discriminate among the forms of separation protest and the conditions which elicit them, following Ainsworth (1972).

Ainsworth differentiates between anxiety following prolonged separations ("definitive separations") and "separation protest" in minor everyday situations. In her 1972 essay and elsewhere, she agrees with other authors that separation protest is a criterion of considerable value in the assessment of human attachments, but in her view it should not be employed as the only criterion of attachment. When separation protest is present along with other behaviors ("following" when mother leaves the room, active contact behaviors, affectionate behaviors, approach through locomotion and the use of mother as a secure base to explore, flight to mother as a haven of safety, and clinging) Ainsworth feels that the judgment of "attachment" can be fairly made.

As we examine our blind infant data on separation we will use two classifications: "minor everyday" separation and "prolonged" separations. We found, as Ainsworth reports, a close correspondence between the occurrence of protest and/or anxiety in both types of separation.

Our data on the emergence of separation protest in "minor, everyday situations" are derived entirely from naturalistic circumstance. We recorded descriptively all occurrences in which mother left the room for a few moments and described the baby's reactions. Until the close of the first year we have no examples in which the blind baby registered in any discernible way an awareness of mother "not present," except in circumstances where hunger or an interrupted game with mother were antecedent conditions. To fairly approximate the "neutral conditions" which provided the base for sighted-child observations of "separation protest" (in which neither need states nor interrupted play were factors), I chose only those examples in our records in which the baby's state would not introduce other variables. (For example, the baby is occupied with a toy, or is listening attentively to conversation between mother and others in the room, and mother leaves the room for a few moments.)

Our data on reactions to prolonged separations (mother employed for several hours a day; mother absent for several days) are derived from direct observation *and* parent reports, since such details as the child's reactions when mother is in the hospital, or the child's reactions when mother is working often had to be filled in by the care-giver's reports to the mother.

We might begin with a general frame of reference for the examination of the blind child's experience of separation: How does the blind child experience what we know as "mother not present"?

BLINDNESS AND THE EXPERIENCE OF
"PRESENCE" AND "ABSENCE"

In the case of the blind infant even the concept of "momentary separation" must be modified and expanded to include a range of experience that may be called "not in contact" and "maintaining contact." It is more difficult in the case of the blind baby to isolate those conditions that mean mother is "absent" in everyday experience. In the case of the sighted child, mother is absent when she is not seen. Vision also permits the sighted child to give meaning to the "goings" and "comings" of his mother, since he can track her with his eyes to the point at which she leaves his visual field (goes to another room, closes a door, and so on).

For the blind child, even when his mother is present in the room, if she is not in physical proximity and refrains from talking or moving, she has left the child's perceptual field. The silencing of mother's voice, however, is not an equivalent in the blind child's experience to the disappearance of the mother for the sighted child. Vision, by its nature, is continuous; visual tracking confers temporal order to events, and a break or closure of the visual record is read as the sign of "gone." Sound, on the other hand, is discontinuous, and for large periods in a blind child's day, things and people do not manifest themselves to him through sound (or touch). Since there is no predictability in events that are experienced through intermittent sound, the breaking or closure of a sound sequence need not by itself connote "separation" or "loss" or "absence."

For these reasons we chose not to define "separation" for the blind baby at the start of our study, but to examine the experiences of "not in contact" and "maintaining contact" with the mother's voice or her person, with the expectation that at certain as yet unknown points in development during the sensorimotor period, the experience of "loss" would be registered in identifiable ways, and the means of perception of loss would be revealed to us.

In the early weeks of life the sighted child maintains contact with the people and the things of his world by fixating on nearby objects and by tracking movement through vision. As recognition memory becomes available to the baby (and he demonstrates this at under three months in the response smile to the configuration of the human face), he scans his environment and can "rediscover" both human and inanimate objects that are momentarily "absent." Repetition of the game of scanning and recovery probably affords a kind of elementary belief in permanence, that things "lost" can be "found" and are somehow at the disposal of vision (Piaget, stages 1–3). Visual tracking of moving objects, both human and inanimate, affords the sighted child the first practical demonstrations that a person or object (sensory picture) located at point A can appear again or be "rediscovered" at points B and at C,D,E, and so on. And long before the child achieves even an elementary notion of causality, visual tracking prepares him for the discoveries at the end of the first year that an object is not bound to place, that it can be subject to multiple displacements (stage 5) and, finally, between thirteen and eighteen months, to the discovery that the displacements of objects can occur independently of his perception of their movements, which then enables him to take account of invisible displacements and to employ an elementary form of deduction regarding an object's probable route (stage 6). At this stage the sighted child conducts a sustained search for a lost object, which testifies to the emergence of a belief in permanence; the person or the object "must be someplace."

The human partner leads the way to these discoveries, as psychoanalysts and Piaget have shown. The person-object sequences which lead to object permanence have been experimentally worked out by Saint-Pierre (1962) and Bell (1972) and in these reports we see that *person permanence normally precedes toy permanence;* that when the search for the not-present mother takes account of her invisible displacements, discoveries leading to belief in the permanence of inanimate objects follow closely in temporal sequence.

For the blind child during most of the first year there is no equivalent for the sighted child's visual scanning or tracking to locate and maintain contact with the mother if she is momentarily out of the child's perceptual field. And where vision guarantees the perception of movement and the "displaceability" of human and inanimate objects, the blind infant cannot attribute movement to objects, or "comings" and "goings," until his own mobility in the second year gives him the experimental conditions for tracking and recovering persons and toys in multiple displacements.

As we have reported in the preceding section of this chapter, acoustical tracking and localization of sound is not achieved by any child in our sample until the last quarter of the first year. And when he reaches directionally for or creeps toward a person or toy on sound cue only, he demonstrates at the same time an emerging concept of permanence, probably on the level of stage 4. The sound "out there" now connotes a person or a toy, and his reach or his locomotor approach signifies that he confers substantiality, a sound-touch unity to the person or object.

This is, I believe, a virtuoso achievement. From all of our evidence, for most of the first year substantiality is affirmed tactually by the blind child. To endow the sound "out there" with meaning, he can employ only one distance sense, hearing, one that was "intended" in the biological program to evolve in synchrony with vision.

This means, of course, that during the first year the awareness and the experience of "mother not present" for the blind child can emerge only under two types of circumstances: In need states, if the cry or signals of distress do not summon her, if there is a delay in answering the signal or satisfying the need, the blind baby may have an acute sense of "loss" or "not present" and when the mother is constituted as an object, at least on the level of stages 4 and 5 (i.e., if her voice and footsteps connote substantiality to the blind child) "presence" and "absence" become open to objective confirmation. Mother is "present" when she manifests herself through voice or sounds of movement and "absent" when she does not. Under all favorable conditions in which the mother has become the central person, the affectively significant person, awareness of "absence" can also evoke protest, distress and anxiety in ways that are entirely analogous to the experience of separation in sighted children.

For both the blind child and the sighted child, then, the manifestations of separation protest and anxiety are linked to the emergence of object permanence, in which the human partner is endowed with objective attributes. If we can employ my provisional crediting of stage 4 to the level of concept development achieved by our blind children at the close of the first year, the emergence of separation protest and anxiety during the same period has close correspondence with sighted-child data which link the emergence of separation anxiety with stage 4.

Next, we should examine the possible relations between the

onset of separation protest and the onset of locomotion in our blind group. See Chapter IX for a discussion of the typical delays in creeping and free walking in our blind group. Creeping was achieved by 9 of our 10 children in the range of ten and a half to sixteen and a half months; free walking in the range of twelve to twenty months. We also describe the relationship between the onset of self-initiated mobility with the coordination of ear and hand. (No child could creep before he first demonstrated reach and attainment of the sound object.) This links locomotion in the blind child to an elementary form of object permanence.

With the onset of locomotion, the blind baby can begin to conduct a large number of experiments which will inform him of the displaceability of human and inanimate objects and he will now be able to use his newly acquired ability to track movement by sound, along with his newly acquired locomotor skills, in a discovery and rediscovery of his mother dozens of times every day. It is even possible that the discovery, in a sense, of his own "displaceability" through locomotion gives some substance to the concept of "movement" which the blind child cannot perceive in any ways that are analogous to the experience of the sighted— that is, as a sequence of pictures. In all these ways, then, mobility plays a central role in the blind child's construction of an object world, and specifically, in the problem under examination, in constituting the mother as object.

ILLUSTRATION: THE COURSE OF SEPARATION AND REUNION BEHAVIOR BETWEEN ELEVEN MONTHS AND TWENTY-FIVE MONTHS

To illustrate the course of separation and reunion behavior I have chosen a set of protocols from Karen's record. Karen falls within the upper half of our group on nearly all dimensions studied. She was blind from birth due to retrolental fibroplasia and was three months premature. She was first seen by us at eight months. (Age is corrected for prematurity in these examples.) Karen was totally blind during her first eighteen months. Light perception (but no form perception) was observed beginning at eighteen months.

Until 0:11:13 we have no observations in our records which show that Karen registered the numerous momentary absences of her mother from the room occasioned by the fact that there was a baby sister (Debby) who required mother's attention. Typically Karen did not interrupt her own activities, did not protest, did not appear to be listening for cues of presence or absence. At eleven months we began to see the first signs of separation protest, now reported by mother and confirmed in our observations.

Karen, it should be noted, began to creep at ten and a half months.

> Karen, 0:11:13 (Mother's report)
> Mother remarked that she can't leave Karen with anyone anymore, which has not been the case until very recently. Karen cries and is unhappy even with her grandmother, whom she has known since birth. Added to Karen's behavior today is her need to always be in contact with mother.
>
> Karen, 0:11:13 (Observer's report)
> Karen let herself down to the floor and started to creep to the box which was about 2 feet away from her. She was somewhat hesitant or cautious, but she was curious. At this moment, mother got up to go to Debby to give her the pacifier because she was fussing. Karen immediately started to whimper, reversed direction, and went back to cling to mother's chair and when mother sat down again, reached to touch mother's arm. Mother reached out and touched Karen's hair.

In the 0:11:13 observation we see that both awareness of mother's absence and distress at that absence have emerged together. But Karen's new-found mobility does not yet lead her to tracking mother on sound cues; her concept of mother as object is illustrated rather in her behavior following loss of mother. *She seeks mother's chair, which is now vacant, of course, and clings to it.* Mother "belongs to" the chair, as it were, and is conceived as having one position in space, the place where Karen had last had contact with her. This is a stage 4 behavior.

Ten days later, we see the same behavior in relation to father.

Karen, 0:11:23
A few minutes later, when father was helping mother gather things up, getting ready to go, Karen suddenly realized that he was not in his seat. She crawled to the empty chair, felt around, stood up, and cried loudly. She would not go toward him when he called her from across the room, but just stood there crying until he came and picked her up.

Father, too, at 0:11:23 "belongs to" his empty chair.
At 0:12:4 we see the beginnings of search for mother after mother leaves the room.

Karen, 0:12:4
Mother offers her visitors coffee. When she leaves the room to start the water boiling, Karen begins to whine. Karen crawls out of the living room into the dining room, perhaps in search of her mother. Mother returns to the room and asks Karen, "Where are you going?" Karen turns around at her mother's voice and crawls to her mother's chair. She smiles and stops crying when she finds her mother's knee. She proceeds to touch her mother's legs again.

Karen's apparent search for her mother (who is at this time actually in the kitchen) leads her to the dining room, which is on the route. If we assume that Karen's mother has, for Karen, left the child's perceptual field, the search to another room must represent an advance in object concept: she does not return to an empty chair, as she did in the 11-month sequence. She searches for her mother in another place, which means that she can conceive of her mother as a "displaceable" object. Analogies with stage 5 behavior suggest themselves.

Two weeks later, Karen is tracking her mother from room to room, and a summary of observations in this session shows also that crying has diminished when mother momentarily leaves the room. One example will illustrate:

Karen, 0:12:19
Mother picks up Debby and carries her into the bedroom talking very quietly to her. Karen, who is busy with a necklace, picks up the distant voice of her mother and, without crying, crawls over all the toys and follows her mother into the bedroom.

In this example Karen can track her mother on sound and use her own mobility to locate and reunite with her. The discovery that a temporarily "lost" mother can be "found" appears to be a potent antidote to separation anxiety, at least within the safety of the home, which is now well mapped for Karen.

One week later the observer's summary statement shows increasing tolerance for momentary separations.

> Karen, 0:12:26 (Observer's summary)
> *Separation from mother:* In this area, too, there was a new Karen. She seemed happy to come upon her mother, but she didn't convey any anxiety when her mother left the room. She did not use as much energy in apparently listening for her mother to move out of the living room. Rather, she was occupied with other people and other activities and seemed comfortable even when her mother was out of the room. She seemed to have grown past following her mother around constantly.

Two observations at fourteen and fifteen months show sustained tolerance for momentary separations.

> Karen, 1:1:23
> Mother leaves the room to get Debby. There is no reaction from Karen when her mother leaves the room.

> Karen, 1:2:7
> Karen came and went, sometimes seeking mother, sometimes on her own, sometimes out of sight, since I did not feel I could follow her around.

Then, at 1:2:28 we have an observation that shows us that separation anxiety will still be evoked under certain circumstances. In this example, we should note, we had inadvertently created two barriers to Karen's search for mother. We were filming at that visit, and our tripod obstructed Karen's path. Also, to make space for filming we had moved one of the living room chairs so that it was not only out of place but partially obstructed the kitchen doorway.

> Karen, 1:2:28
> Mother leaves the living room to see why Debby is fussing in the bedroom. Karen crawls after her, gets tangled up with the tripod, but

manages to make her way through anyway without tipping it over. Here is a problem for Karen. She is not quite sure where mother is and goes to the kitchen for her first try. We have moved one of the living room chairs, so that it is in the dining room, almost in the kitchen doorway, not at all where it should ordinarily be. Karen has to move around it in order to get to the kitchen. She makes the detour, goes into the kitchen, then hears her mother in the bedroom. Karen is crying by the time she gets to her mother.

We had inadvertently created barriers both to memory and to locomotion. Assuming that some form of mental representation of mother is available to Karen as she conducts her searches during this period, the tripod and the chair may constitute distractions or obstacles to memory by introducing competing problems for attention. Assuming that Karen can, for short intervals, sustain a mental representation of mother in spite of barriers to perception and memory, the tripod and chair were obstacles to locomotion and, therefore, to her recovery of mother. Karen, who has been able to track her mother accurately from room to room for the past three months, becomes slightly disoriented. Like Ariadne in the labyrinth, she must find her path by a thread, but Karen's thread has become tangled in barriers. Under these conditions mother becomes "lost" again, in her own house, and Karen, by the time she picks up the voice thread again, is crying.

Between fifteen and twenty-six months Karen (who began free walking at fifteen months) has a variety of ways in which she "keeps in touch" with mother, and anxiety at momentary separations is no longer recorded.

At sixteen months she is still experimenting with her new freedom in walking and stays in close touch with her mother.

Karen, 1:4:9
Karen is extremely and insistently independent in walking, while at the same time staying very close to mother, constantly renewing physical contact with mother if a stranger or a disliked adult is present.

At nearly two years of age, Karen has begun to make more and more use of language to locate her mother. The word "mama" can now be used as a probe to take soundings of her mother's where-abouts.

Karen, 1:11:25
Mother was busy in the kitchen. An interesting interaction between Karen and her mother followed. Karen would be ordered into the living room, she would go to the dining room, pause, then return to the kitchen where she would maintain contact with her mother by saying, "mama." Her mother would answer, "what?" and Karen would say, "mama" again. This was repeated to the distraction of mother, who would order her out to the living room again. During the dining room sojourns of Karen, she seemed to be waiting a decent interval before she could sneak back into the kitchen.

At twenty-six months another example:

Karen, 2:2:26
With form board: She held the triangular piece in her left hand and felt the board with her right hand. She couldn't find the right hole and called "mommy" in frustration but was finally able to fit the piece in by herself. Karen removed the circle and triangle and clapped them together. She called to her mother, "doing?" and her mother answered "nothing, what are you doing?" Karen briefly felt the holes on the form board while holding the pieces and repeated "doing?" This time her mother replied, "sitting here."

By the close of the second year examples of anxiety at momentary separations are rare for Karen. We do not see distress again, except during periods of prolonged daily separation during a period when her mother is working part-time.

The illustrations from Karen's record of momentary separations fairly describe the process for our group of blind children: (a) awareness of loss of contact with mother; (b) distress; (c) tracking and locating mother on voice or sounds of movement; (d) following; (e) accounting for mother as a displaceable object; (f) diminution of distress; (g) use of language as a probe (a "radar device" as Lyle Warner of our staff called it) to locate and to keep in touch with mother.

The Development of Human Attachments

Our next question brings us to an area of this study which is of very great interest. What happens when the blind child's tracking and locomotor pursuit do not lead to a "rediscovery" of mother? In the early examples from Karen's record of momentary separation, we saw distressed crying, even though she was in her own home, and something close to panic when she lost touch with her mother, tried to find her in the kitchen and could not locate her on sound.

It happened that all of our children, in the first half of the second year, experienced prolonged daily separations from mother (mother working part-time was the most frequent reason), and 5 of the children were separated from their mothers for more than 3 days when either child or mother was hospitalized or a crisis required mother to be away from home. In all these cases, an examination of individual protocols showed that *extreme* forms of distress emerged in minor, everyday situations (mother leaving room) during the period that included prolonged daily separations or prolonged day and night separations. It appeared, then, that the anxiety and panic states seen in these children during the second year were forms of anticipatory anxiety in which "mother not present" signaled the danger of losing mother, which had become actual through the experience of prolonged separations.

In 5 cases, where separation of mother and child lasted for 3 or more days, we saw forms of regression and panic states that I have rarely seen in otherwise healthy children who are sighted. (Clinical examples appear in Fraiberg 1968, 1971a.) Day-and-night screaming, inability to be comforted, and loss of newly acquired achievements in language or mobility appeared during the separation, and persisted even after reunion with the mother. But also, with reunion, we saw forms of clinging to mother which were chilling to witness. The child would press himself against his mother's body in a ventral clasp which united every surface with his mother's body. "He plasters himself against me," one mother said in despair as we witnessed this. We saw primitive forms of clawing at the mother's hands, arms, and face, which the parents, quite naturally, thought was hostile. But it happened, more than once that I, too, held a blind baby who was in a panic state, and I experienced the clawing. To me this was not "hostile." It was an archaic form of anxiety, and I felt that the baby was grasping me, clutching me, digging into me, holding on in a desperate terror. The only analogy which comes to mind is the nightmare experience, in which the dreamer is hanging from a cliff, his hands clutching a ledge, his body pressed against vertical rock—with the void below.

All of the children who experienced these traumatic separations recovered, and we provided much help to the families during these critical periods (Fraiberg 1971b).

In only one case do we have no examples of separation distress or anxiety. This was Robbie. It was Robbie also who never showed stranger avoidance in the first year. As late as three years of age we have no examples of separation distress in his own home. He was, at three, very adequate in language, adaptive hand behavior, and motor skills. There was no question that self- and object-differentiation had been achieved at earlier stages, and that his ego organization was appropriate to his age. But, by all criteria known to us, Robbie could be discriminated from other children in our group as being a child who was not "securely attached" to his mother.

Chapter VII

SELMA FRAIBERG

Prehension

IN THE biological program it is "intended" that vision and prehension evolve in synchrony. The story of prehension is not the story of the maturational and adaptive functions of the hand alone, but the story of hand and eye, eye and hand. At four and a half months when the sighted child demonstrates that he can reach and attain an object "on sight" he has achieved a coordinated function of hand and eye which evolved in a biological sequence, assured under all normal environmental circumstances.

For the blind baby at four and a half months there is no equivalence in prehension. There is no adaptive substitution of the ear for the eye available to him. The coordination of ear and hand in reaching and attaining an object is achieved by the babies in our study at the median age of 8:27.

Since in our intervention program we also employed educational strategies which, we believe, facilitated the coordination of ear and hand, this "late achievement" by sighted-child standards must be examined in the light of the unique adaptive problems for the blind child in the substitution of hand and ear for hand and eye.

In all those ways, then, in which the hand unites the infant with a world "out there," in those ways in which the purposeful reach gives intentionality to action and a sense of voluntariness in the formative period of the ego, the blind child is deprived for much of the first year. In cruelest irony, these hands, quite literally groping in the near void of the blind child's world, derailed in their progress by a deficit in the biological plan, must come to serve the blind child as primary perceptual organs—something not "intended," either, in human biology.

In this chapter we will examine the unique course of adaptive hand behavior in the first year of the blind child's life. Part I will compare the developmental characteristics of prehension in sighted and blind children using a sighted-infant profile derived from the Bayley Mental and Motor Scales and a profile of a blind child at five and a half months who has had no educational intervention. Part II will describe our intervention program. Part III will summarize our findings for the 10 children we studied in the developmental sequence which leads to coordination of hand and ear in reaching and attaining an object. In Chapter VIII we will present a detailed descriptive analysis of this sequence through the study of 1 child, Robbie.

DATA SOURCES

As described in Chapter III our primary source of data in the study of prehension was the 16mm film record together with our analysis of the film by our team of senior investigators using a variable-speed projector. At one-third speed and, often, a frame-by-frame analysis we were able to examine hand behavior in fine detail. At team meetings one of the senior investigators dictated a narrative during the slow-motion review, which then gave us a transcript which could be employed for qualitative analysis and for coding.

Our code schedule included prehension items from standard scales (Gesell and Cattell were the two scales available to us during those years). We did not score these items. We described in detail the behavior observed. The film, the film narrative and the descriptive protocols gave us a bank of data for the deferred comparison with sighted-child achievements at the conclusion of the study. By 1969 the Bayley scales were available to us, and where comparison was possible in both prehensile mode and adaptive hand behavior we attempted to match our items with Bayley items using her ranges and medians.

For the study of "reach on sound" we employed experimental procedures which will be described in Part III. We were equally attentive to spontaneous demonstrations in naturalistic circumstance, and the stage-specific characteristics were derived from both sources.

Part I
Profiles: A Sighted Child and a Blind Child

It was our original intention in the data evaluation plan to select prehension items from the Bayley scale which could be fairly applied to the blind infant as well as to the sighted infant, to find the matching items in our films and protocols, to score these items and work out tables in which the age of attainment of each could be placed in relation to the ranges and medians for sighted children. This plan would then be consistent with our plan for comparative study in other areas of the investigation, which had, in fact, been found workable and useful in the areas of human attachment, gross motor development, and language.

But the plan was unworkable in the area of prehension. In an item-by-item comparison we saw qualitative differences between the hand behavior of our blind children and that of sighted children which raised serious questions in scoring. Finally, I decided that it would be more profitable to examine these qualitative differences, to present the ambiguities, and to follow the course of prehension through another mode of presentation.

For purposes of comparison, and to highlight the differences and ambiguities, I propose to construct 2 profiles. The prehension profile for the sighted child outlines the normal course of hand-eye development in the first six months, using selected milestones from the Bayley Mental and Motor Scales and, for quick reference, the Bayley medians (rounded to the nearest half month) are employed to construct the profile. The profile of the blind baby is derived from our own records and, for purposes of illustration, this baby is presented as he appears to us at five and a half months of age, our first visit, first observations, and with *no previous intervention*.

THE SIGHTED BABY'S PROFILE

At four and a half months of age, when the sighted child has achieved a co-ordinated reach for nearby objects, he has traversed a developmental route in which neurophysiological maturation and visual experience have united to produce this monumental step.

In the biological sequence, the fisted hands of the newborn begin to unfold in the early weeks, and at approximately three months these hands are mainly open. During the same period the tonic neck reflex (t-n-r) which has disposed the baby to a posture in which the head is rotated to one side with one arm extended, gives way to a midline orientation of the head which expands the range of his vision. Now, the t-n-r attitude, as Gesell (1947) is careful to emphasize, channels visual fixation to the extended hand and by gradual stages leads to hand inspection, active approach upon an object, and to manipulation of the object. This early alliance of hand and eye, which is biologically insured to promote the later complex coordinations of eye and hand, is already lost to the baby who is born blind.

At approximately three months, as the head begins to "prefer" the midline position and the range of the sighted baby's vision widens, the early alliance of eyes and hand promotes further discoveries and experiments on the baby's part in which hands and eyes advance him toward complex performances. In the supine position the hands come across the child's field of vision for close inspection. Chance encounters at first bring the fingers together for new discoveries—rudimentary discoveries—of self, in a certain sense. From the baby's fascinated inspection of hands and the sustained experiments in bringing the hands together we infer something new in his experience—novelty in sensation, novelty in a spectacle which he can produce for himself, and the beginnings of voluntariness, through the command of an elementary exercise in touching and the coordination of hands and vision.

His experiments at three months lead the baby to a game in which the hands at midline engage in mutual fingering. The sighted baby entertains himself tirelessly with his new discovery and from the rapturous look upon his face and his smiles, we infer that the game of mutual fingering is sustained by more than a biological urge. There is a large pleasure bonus for him. He doesn't know it, but the game will lead him into new discoveries within a few weeks.

The new sense of voluntariness in his hands—and the early alliance of hands and eyes—now leads him to approach objects "out there" with his hands. The earliest attempts are off-target, of course, but chance encounters win him rare rewards. He is persistent, a gambler who is always ready for another try. By four and a half months his errors drop out. If we place an object within easy reach of his hands he will pick it up with one or both of them. His grasp may still be ulnar-palmar, but he is moving toward partial thumb opposition (radial-palmar) which he will achieve before five months.*

As reciprocity between the hands develops during this four-to-five-month period the baby demonstrates in testing that he can retain 2 cubes simultaneously, one in each hand, and very soon after, at five and a half months, his proficiency in reaching and attaining objects extends to reaching for a second cube while retaining the first one in his hand.

At five and a half months the reciprocity between the hands

* Bayley (1969) defines ulnar-palmar prehension as holding an object by the fingers alone against the heel of the palm (p. 84) and radial-palmar as holding an object with thumb partially opposed to fingers, using the palm as well as the thumb and fingers (p. 86).

leads the baby to another milestone in prehension: he can transfer from hand to hand.

Before six months of age, then, the sighted baby is in possession of the primary eye-hand schemas for reaching and attaining objects. In the period between six and ten months, hand proficiency will be accelerated as grasping itself undergoes refinements leading to the efficient, fine pincer grasp at nine months. The biological sequence promotes capability; the experience and experimentation of the baby leads him to exploit his hands in increasingly complex manipulative tasks. By thirteen and a half months, the sighted baby in a testing situation can combine visual discrimination and manual dexterity by placing a round block in a round hole on the form board, and in discriminating between square blocks and square recesses. Some precocious babies at this age may sort and place correctly all the round and square blocks after the simple instruction from the examiner, "Put the block in its hole." At almost the same age, the baby can build a tower of two blocks after a demonstration by the examiner.

In the first year, then, we witness the development of prehension in a normal child as a sequence of increasingly complex schemes in which a single theme is elaborated: *eye and hand; hand and eye*.

THE BLIND BABY'S PROFILE

Prehension and vision were "intended" to evolve together in the biological program. But when a visual deficit is present from birth, what are the effects upon the course of prehensile development?

At five months of age, the sighted child has proficiency in reaching for and attaining an object. This is *not* what we see in a blind baby who has had adequate nurture and who would be assessed by us as "well within the middle range for blind children in his hand capabilities." For illustration we will construct a profile for a blind child who has come to us for the first time at the age of five months and who has had *no prior educational intervention*.

Prehension

We visit him in his home. The baby, seated in his mother's lap before a table, shows fair to good control of his head, and the head is oriented to the midline position. His hands, however, are maintained at shoulder height in the neonatal posture. The hands are open, and in the course of a one-hour observation period, the empty hands are seen to execute occasional grasping-ungrasping motions or to engage in inutile fingering in mid-air. If his mother or the examiner touches a rattle to his hand, he will grasp it firmly and retain it. If a second toy is introduced to the other hand, he will drop one toy. If a favorite toy is in his hand and he drops it, his face registers no emotion, and he will not make a gesture of search for it.

If we guide his hands to the table surface which is provided with 2 or 3 toys he will show some alertness and interest when he makes contact with the toy. If he makes contact with a cube, he will grasp it clumsily, but we note partial thumb opposition, as if the biological pattern has emerged but is unpracticed.

When interest wanes, or when the hands are empty, they return to their station at shoulder height. Our clinical eyes are riveted on those hands. *There is virtually no engagement of the hands at midline*. If, by chance, the two hands encounter each other at midline, we may see brief and transient mutual fingering.

To test the baby's optimal capacities in responding to a sound toy, we invite the mother to bring us one of his favorite toys. She is doubtful. He doesn't really like toys very much. But maybe his musical teddy bear. She will get it. It is soft and cuddly. Its music is Brahms' Lullaby. It is wound up and placed in the baby's hands. He holds it close, listens attentively to its music. At one point we ask mother to remove the toy from his hands for a moment. She gently takes it from him and places it on the table within easy reach of his hands. The baby registers no emotion and does not make even a gesture of reach or recovery as the toy continues to play its music. It is as if the musical bear that he had just held in his hands is "not the same bear" when it is "out there" and only one of its attributes, sound, is manifest to him.

"Is he deaf?" the mother asks worriedly. No. We have tested his hearing throughout this session. "Is he retarded?" the mother asks. And in response to this anguished question, which we have heard many times, we can now assure the mother that what we have seen is characteristic of blind children at this age. We begin to sketch for the mother the extraordinary problems for the blind baby in the coordination of ear and hand and weave in suggestions which will facilitate this development.

What we have seen in this typical profile of a blind baby at five months of age is a biological program that has been derailed and for which adaptive solutions have not yet been found.

As we examine the prehension items recorded in this profile of a blind child, we can see that there is no possibility of comparing the blind and sighted child in an item-by-item inventory of prehension and no possibility of fairly scoring these items using sighted-child criteria.

If, for instance, we examine the items of hand behavior that are normally regarded as milestones in a biological sequence, we find a disordered picture. As we have said, the head has found its midline orientation but the hands have not. Our eyes are riveted upon those hands which "prefer" a station at the shoulders. The hands are "open" but mainly empty and as we watch them at shoulder height in their inutile fingering, or grasping-ungrasping motions, we see a reflex pattern, ordained in the biological program to lock in with hand-eye experience in an orderly sequence. In the absence of vision, the reflex is exercised in a void. Or a near void.

In the profile we see that chance encounter of the two hands at midline results in brief, automatic mutual fingering. Shall we credit the blind baby with "mutual fingering"? If we should, he would be nicely aligned with sighted babies on a table, but if we make a qualitative comparison between this behavior in the blind infant and the mutual fingering of a sighted child we see very significant differences.

In the sighted child we see a sustained, fascinated finger game played before the eyes. The game of mutual fingering appears to be augmented to a very large degree by the visual spectacle. The baby's intense and often rapturous facial expression suggests a pleasure bonus for the sighted child in which he is both performer and spectator. There is an element of *voluntariness* in his finger game. He can produce the game and reproduce it. He can sustain the game for several minutes.

The blind baby in our five-month profile, who has had no educational intervention when we meet him, does not engage in a sustained game of mutual fingering. What we have described is only a *chance* encounter of the hands at midline, brief and transient fingering, no voluntary or involuntary repetitions. What we see is a part-pattern of a biological mode at four months which is a component of the sequence that normally leads to midline organization of the hands, reciprocity between the hands, and the coordination of hand and eye in intentional reaching. But in the absence of vision there is no pleasure bonus for the blind baby. The part-pattern remains static in its nascent form.

This lengthy exposition on the subject of an infant game of mutual fingering may strike the reader as an extraordinary amount of attention to detail. (In lectures, for example, we begin to feel restlessness in the audience as we pursue this point. A restlessness that speaks for "Come now, get on with the story!") But the problem is that neither we nor the blind baby can "get on with the story" until we get those hands together at midline: the hands sustained at shoulder height are inutile hands. And they are the hands which in the blind child's unique program must serve as primary perceptual organs, a function *not* "intended" in the biological program.

Question from the audience: "How do you *know* that this failure to achieve midline organization of the hands is not a sign of CNS (Central Nervous System) damage?" We couldn't know, of course, even with preliminary neurological screening of our babies. But it is a fact that for every baby in our primary research group our prehension intervention strategies (to be described later) brought about midline organization and coordination of the hands with rapid and favorable effects upon prehension.

As we pursue the comparison between prehension in the blind and sighted child, we encounter further problems. In grasping mode, for example, we see that the blind baby makes contact with a cube using partial thumb opposition, but the grasp is clumsy in comparison to the sighted child. Again, it appears that the biological pattern has emerged, or at least a part-pattern has emerged, but the pattern is unpracticed in the blind child while the sighted child exploits his biological capability in hundreds of experiments in reaching and grasping each day.

To cite another example at a later stage of development, we will see that at nine months of age the blind child will employ his index finger in exploring the holes in the peg board, and he will employ pincer grasping to attain a cube. This tells us that the genetic timetable for this mode of prehension is similar for both blind and sighted babies. But the grasp is not precise, "neat," as we expect to find it in the sighted baby of this age. Moreover, when the blind baby is confronted with the task of picking up a pellet, or a cereal tidbit from his tray, he will *not* employ thumb and forefinger. He reverts to a raking mode or palmar clutching, an early mode which is actually more adaptive and efficient for a blind baby when confronted with the task of finding and attaining a pellet-sized morsel. (If a sighted adult loses a coin in a darkened movie theater, he will also use a raking mode of prehension for search and may find that four fingers and his thumb will be more efficient than thumb and forefinger in attaining the coin in the dark.)

There are enough differences, then, even in the grasping mode, which caution us against making strict comparisons between the blind and sighted child using standard scale items. We cannot fairly credit these part-patterns in mutual fingering and grasping mode which appear in blind children.

The five and a half-month-old blind baby in our profile has not yet demonstrated that he can hold two cubes simultaneously, one in each hand (Bayley median 4.7) and he has not yet demonstrated transfer (Bayley median 5.5). Both tasks are normally facilitated by vision. Both stem from the forms of reciprocity between the hands, and midline symmetry, which are normally established at four months of age.

Finally, for the item "reaches for and attains an object" all comparisons between the blind baby and the sighted baby collapse at the crucial milestone. The sighted baby median age for the coordination of eye and hand is 4.6 (ranges three to seven months). In our group, the blind child's median age for the coordination of *ear and hand* in this task is 8.27 (range six and a half to eleven months). Moreover, even this "late achievement" by sighted-child standards has probably been advanced by our intervention program.

The unique adaptive problems for the blind child in the coordination of ear and hand are described in a later section of this chapter, and examined in some detail in Chapter VIII.

PREHENSION AND THE WORLD "OUT THERE"

A comparison of the sighted and blind developmental profiles in prehension speaks eloquently for the function of vision in the biological program and in adaptive hand behavior. In the blind infant we see that both the biological mode and adaptive hand behavior are affected by the visual deficit. In the crucial milestone of "reaching and attaining an object" we witness the extraordinary problem for the blind child in finding an adaptive substitution for vision in the coordinated reach for an object "out there." We shall illustrate in this chapter, and in Chapter VIII, that when the blind child at nine months of age reaches for and attains an object on sound cue only, he has achieved an adaptive feat.

To begin with, we must ask the question, *"What is 'out there' to a blind infant under six months of age?"*

For a perilously long time in the first year of life, the blind child lives in a near-void compared to the sighted child. When he is in his mother's arms he experiences enclosure and tactile intimacy and her voice. When he is not in tactile contact with his mother we infer from his behavior that she has evanesced for him (see Chapter VI). There are no contact-seeking behaviors, no gestures of reach. In this world without pictures, persons and things manifest themselves in random fashion, emerging from the void as transient tactile-auditory experiences, returning to the void as they remove themselves, or as they are removed from the near space which is his "space." Sounds and voices register from "out there," but sound is discontinuous, intermittent, and the behavior of the blind baby in the first six to nine months tells us clearly that sound does not yet connote a person or thing "out there."

In contrast to the visual panorama, the endless spectacle of sensory pictures which furnish the sighted child's world from the moment he opens his eyes, the blind child's space is empty or sparsely furnished. In fact, to our perception as seeing persons his space may be richly furnished, but the toy we see in his crib or his playpen is "not there" to him unless he makes accidental contact with it. When he loses contact with the toy it is "not there" again, and he will not search for it. His is, then, a world of evanescent objects, a world of magic, in which persons and things are subject to a capricious causality.

To reconstruct this world in our imagination is a formidable task. Perhaps the blind baby registers these occurrences and non-occurrences as the dreamer does, when the events of the dream produce a voice or a sound without context which then recede to nothingness as the dream transports the dreamer to another realm, other voices, other places. And even as we, in our dreams, do not reflect upon the occurrence and the nonoccurrence of the ghostly disembodied voice or sound, the blind baby at six months cannot find meaning in the sound that comes out of nowhere, the tactile engagement that now is here and now is not.

In the everyday life of the sighted child the picture would unite these experiences of sound and touch for him long before four months of age. At three months of age, the sighted child turns to the source of sound with the "expectation," as Piaget puts it, that a "spectacle" will present itself. This turning toward the source of sound manifests itself in the neonate as a reflex eye movement to the stimulus of sound, a reflex which is fortified and rewarded through visual experience. I have seen this reflex-turning of the eye toward sound in a totally blind baby at two months of age and have also seen, within a few months, that the reflex had been extinguished, and the blind baby, like all other blind babies at six months, did not turn to the source of sound.

So the blind baby at six months does not locate persons or things through sound. What is equally important—and potentially ominous for development—is that he cannot yet attribute substantiality to objects that manifest themselves through sound alone. It is a *conceptual* problem for the blind infant: he must infer the identity and substantiality of an object "out there" when only one of its attributes, sound, is given. The sighted baby, who reaches for and attains an object "on sight" at four and a half months, does not *need* a concept of the object for this coordinated task. Vision has conferred identity on the person or object, and vision, the synthesizer of sense experience, has united the attributes of the object. Vision insures that the toy or the person "out there," within reach, can be grasped.

And, finally, we are struck by the mundane fact that visual experience lures the sighted child in his hand pursuits at each step in his progress toward the coordinated reach. What constitutes the "lure" in exteroceptive experience for the blind baby's hand? What constitutes the target in this darkness?

Astonishingly, against all odds in this cruel game of chance in which a baby's hands must find targets in the dark and must construct a map in a labyrinth, all of the babies in our group found their way, in the first year, aided by their parents and by us.

Part II
Intervention

Through our pilot work in Ann Arbor (1963–64) we were able to identify the unique adaptive problems for the blind infant in the area of prehension. As we have seen in our comparative analysis in the preceding section, at every point where vision normally provides incentives and lures in prehension, the blind infant reaches a developmental impasse; sound does not provide an alternative adaptive solution in the early months.

Our problem in devising "an education of the hands" in the guidance program was to facilitate adaptive hand behavior by exploiting the intact systems, by providing exteroceptive "lures" to substitute for those normally provided by vision.

In the area of prehension, as in all other areas of our guidance program, there was no formal program or "curriculum." Each baby and his family constituted a unique entity; the parents, with our help, were the educators. While we can summarize the principles of this program, the program itself was highly individualized, allowing for much invention on the part of the parents and baby and capitalizing upon the assets of each family, each baby, in seeking adaptive solutions.

In the following summary the principles and some of our educational strategies are described. (For more detailed exposition of the guidance principles the reader is referred to Fraiberg, Smith, and Adelson 1969 and Fraiberg 1971a.)

The adaptive problems, in concise summary, we have already identified: (1) Blindness as an impediment to midline organization of the hands; (2) Blindness as an impediment to hand experience (no lures); (3) The emptiness of "the world out there" when sound does not yet connote substantiality.

To promote midline organization of the hands, we and our parents developed strategies to bring the hands together. Where vision normally provides the lure, we found substitutes in everyday experience. In feeding, we encouraged our mothers to place the baby's hands on the bottle. (Typically, the blind baby's posture during a bottle feeding was passive, with dropped hands, or occasional fingering of the mother's hand or her clothing.) With the hands placed upon the bottle we provided one lure to midline engagement of the hands with a "pleasure bonus" in the experience of feeding itself.

Prehension

We encouraged patty cake games and other hand-clapping games with rhythmic chants, which provided their own "pleasure bonus" for midline engagement of the hands (where vision would have guaranteed the spontaneous untutored engagement).

We created an "interesting space" at midline—"furnishing" a space that is empty for the blind baby when he is not in immediate contact with a human partner. For the baby still mainly supine, we encouraged the use of cradle gyms and dangling toys in which a midline reach guaranteed contact with a toy "out there." Both the cradle gym and the dangling toy were selected to give sound as well as tactile experience. For the baby who was capable of supported sit or independent sit, we encouraged the use of a stable, low play table, which also served, of course, as a feeding table. The tray top on such a table provided a 100° arc for exploration and mapping; the tray itself had a rail which defined its boundaries (and kept objects on its surface). The tray was furnished at any one time with two or three interesting toys of tactile interest and of tactile-auditory interest. A midline reach by the baby virtually guaranteed contact with one of the toys. The tray top became "the place" where interesting objects could be found.

By enlarging and expanding the blind baby's tactile-auditory experience, we began to see the hands in exploration of toys, and other objects; we began to see the fingers making sensitive discriminations, finding the unique tactile characteristics of objects. And through a more and more efficient scanning with the fingers, we saw clear signs of recognition and preference. We saw our babies experiment with toys and other objects, listening attentively to the sounds and creating sound through voluntary hand movement.

Similarly, when the baby achieved independent sit, and enjoyed sitting on the floor, we "furnished" the near space of the floor with interesting and intriguing objects which could be "found" at midline, and also at various points in the arc which represented his reach space. In this way and in others we began to build into the blind baby's experience an elementary form of recognition of the "displaceability" of objects. The toy that is "found" on the tray top can be rediscovered in other places. All this was still in the realm of "magic" for the blind baby during most of the first year, but we were facilitating for him a developing concept of "displaceability" which is very largely impeded by the absence of vision. (For the sighted child, who can track the movements of objects with his eyes, vision provides such elementary lessons in the displaceability of objects.)

By furnishing the blind baby's near space we saw that we could create incentives for mobility in sit, in prone, and later in cruising and free walking. The lure of "something out there" which is normally provided by vision and serves as an incentive for reach and mobility, could be provided for the blind child when we furnished his near space and offered lures in a space which he had learned to map.

To facilitate the coordination of ear and hand, leading to "reach on sound cue only," we did not need to augment the educational strategies outlined here. By providing the blind baby with a vastly expanded range of experience with persons and toys in which the sound-touch-identity of human and inanimate objects could be established and reestablished in hundreds of everyday connections, we began to see the schemas of sound and touch come together in a two-stage process: (1) Reach on sound cue following tactile cue; (2) Reach on sound cue alone.

The coordination of ear and hand in intentional reach and attainment will be the subject of the next section of this chapter.

Part III
The Coordination of Hand and Ear

DATA SOURCES

As described earlier, our primary sources of data for the study of the coordination of hand and ear were the 16mm film records and our detailed descriptive protocols. We were not only interested in the demonstration of "reach on sound cue only" and the age of attainment. We wanted and needed the story which must include all the antecedent behaviors in a sequential development from "no hand response to sound cue" to "reach and attainment of an object on sound cue only."

We examined this process through both naturalistic observation and experimental procedures.

The experimental procedures were worked out in our pilot study in 1963 and, as one or another of the strategies proved unproductive, these were dropped until we had obtained an economical and simplified set of procedures which elicited the highest level of response from the baby under circumstances which were least stressful to him.

In the sound-toy experiments we employed both the baby's own familiar or favorite toys or a standard test bell from our own kit which, as it happened, was almost uniformly attractive and interesting to the blind babies in our group. The examiner alternated with the baby's own mother in presenting the toy in a prescribed sequence, in order to provide the most favorable circumstances for the baby. The mother was fully aware of the purposes of this study and, in order to allay her own anxieties, we explained that many of the "games" we were playing with the baby could not be "passed" until he was older; we only wanted the baby to teach us how he solved the problem over a period of months.

The setting was almost always in the child's own home. We chose those moments in the hour's observation period when the baby was most alert and responsive, and limited our testing according to the baby's own tolerance. (In the early months, this might be less than a minute, yet sufficient for our purposes.)

In our pilot work with 4 children in 1963 (Ann Arbor study) we had identified 2 major stages in the coordination of ear-hand schemas (with sub-stages which will be described later and illustrated in Chapter VIII).

Stage I. *Midline reach on sound cue following tactile cue.* Demonstration: The blind baby attempts to retrieve the toy on sound cue which has been experimentally removed from his hands, if he has had an immediately antecedent manual contact with the toy. He cannot yet retrieve the toy on sound cue only.

Stage II. *Midline reach for the toy on sound cue only*. Demonstration: The baby retrieves the toy sounded at midline, without having antecedent manual contact with the toy.

PROCEDURES AND SCORING

Stage I. *Reach on sound, following tactile cue*.

1.   The baby is seated at his play table. One or another of the sound toys which are demonstrably favored by him are given to him to hold in his hands and explore.

2.   The sound toy is then gently removed from his hands by the examiner or the baby's mother and sounded at midline within easy reach.

3.   The baby's affective response and his hand behavior are recorded in descriptive detail. (E.g., no protest; protest. Hands motionless. Fingers activated. No search. Search without localizing sound. Search with approximate location of sound. Direct reach at midline, localizing sound. Retrieves toy.)

4.   If there is no hand response of seeking or reaching, the toy is returned to the baby's hand for further play, and the sequence of removal and sounding at midline is repeated. Several trials are given if the baby's tolerance and interest can be maintained.

Credit: If the baby retrieves the toy at midline he is credited with achieving "reach on sound cue following tactile cue." Credit is also given for a spontaneous demonstration of a stage I achievement observed and recorded outside of the experimental situation.

Interpretation: The baby who has achieved this stage demonstrates that the tactile-auditory schemas are beginning to unite, that the sound attributes of the toy and its tactile attributes are unified under the restricted circumstances in which he has had immediately antecedent tactile contact with the toy. The toy in the hand, then, can be mentally represented for a brief interval when it leaves his hands and his search is probably guided by the magical expectation that it is "out there" and can be recovered. If he has not had antecedent manual contact with the toy, he will not yet make a gesture of search or recovery upon hearing its familiar sound. He cannot yet reconstitute the unity of the toy in space when only one of its attributes is given him without the tactile cue.

Stage II. *Midline reach on sound cue only*

1. A familiar toy is sounded at midline by E. or mother without giving the baby antecedent manual contact with the toy.

2. The observer records affective and motor response in descriptive detail. (E.g., alert, attentive, unattentive. Activation of fingers, grasping-ungrasping, reach-no reach, brief search-sustained search, direct reach, reach and attainment of the toy.)

3. If there is no success in reaching and attaining the toy on sound cue only, the procedure is repeated with other toys. In order not to strain the tolerance of the baby, ad hoc trials following the same procedures are conducted at favorable intervals throughout the observational session, capitalizing on the baby's playfulness and rapport with mother or E.

Credit: If the baby reaches for and attains the object at midline on sound cue only, he is credited with achieving stage II. A spontaneous demonstration observed and recorded in naturalistic circumstance, which fulfills this requirement, is fully acceptable to us for credit.

Interpretation: The blind baby who can demonstrate a coordinated midline reach for and recovery of the toy on sound cue only has inferred the substantiality of the object when only one of its attributes (sound) is given, and he has emancipated himself from the previous mode in which the unity or identity of the object was strictly related to its antecedent tactile-auditory experience.

His level of object concept is now approaching Piaget's stage 4, or may even be interpreted as having some correspondence with Piaget's stage 4. He appears to attribute some degree of objectivity to the toy sounding "out there." His reach into space on registering the toy's sound implies that it is represented as a unified auditory-tactile object with a substantiality that is independent of his own tactile experience and can be recovered in another space.

Results

For ten infants "midline reach for the toy on sound cue only (no antecedent tactile contact)" is recorded in the table below which was prepared for this text by Edna Adelson:

TABLE 3 *
Midline Reach and Attainment on Sound Cue Only

1.	Kathie	0:06:18 †
2.	Ronnie	0:08:21
3.	Carol	0:08:22
4.	Jackie	0:08:26 †
5.	Karen	0:08:27 †
6.	Jamie	0:08:27
7.	Joan	0:09:07
8.	Toni	0:10:09
9.	Paul	0:10:22
10.	Robbie	0:11:01
	Range:	0:6:18–0:11:1
	Median:	0:8:27

* This table supersedes a preliminary table and summary reported in Fraiberg (1968).
† Age corrected for prematurity

Discussion

If the coordination of ear and hand in attaining an object strikes us as a "delayed achievement," this is only because in our minds we are comparing the coordination of eye and hand in the sighted child with the coordination of ear and hand in the blind child. For a fair comparison it would be more profitable to ask ourselves: "If a sighted child is presented with the problem of recovering a sound toy that is screened from vision, at what age will he remove the visual barrier and recover the sound toy?"

Piaget (1954) recorded observations of Laurent at 0:7 (Obs. 30) and Lucienne at 0:8 (Obs. 32) in which Piaget experimentally sounds a familiar toy under a visual screen. Neither child removes the screen to recover the toy in these two experiments.

Laurent's seven-month protocol records:

> He taps on the little bell with his index finger *through the cloth* (italics mine) and the little bell rings; Laurent watches this phenomenon with great interest, then his eyes follow my hand as I withdraw it open, and looks at it (Piaget's hand) for a moment (as though the little bell were going to arise from it. But he does not raise the cloth).

The protocol for Lucienne at eight months of age records:

> When I hide her rattle under the coverlet and make it sound she looks in the right direction but merely examines the coverlet itself, without trying to raise it.

Freedman, Margileth, Fox-Kolenda, and Miller (1969) replicated the Piagetian task with an N of 33 sighted babies between the ages of five and twelve months. The results reported show that the sighted children in their sample search for a toy that is sounded beneath a visual screen in the age range eight to eleven months!

These ranges correspond almost exactly with the ranges we have given for our blind infants in the attainment of an object on sound cue only.

These findings for a sighted-child population tell us that *for the sighted child as well as the blind child, "search for the sound toy when a visual barrier intervenes" is a conceptual problem.* When we consider that the sighted child is vastly advantaged in this task which involves a mental reconstruction or reconstitution of the toy when only one of its attributes (sound) is given, the achievement of the blind infants in our group who have no visual representation of the toy to aid them in the task, strikes us as a virtuoso performance.

Is the blind child's demonstration of "reach on sound" a Piaget stage 4 achievement in object permanence? Here we are bedeviled by problems of "equivalence of the task" and scoring. Since the tasks, as we presented them, involved a midline presentation of the sound toy in a space that was mapped for our blind children (midline is "the place where toys can be found"), the most conservative judgment may be only that the child has demonstrated that he can coordinate ear and hand schemas, with the magical expectation that a reach at midline on sound cue will unite the hands with a substantial "something." On this level of coordination of schemas he would be credited with a stage 3 performance on a Piagetian scale. On the other hand, if he has united sound with substantiality in the absence of vision, he has inferred the substantiality of the toy from only one of its attributes (sound) in which case the level of inference required for this task might fairly place him at stage 4.

To avoid the ambiguities of scoring "midline reach" we should, ideally, add another item to the experimental sequence in the blind child's scale of prehension, "directional reach on sound cue." In this case the toy is sounded to the right or left of midline and "in the air," in a space removed from midline or from the tray surface with its built-in "magic" as "the place where things can be found." The blind baby's directional reach for the toy more fairly tests his level of inference. The child who reaches directionally and attains the sound toy is no longer searching for the toy in the "expected place" but localizes sound at its variable source and infers its substantiality from its sound attributes—which we may take as an elementary demonstration of the toy's "permanence" and so with greater confidence credit this performance as an equivalent to Piaget's stage 4.

But now, to our everlasting regret, we must report that our data for age of attainment of "directional reach for the toy on sound cue only" are incomplete and will not advance our inquiry.

Prehension

We were well advanced in data evaluation when Edna Adelson discerned that in naturalistic circumstance, in some instances caught by the camera or recorded exactly in the descriptive protocol, there was a third stage in "reach on sound." Following "midline reach and attainment on sound cue only" which we had systematically studied, there was an interval of growing proficiency—and then, a third stage, "directional reach on sound," emerged within the following weeks.

It was a very important finding. But since we had not anticipated this stage in our research design and did not test for it in our experimental procedures, we do not have uniform data on the attainment of this stage for our 10 children. It was too late in our study to incorporate "directional reach" into our data collection procedures (the tenth baby had already passed this milestone) and we could not recover the data retrospectively from analysis of films or protocols.

This loss for us may be of value to other investigators who may wish to pursue the development of prehension in blind infants in further studies.

Since there are no other studies of blind infants in which the coordination of ear and hand has been systematically studied and recorded, we do not have comparison groups available to examine the scores of our 10 blind infants in the primary research group in relation to another group, independently studied, in which no intervention was available.

Summary

In this chapter we have examined the unique adaptive problems in prehension for the infant blind from birth. On the basis of comparison profiles of sighted and blind children, qualitative differences in prehension were discerned. Our study of the coordination of hand and ear in a largely advantaged blind infant population has been summarized. In our group the criterion "reach and attainment of an object on sound cue only" was attained in the range 0:6:18–0:11:1; median age 0:8:27.

In the following chapter we will examine in fine detail the sequence and stage-specific characteristics of prehension by means of an individual case study.

Chapter VIII

SELMA FRAIBERG, BARRY L. SIEGEL, M.D.,
RALPH GIBSON, PH.D.

Stage-Specific Characteristics of Prehension: The Profile of a Blind Infant in the First Year[*]

FOR THE STUDY of the stage-specific characteristics of prehension in the blind child we will present a detailed analysis of the films and protocols of Robbie. This chapter is based very largely upon an earlier paper by the authors (Fraiberg, Siegel, and Gibson 1966). This report, now viewed from the perspective of 1975 and the completed study of 10 infants, has stood the test of time very well. The original paper has been modified for this volume chiefly through deletions of the extensive introductory material and content which are covered elsewhere in various chapters of this book. Other modifications include explanatory notes by

[*] This chapter appeared, in slightly different form, as S. Fraiberg, B. Siegel, and R. Gibson, "The Role of Sound in the Search Behavior of a Blind Infant," *The Psychoanalytic Study of the Child* (New York: International Universities Press, 1966), 21:327–357.

S.F. which widen the perspective following a decade of experience. These are indicated in the text.

Robbie, the subject of this study, was the first baby in our Ann Arbor series, and the only one of 4 babies in the period 1963–65 who, after extended study, satisfied our strict selective criteria. While every aspect of his development was thoroughly studied following the procedures we have outlined in Chapter IV, the area of prehension was given the most intensive film analysis at this stage of our work, when prehension was the least understood of the areas of our study of blind infants. It was Robbie who taught us the stage-specific characteristics of prehension leading to "reach and attainment of the object on sound cue only."

In 1975 we can say that the sequence which was established for Robbie has been confirmed in the study of each of the later babies in our series.

Since Robbie was, in a sense, our teacher in the area of prehension, we did not have the information that would lead us to intervention strategies for the facilitation of prehension in his first year. This means, of course, that Robbie provides us with a picture of the prehension sequence and its timetable which more fairly states the unique problems in adaptive behavior for a blind infant than the profiles of the later babies which reflect our intervention strategies.

Robbie, we note in consulting Table 3, achieved midline reach and attainment of an object on sound cue only at the age of 0:11:01 and on this item is the lowest ranking child in our series. Yet, as we follow his progress in the text, we shall see that he was a very adequate child. In manual discrimination, in gross motor development, and in language he ranks in the upper half of our group of 10. In human attachment, however, he is described in Chapter VI as a child who did not demonstrate a strong, secure attachment to his mother in the second year. His rank in "reach on sound" may reflect instability in the mother-infant relationship, as well as our own limitations at that time in intervention strategies. However, our experience with blind children in our consultation program tells us that Robbie's eleven-month achievement places him well ahead of the average child in a blind child population.

DATA SOURCES

The data which we present from the study of Robbie are derived entirely from film study and the protocols. Through the slow-motion film study we were able to trace in fine detail the subtleties in hand behavior, the fleeting first intimations of search, and the development of intentional reaching. The transcript of these developments in a written report cannot, of course, reproduce the effects of viewing the film, and our descriptive language for the subtleties of hand behavior cannot do justice to the story told by the hand alone during the first year of Robbie's life.

The test procedures are described in Chapter VII.

ROBBIE: PERTINENT BACKGROUND DETAILS

Robbie was first seen by us at 23 weeks of age following the diagnosis of bilateral agenesis of the optic nerves which was made by our Department of Ophthalmology. Pediatric and neurological examinations did not reveal any other congenital defects. The parents had suspected blindness earlier and told the social worker who spoke with them after the examination that the diagnosis was only a confirmation of what they already knew. They warded off the social worker's tactful allusions to feelings and only gradually, in the months that followed, were they able to speak of their fears for the child's future and of their guilt: "Could we have done something . . . ?" "Is it bad blood in the family?"

The parents were both young, and Robbie was their first child. The father was a factory worker, and both parents had had limited educations. In spite of their pain and self-reproach, they demonstrated a considerable capacity to come to grips with the child's blindness; their tenderness for the baby and their pleasure in him were evident when we first visited the family.

Robbie, at 23 weeks, was alert, responsive, attentive to voices and domestic sounds. He smiled joyfully in play with his parents and displayed a good range of vocalizations. He was able to sit for long periods in a propped position and enjoyed the sociability of the living room. He had two brief naps, morning and afternoon, and the long and sustained waking periods spoke well for the amount of stimulation he was receiving. His adaptive hand behavior was very superior for a blind baby. He explored objects with his hands and used his mouth minimally for getting information about objects.

Robbie's development throughout the first year (the period covered in this paper) was consistently superior as judged by existing scales for blind infants.* While we should note that none of the available instruments for testing blind preschool children is satisfactory to us and that we have no confidence in a developmental quotrent based upon these tests, an analysis of each sector of development over the period five to eleven months showed consistent and stable gains for Robbie and a harmonious profile. Robbie's overall achievement placed him in the superior range for blind children on scales that were standardized for children with varying degrees of visual loss. In general, the examiner can have more confidence in the assessments of blind children who maintain their leads in the superior or very superior range than in the assessments of those blind children who show unevenness and even great disparities in their developmental achievements at any given test period.

Robbie's development testified to adequacy in mothering—that he was being stimulated by his human environment. Yet it is important to note that Robbie's mother had depressive features in her personality which concerned us as clinicians, and we had reason to believe that they antedated the birth of the blind infant.

* Scales available to us in 1963 were the Maxfield-Fjeld Social Maturity Scale adaptation of the Vineland Social Maturity Scale for visually handicapped children and the Cattell Infant Development Scale adapted for blind preschool children by Norris, Spaulding, and Brodie.

She tried to ward off depression by eating and by defenses against painful feelings. We were impressed to see that as long as she succeeded, there were no apparent impediments to Robbie's development. This means that, for the age period four to eleven months covered in this essay, the quality of mothering was at least adequate, and the language and social sectors of development, which are clinically relevant in the evaluation of the mother-child relationship, showed no impairment. (In the second year, by contrast, there was a 4-month period during which the mother's withdrawal and loss of rapport with Robbie showed immediate effects in the language sector and a slowing down of the rate of development in all areas. With guidance and support, the mother was able to reestablish her relationship with the child, and Robbie's language and overall development leaped forward again.)

At the time this was written (1966), Robbie was two years, three months of age. His mobility (running, climbing, walking up and down stairs, playing ball), his skill in the use of his hands for fine perceptions, his speech development (good simple sentences), his lively interest in people and objects, were within the top range for blind children. He was not easily identified as a blind child either on the playground or in our office waiting room.

When we now describe the slow and laborious route that brought Robbie at eleven months of age to reach for objects on sound cue alone, we need to place this achievement in the context of his overall development, which in this blind child was superior.

With this background we now propose to describe the patterns of search behavior over a period of from six months to eleven months of age which brought Robbie to recover an object on sound cue alone.

Six to Seven Months

If a sound-making object or a soundless object is removed from Robbie's hand, there is, typically, no vocal protest, no expression of displeasure on the face, no attempt to reach out and recover the object.*

Hand behavior: Typically, the hands remain motionless after removal of the object, but we begin to get isolated examples of a new behavior. In the slowed-down film we can see that after the object is withdrawn from the hand, the hand sometimes executes a brief pantomime of the action previously employed in holding the object. The pantomime will occur only when there has been tactile contact with an object the moment before and will occur with the same frequency for a sound-making object as for a soundless object.

On sound cue only: In repeated experiments we demonstrate that if the bell or the squeaky toy or one of the child's own noise-making toys is manipulated by the examiner to make sound, and if there is no antecedent contact with the object, the hands remain

---

* The examples cited in the text were selected from hundreds of items analyzed by us to trace the characteristics of each phase. Observations of search behavior covered spontaneous demonstrations of the child in play as well as the structured test situation. To encourage the child's best performance and to test the full range of his performance we varied the conditions in these ways: the mother herself was invited to present a favorite toy to the child in parallel search problems. When the examiner tested, he employed the child's own toys as well as test objects to obtain the most favorable conditions for search. The child was offered as many trials as he could tolerate within the range of his attention span. (Typically, there were five to ten trials for each sound object each session.) Such factors as duration of the sound stimulus and continuity or interruption of sound were experimentally varied. Not one of the variables introduced elicited search and recovery on sound cue alone until eleven months.

One example may be cited here which covers all the variables mentioned: Robbie's musical dog, one of his oldest and most treasured toys, was offered to him in nearly every session; the toy playing its music was within easy reach of his hands. Whether mother or father presented it, or the examiner, whether the music played for a few seconds or a few minutes, there was no reaching, no gesture of search, no attempt at recovery under eleven months.

motionless. The sound of neither bell nor rattle activates the hands in any way, although the child shows alertness and concentrated attention when he hears the sound. There is no orientation of the head toward the source of sound.

Pertinent developmental data: Robbie is sitting well, with slight support; in the prone position he elevates himself on hands, elevates the trunk. There is good coordinate use of hands in holding objects. He smiles in response to mother's and father's voices and tactile stimulation. He is generally attentive and alert to voices and domestic sounds. His language development is good; he coos, vocalizes vowel sounds. His favorite toy is a musical dog, which he embraces, brings to his mouth, and explores with his hands. Rocking is noted during periods of nonstimulation.

EXAMPLES OF TEST BEHAVIOR ON REMOVAL OR LOSS OF OBJECT

1. A soundless object
   Age: 0:5:28
   Robbie is given a small ball of yarn and is allowed to play with it on the tray of his low chair. With yarn in hand he moves his hand along the surface of the tray in a bouncing motion. He drops the yarn on the tray and makes no attempt to recover it. The hand, still formed as if grasping the lost object, begins to move along the surface of the tray in a bouncing motion, continuing the action employed during the interval that he had held the ball of yarn in his hand.

2. A sound-making object
No tactile cue
   (a) The examiner rings the bell and places it on Robbie's platform. Robbie has not been given prior tactile contact with the bell in this trial. At the sound of the bell Robbie is attentive and motionless. There is no movement of the hands or articulation of the fingers.

With tactile cue
   (b) The examiner touches the bell against the back of Robbie's fingers. The tactile contact now activates the hand. The hand makes

an exploratory gesture, makes contact with the bell handle, and grasps it firmly. Robbie moves his hand back and forth ringing the bell.

(c) Immediately following sequence (b) in which Robbie held the bell in his hand and rang it, the examiner removes the bell from Robbie's hand and rings it within easy reach of Robbie's fingers. The hands remain still. There is no gesture, not even a flexing of the fingers in response to the bell sound, although Robbie held the bell in his hands and rang it only a few seconds before.

These experiments are repeated using a variety of test objects and the child's own toys. On sound cue alone there is no behavior of the hand that shows recognition or search; the hand remains motionless. Following tactile contact, the removal of an object will sometimes elicit a hand behavior that suggests continuation of the interrupted action.

From these observations we can see that sound alone does not confer substantiality on the object. Even after Robbie has held the bell in his hand and rung it, his behavior toward the bell sound in sequence (c) tells us that holding the bell and hearing the bell do not evoke the schema of grasping, as evidenced by the stillness of the hand and the absence of an exploratory gesture.

In these and repeated observations during this period, however, we see that tactile contact with the object, whether it is sound-making or soundless, will activate the hand. In the yarn sequence, for example, when he loses the object, he does not yet search for it in the place where he lost it, but reproduces the previous action when the ball of yarn was held in his hand (bouncing the hand along the surface of the tray).

By reproducing the previous action in holding the yarn we can see that for Robbie the substantiality of the object is still dependent upon his own actions; it is "there" when he holds it in his hand; when he loses tactile contact with the object, it ceases to "exist"; hence, no search behavior. (At this age the sighted child will make a sure reach for the object on sight. When the object is removed before his eyes and concealed, he will not search for the object—it ceases to "exist." But his visual tracking of the object in this stage will lead him in the next stage, at about eight months, to search for the object behind the screen.)

Seven to Eight Months

The beginning of search for the tactile object occurs. Following tactile contact with either a sound-making object or a soundless object Robbie begins to make exploratory motions with his hands and actually conducts a random search on the tray top or the table top.

Hand behavior: Following removal of the object from his hands Robbie will now give occasional demonstrations of the beginnings of search. The hand moves radially across the tray from the periphery, a global search which does not take into account sound cues created when the object makes contact with the surface. Since the tray is his play table, his search at this time tells us only that now there is an expectation that the object lost may be discovered again within the circumscribed space of the tray. Moreover, since we ourselves usually return the object to the tray top, we reinforce his expectation that this is the place where the object can be found. On the other hand, the boundaries of this small space are not organized or mapped by him; his search is therefore unsystematic and he can easily bypass an object that is on the tray. When his random search does not rediscover the object in a brief trial, he makes no attempt to extend the search. If he makes accidental contact with the object on the tray, he grasps it surely. If the bell is rung by the examiner immediately after Robbie has held it in his hands, we then see the hand activated in a grasping motion. There is no search, but the hand executes a pantomime of opening and closing, grasping and ungrasping—or sometimes only a brief fluttering.

On sound cue alone: If the bell is rung without giving Robbie prior tactile contact with it, there is no gesture of reaching, no searching, no hand pantomime. One new behavior is promising.

We begin to get isolated incidents in which Robbie orients his head to the sound, turning toward the source of sound.

Pertinent developmental data: At 0:6:9 Robbie sits well unsupported; he can pull himself to standing position with assistance. He now transfers. He imitates banging the cup with spoon, after examiner demonstrates, using child's own hands in his. At 0:7:4 he patty cakes in response to verbal request. He shows recognition of the tin cup (test object) when his hand makes contact with the handle, by grasping the cup and bringing it to mouth.

EXAMPLES OF TEST BEHAVIOR ON REMOVAL
OR LOSS OF OBJECT

1.   On sound cue alone
     Age: 0:6:28
     Robbie is seated before a small table on his mother's lap. The bell is rung by the examiner and placed on the platform within easy reach for Robbie. There is no gesture of reaching, no special behavior of hands; the hands remain at rest.

     Age: 0:7:11
     A squeaky toy fish (a test object) is squeaked by the examiner, a few inches away from Robbie's hand. The hand remains still. There is no gesture of reach or recovery.

     Age: 0:8:23
     (a)   Robbie's own squeaky hammer is made to squeak by the examiner in a range within easy grasp for the child if he could reach. Robbie is attentive, blinks his eyes each time he hears the sound, makes no gesture of search or recovery.
     (b)   Robbie's own beloved musical dog is made to play its tune within close range of Robbie's hand, but without touching the hand. Robbie appears to recognize the sound, stops what he is doing and attends. He does not reach for the toy; shows no attempt to search.

Repeated tests during this period demonstrate that *sound alone* will not elicit any behavior of reach or recovery. The hands themselves remain still; there is no motion of the hand or activation of the fingers that can tell us that the sound is meaningful to the child. There is no difference in his behavior toward the sound of his own toys or the sound of test objects. The squeaky hammer and the musical dog are two of Robbie's favorite toys, frequently handled, tasted, manipulated, and experienced as sound toy objects. He himself can squeak the hammer to make its noise. But when the toy is made to produce sound which is independent of his own immediate tactile experience of it, he behaves as if it had no identity for him. Nothing in his hand behavior yet tells us that the sound elicits a tactile-motor recognition of the object.

2. Sound cue following tactile cue
   Age: 0:6:28
   (a) The bell is placed in Robbie's hand, then removed and rung in front of him at midline. The face shows alertness and attention. There is no gesture of reaching, but the hands open and close, in a gesture of grasping. (The experiment is repeated several times with the same reaction.)

Here we see a behavior that is, properly speaking, only an extension of hand behavior in the 23- to 28-week period when, following loss of the object, the hand reproduced the action previously employed in holding the object. Now, however, something new is emerging. The bell sound now elicits the motion of grasping when there has been an antecedent tactile experience with the bell and when there is temporal contiguity of the two experiences. (On sound cue alone, without prior tactile contact, there is no specific hand behavior, as we have shown in 1.) But there is not yet any behavior (reaching or search) that tells us that the bell sound is interpreted as a manifestation of the object bell in space.

Age: 0:7:11
   (b) A cube is placed in Robbie's hand, then removed and tapped on the table. Robbie makes a tentative search on the table, makes accidental contact with it and recovers it. The experiment is repeated several times, but after this first success Robbie does not attempt a search.

Typically, during this period Robbie cannot employ sound to trace an object's trajectory or find an object's place through its sound as in (b). This means, of course, that if search is initiated at all following the removal of the object, it is tentative and exploratory, and recovery of the object is almost accidental. Even when we increase his chances of recovery (as we always do) by narrowing the field of search and bringing the object either to the tray or table or within a range of a few inches from his hand, the encounter with the object is a matter of chance, as we see in (b).

When we consider that in the sighted child of 24 to 28 weeks, hand-and-eye coordination brings about a sure reach and recovery of objects, the problem for the blind child seems formidable. Before the blind child can "place" an object on sound cues, recovery is accidental, search will bring only rare rewards, and reaching is virtually purposeless.

Eight to Eleven Months

Search patterns for the tactile object become organized. The tactile and auditory schemas begin to unite toward the end of this period. As late as 48 weeks he will not yet search for an object on sound cue alone, but we can predict from his hand behavior that he is nearly ready to take the step.

Hand behavior: The radial, global exploration of the table surface or space gives way to intentional reaching when there are cues for locating the object or following its trajectory. When the examiner removes an object, we begin to get more frequent demonstrations of reaching or searching in the place where he last had contact with it. Following tactile contact with a sound-making object, he occasionally is able to trace it through sound cues and to recover it.

On sound cue only: There is still no gesture of reach or search for either a test object or familiar toy on sound cue only; but on sound cue alone we now see the fingers activated in a pantomime of grasping.

Pertinent developmental data: At o:8:8 he fingers the holes of the peg board. He protests the removal of objects. At 0:9:8 he is supporting himself well on hands and knees, rocking back and forth; at 0:10:10 he is bridging, balancing well on hands and one leg. He is standing with slight support, takes steps while supported; pincer grasping is demonstrated. He hits two spoons together. Robbie examines the interior of the bell and clapper with interest, reorients the bell in order to hold it by hand, rings it. He holds his own cup and drinks from it. He discriminates and shows preference among toys and test objects. He imitates sounds, "mama," "dada," "no." He reacts to strangers' voices by motionless attention; there is no manifest anxiety.

EXAMPLES OF TEST BEHAVIOR ON REMOVAL
OR LOSS OF OBJECT

1. On tactile cue alone
    Age: 0:8:8
    (a) Robbie is seated before a small table. The examiner touches a cube to Robbie's fingers. Robbie grasps it. The examiner attempts to withdraw the cube and the hand grasping the cube is pulled forward in resistance. The examiner removes the cube from Robbie's hand and holds it in mid-air within reach of the child's hands. Robbie withdraws his hand, then makes a sure reach in the direction and the area where he last had contact with the cube and recovers it. The reach itself reproduces the motor pattern in which the hand was pulled in resistance to the examiner's attempt to remove the cube from his grasp.
    (b) A peg board is placed before Robbie on the table. Robbie is helped to find one peg that is placed in a hole. He grasps the peg and removes it. The examiner removes the peg from Robbie's hand and places it in the same hole. Robbie makes a direct reach to the place where he last found the peg and grasps it. (There is no guidance from the examiner at this point.)
    (c) Immediately following (b): Robbie is holding peg A with both hands at mouth level. The examiner places another peg, B, in the peg board and removes peg A from Robbie's grasp. Robbie makes a sure reach for a hole in the peg board where he last encountered peg A and retrieves peg B. (Note: This was not, of course, the place where he had lost contact with peg A, which was at mouth level.)

These are examples of purposive reaching following *tactile* experience with the object. Before reaching became purposive, however, we caught glimpses in our early films of its origins. At an earlier stage, when the examiner attempted to remove a toy that Robbie held fast, the hand was pulled gently forward in the act of resistance. Here the motor pattern for reaching was established before reaching became intentional. (There is a parallel in the development of reaching in the sighted child during the period that precedes intentional reach.) Before intentional reaching appeared in Robbie's case there was a transitional behavior. We would sometimes see Robbie's hand reach out in space after an object was removed, reproducing the action in which the hand and arm were extended in resistance to the examiner's attempts to remove the toy—a continuation of the interrupted action. This act of reaching, not yet intentional, sometimes led to contact with the object and recovery.

In order for intentional reaching to take place, Robbie needed to have some notion that the object lost was still to be found "someplace." This step in the development of intentional reaching has no parallel in the sighted child. When vision and prehension are coordinated, the child reaches on sight; the object is "there" because the child can see it. In this way vision confers an elementary form of "permanence" to the object months before the child searches for the hidden object (the demonstration of the emergence of an object concept). But when Robbie makes a purposive reach for an object he is not informed by vision or hearing. How does he do it?

In the examples (a), (b), and (c) and in a number of other examples in this section, it is clear that Robbie will conduct some kind of search following manual tactile experience with the object removed and that he is employing directional cues for the purposive reach. Earlier, in the seven- to eight-month period, search was random, that is, a global search of the tray top or a gesture in space. Now at eight months, search patterns take into account the place where the "lost" object had been tactually experienced. The antecedent tactile experience with the object confers the beginnings of "permanence" to the object. In this respect, there is a striking parallel with the sighted child.

Piaget (1954) records a number of examples in which the sighted child at eight months will search with the hand, following a tactile experience, for an object lost or removed without employing vision in the search. This search is demonstrated only when the child has had an antecedent tactile contact with the object. Through these examples Piaget demonstrates how the child attributes the beginning of permanence to tactile objects. At a slightly later stage, eight to ten months, the concept of permanence emerges with regard to visual objects; the child will conduct a search for the hidden object when he has seen it disappear before his eyes.

In examples (a), (b), and (c) we can see typical search patterns for this period. In (a) Robbie makes a sure reach in the direction and the area where he last had contact with the cube (a point in mid-air between him and the examiner). While the action places this behavior in part as belonging to the pattern of "interrupted prehension," this is a big advance from the behavior of the earlier period, six to eight months, when the search did not take into account the point at which he lost contact with the object. The sure reach of this period contrasts with the random search of the earlier period and tells us that there is some belief that the lost object can be recovered, that it is "someplace." In (b) and in (c) he searches for the peg on the peg board, accurately locating the hole where he first encountered a peg and removed it. There is not yet a deduction involved in this search behavior; there is only the expectation that the object can be recovered in a certain place, the place where he first found it. (Here there is some correspondence with the sighted child of the same age who searches for the lost object in the place where he first encountered it. As Piaget points out, the child conceives of the object only in a special position, the first place in which it was hidden and found.)

2. Sound cue following tactile cue
    Age: 0:8:8
    (a) Robbie is given a squeaky rubber toy (test object) and is given

time to explore it manually and by mouth. He squeezes it to make it squeak. The examiner removes the toy. Robbie reaches directly to the place on the tray where he first encountered it. He does not recover it. He does not conduct a further search.

(b) Immediately following (a) the examiner squeaks the toy to give Robbie a cue if he can use it. He begins to kick his feet. Hands are held together. No gesture of reach or search.

In this sequence we see that Robbie cannot yet use sound to guide his search. In (a) he disregards the sound cue given by the examiner and conducts his search along the lines of search for the tactile object which we described in 1(a). He confers a position on the object, the place where he first made his tactile encounter with it. In (b) when the examiner gives him another sound cue, he makes no attempt to reach or search for the object following failure in (a) to recover it in the first position.

Age: 0:9:8
(a) Robbie is lying supine in his crib, fingering his cradle gym. (The trapeze is composed of rings and a bell toy, a clown.) Robbie reaches up surely to grasp the rings and sets the trapeze in motion, smiling joyfully as he engages the trapeze again and again.

(b) Immediately after (a) he is lying quietly, *not* in touch with the trapeze. The examiner rings a bell toy on the trapeze which Robbie engaged only a few seconds earlier. Robbie is attentive. He makes no attempt to reach out toward the bell toy, but his hands go through the pantomime of grasping.

Here we see that the bell sound from his oldest and most intimate bed toy does not yet elicit a gesture of reach or search. The bell sound is still linked to his own actions; he "causes" the sound through his manual contact and manipulation of the toy. He cannot yet conceive of the objectivity of the toy through the sound which he has not "caused."

But in this example and a number of others during this period, we see that following tactile contact the bell sound activates the hands; the hand goes through a pantomime of grasping, which tells us again that bell sound and bell-in-hand are slowly uniting.

Stage-Specific Characteristics of Prehension

3.   On sound cue only
    Age: o:8:8
    The examiner presents Robbie with one of his own toys, the musical dog. Without giving Robbie prior tactile contact with the toy, the music is started. Robbie makes groping gestures with both hands, but there is no intentional reaching or search. In random movement of his hand he makes accidental contact with the toy animal. He immediately grasps it and brings it to his mouth.

Here, for the first time in our observations, we have an isolated instance in which the sound of the object activates the hands in a groping gesture. There is not yet purposeful search or reach, but the hand behavior tells us that the sound of the familiar toy and a tactile-motor memory of the toy are beginning to converge. Here, there was no antecedent tactile experience with the toy dog. Yet, for nearly 2 months this remains our only example of a specific hand behavior on sound cue without prior tactile contact.

We have demonstrated that, for Robbie, at this stage sound alone does not yet confer substantiality upon the object. There is no gesture of search or reach even when the object is a familiar toy. However, we cannot attribute this behavior to absence of vision alone. Once again we have an interesting parallel in the behavior of the sighted child of eight months as recorded by Piaget (1954). In a typical example Piaget hides Lucienne's rattle under the coverlet and makes it sound. Lucienne looks in the right direction, examines the coverlet, but makes no attempt to raise it. Sound alone does not confer substantiality upon the object when it disappears from the visual field of the sighted child. This is a conceptual problem for the child of this age, sighted as well as blind. (See also Chapter VII.)

The sighted child, however, has an enormous advantage in building the concept. As early as the second month in Piaget's samples, the child coordinates sound and vision, he searches with his eyes for the source of sound, and there soon develops an expectation that sound will evoke a visual experience. The sound of the mother's voice and the visual experience of the mother will be united. By the third month the sighted infant is practiced in localizing sound.

At eight months Robbie has just begun to orient his head to the source of sound, but in the absence of vision he cannot locate the source of sound with any degree of accuracy, and he cannot, of course, locate an object on sound cue alone. In order to place an object on sound cue alone, in order to reach for and recover an object on sound cue, he will need a concept of the object in space. And he will need to build the concept without the visual experiences that organize and synthesize sense experience for the sighted child.

Robbie will need to construct an object's trajectory in space without having *seen* movement. He must come to believe that an object can undergo various displacements in space that are independent of his own activity and his own manipulations, and that it remains the same object. But what is movement to a blind child? He can only discover movement through analogues of his own motor and kinesthetic experience which tie the discovery of objective phenomena to his body image in ways that can imperil the construction of an object concept. This is an intellectual feat for the blind infant. Some blind babies never find the route, and we see in certain deviant children a developmental arrest which, by all signs, reveals a failure to differentiate self and non-self, an inability to go beyond the self and construct a world of objects.

4.   No stimulus for the initiation of the creeping pattern

The inability to reach on sound cue retards the development of locomotion during this period. As early as nine months Robbie has demonstrated postural readiness for creeping, supporting himself well on hands and knees, bridging, and rocking back and forth. But for Robbie (as we have seen in all of our blind babies [S.F.]) the creeping pattern cannot be initiated in the absence of an external stimulus for reaching. In the case of the sighted child the visual stimulus provides incentives for reaching, and the reach propels the child forward. The blind child typically comes to an impasse at the point where there is postural readiness for creeping. Many blind babies do not creep at all, and developmental data for blind infants in the larger blind population show a lag of one year in establishing independent locomotion. (See also Chapter IX.)

In the following sequences we are attempting to find experimentally whether an attractive object, sound-making or soundless, can provide incentives for reaching while Robbie is supporting himself on hands and knees.

Age: 0:9:8

(a) Robbie is on the floor, supporting himself on hands and knees, rocking and inching forward. Now he elevates his trunk and bridges on hands and feet. Someone brings his musical dog to him, touches his hand to it, removes it a few inches from his extended hand, well within his reach. He makes no attempt to reach for it.

(b) Robbie is again on hands and knees, rocking back and forth. His squeaky hammer is given to him. He mouths it. Now he loses it and somehow propels himself backwards. He does not reach in the place where he lost contact with it, but makes swiping motions of his hand in an area a few inches from the object. He makes no further search. Now he reverts to a passive prone position on the rug, face down, quite immobile.

Age: 0:10:10

(a) Robbie is on hands and knees, rocking. The squeaky hammer is placed a few inches from Robbie's elbow and squeaked by the examiner. No gesture of search or reach.

(b) Following (a) the examiner brings the toy in contact with Robbie's hand, removes it, and places it within easy grasp for Robbie. Robbie elevates himself, is poised in a bridging posture, elevates one leg for a few seconds, and maintains this three-point posture with beautiful balance. In moving his hand he actually makes contact with his toy but makes no effort to retrieve it. He continues rocking, actually moves back from the object.

(c) Robbie is given a large patent leather handbag to play with on the floor. He moves to hands and knees and the bag is moved directly in front of him. The examiner taps the bag to give him a cue. Robbie reaches both hands forward and makes contact with the purse.

(d) Following (c), while Robbie is rocking, bridging on hands and toes, the examiner gives him contact with the handbag. There is no reach. The examiner alternately touches the bag to Robbie's hand and moves it a few inches in front of him. Robbie makes no attempt to reach for the bag. (The examiner during this sequence is seated on the floor, parallel to Robbie's position, and there are no directional cues from the position of the examiner.)

It is interesting that even though Robbie has demonstrated reach for the tactile object since 34 weeks, he behaves as if this were a new problem for him when he is on hands and knees. This is not a problem of maintaining his balance because he has demonstrated for us that he can use one hand freely and still maintain his balance, and can even maintain balance on one leg and two hands. We have the impression that this problem has to do with the blind child's "space." In the circumscribed space of the crib, the play table, and the playpen, he can believe that an object can be found through one or another of his search patterns, but on the floor he behaves once again as he did at 24 weeks when lost objects were swallowed up in a void. Until he can creep, the floor and room space cannot be mapped by him. But until he can locate and pursue objects, he will not be able to creep!

In the examples cited we see that on hands and knees he does not employ search patterns that he has already learned and demonstrated. On tactile cues he does not pursue the object with his hand. He does not search in the direction of the examiner. When he himself loses the squeaky hammer, he does not search for it in the place where he lost it but makes swiping motions with his hand a few inches away. There is also a problem of relativity involved for him. When he loses the hammer and somehow propels himself backward, he cannot make the necessary correction based on his movement backward and the object's position.

In one of the ten-month examples he reaches for the patent leather handbag when the examiner taps it to give him a cue. He has had prior tactile contact with the bag when he was playing with it the moment before. The bulk of the bag made contact virtually inescapable under these circumstances when Robbie reached out. It remains the only sample we have during this period of reaching for an object while on hands and knees.

Clearly he needs time to transfer the search behavior from one plane and one kind of space to another plane and a new unmapped space. But search on tactile cue alone is a highly unsatisfactory method for the recovery of lost objects in unlimited space. Until Robbie can place objects on sound cue he will have no directional cues for search that can lead him into creeping.

5. Toward convergence of the two schemas

In the following sequence, we have good samples of Robbie's search patterns at 0:10:10 and the convergence of the tactile and auditory schemas.

Age: 0:10:10

(a) Robbie is seated in his little chair. The examiner rings the bell without giving Robbie prior tactile contact with it. Robbie rocks back and forth. The hands are immobile. No gesture of search or reach.

(b) Following (a) the examiner brings Robbie's hands to the bell. Robbie grasps it at the handle, pulls it away from the examiner, and rings it himself. As the right hand rings the bell the left hand goes through the pantomime of ringing. Now Robbie transfers the bell to the left hand, rings it, explores the rim, and appears to be exploring the interior of the bell with his finger.

(c) Following (b) the examiner removes the bell, brings the bell very briefly in touch with Robbie's fingers, and moves it about six inches from Robbie's hand at this moment. Robbie now begins to make a tentative search in the area where he last encountered the bell on touch. (The bell is actually a few inches away from this place.) Robbie now moves the fingers across the board a few inches until he makes contact with the bell, accidentally pushes it further across the tray; now with his finger and thumb around the bottom, he lifts it, clasps it by the handle, and begins ringing the bell in his right hand. Again the left hand goes through the pantomime of ringing. He transfers the bell back and forth between both hands, examining the rim of the bell, and appears to be examining the clapper too.

(d) Following (c) the examiner attempts to remove the bell. Robbie is holding fast to it and the arm is extended toward the examiner as it resists the attempts of the examiner to remove the object. The examiner removes the bell from Robbie's hand and places it on the tray.

Robbie begins a search, again in the area where he last encountered it. He does not find it, withdraws his hand, does not pursue the search, begins rocking in his chair.

(e) Following (d) the examiner rings the bell, touches it briefly to Robbie's hand, and places it on the tray. When Robbie hears the bell, his hands move slowly toward the bell and he grasps it.

(f) The examiner removes the bell, touches Robbie's hand to it, and places it on the tray close to Robbie's hand. Robbie reaches in the area where his hand was touched and recovers the bell. Robbie rings the bell, now holding it in both hands; again begins to reexplore the interior of the bell with much interest.

(g) Following (f) Robbie drops the bell on the right side of the tray. He fingers the air briefly in the place where he lost it, but when he does not recover it, makes no further search.

In (a) when Robbie hears the bell without having had prior tactile contact with it the hands remain still, there is no gesture of search or reach. But now in (b) and throughout this sequence we see a new kind of investment in the bell and active search following loss.

In (b), (c), and (f) he examines the bell's interior and exterior surface, ringing it, transferring it from one hand to the other. He grabs it from the examiner's hand in (b), resists the examiner's attempts to remove the bell in (d). His exploration and manipulation of the bell tell us that he is interested in the qualities of the bell, that there is now an investment in the bell as an object. It is a thing which has qualities of its own, independent of his own activity.

This investment of the bell with qualities has correlates in Robbie's behavior toward the bell in his search. Following loss of the object his reach is intentional, his pursuit of the bell is purposeful, and his search patterns demonstrate that he has some belief that the object can be rediscovered. His search in (c), (d), and (f) is in the area where he last had tactile contact with the bell, which means, of course, that the object is still conceived as if it had only one position in space. When he is unsuccessful in finding the object in this position, he does not pursue his search.

Stage-Specific Characteristics of Prehension

When he himself drops the bell in (g), he fingers the air in the place where he last had contact with it, then gives up his search. The trajectory of a falling object cannot yet be reconstructed by him through any cues available to him at this point. Until sound can be utilized to construct an object's movements in space he cannot have the experience of "movement" as an objective phenomenon.

In this ten-month-old sequence, however, we see Robbie beginning to place an object on sound cue. In (a) following brief tactile contact with the bell, he does not direct his search to the place where he last had tactile contact with it, but searches in the area where the bell *sound* was heard. He recovers the object.

At the same time he showed a parallel development in his behavior toward persons:

> Age: 0:10:10
> Robbie is supine on the floor. The examiner is talking to him. Robbie raises both hands to the examiner's face, feels it, touches it, and at the same time begins to kick his legs with excitement.

This reach toward "the human source of sound" is slightly more advanced than Robbie's behavior toward the bell in this session. Robbie locates and reaches for the bell (following tactile cues) through its sounds. But in this instance Robbie is clearly reacting to the *voice* of the examiner, he is *not* in tactile contact with him, and he reaches for the face in response to sound.

It should be mentioned, too, that in all of our testing the examiner talked with Robbie during the test and usually spent time playing and talking with him at the beginning of each session. This was the first time in our observations that Robbie reached for the examiner at the sound of his voice. We have no earlier examples of his reach for either of the parents upon hearing their voices.

We cannot generalize further from this experience in the observational situation. It is entirely possible that this behavior toward human objects, particularly the parents, had appeared earlier than the time of our observation and was already beginning to emerge as a generalization to inanimate objects, such as the bell, at the time we saw it. We lost the opportunity to study the evolution of this behavior because the summer vacation schedule gave us only one observational session, August 13, the month preceding the 0:10:10 observation on September 15. We are able to say only that all of our own observations up to September 15 had shown that there was no *reach* for the human object, parents or investigators, in response to voice alone. The behavior elicited by the sound of the human voice was "attentiveness," orientation of the head toward the source of sound and smiling in recognition. There was no manifest anxiety at the sound of the stranger's voice, but typically Robbie would become very quiet and cease activity when he first heard the voices of strangers.

The location of bell and person on sound cue is an important transitional behavior at this point, but we note that the search for the bell was still dependent upon an antecedent tactile experience which granted it substantiality. The reach for the examiner on voice cue was independent of a tactile experience of the examiner and may be considered a more advanced behavior.

Eleven to Thirteen Months

Robbie at eleven months begins to reach for and recover objects on sound cue alone. Two days after this demonstration he begins to creep in pursuit of sound-making objects.

EXAMPLES OF TEST BEHAVIOR
ON REMOVAL OR LOSS OF OBJECT

Age: 0:11:0
(a) The examiner rings the bell in front of Robbie (without giving him prior tactile contact with it). Robbie extends his right hand directly to the bell and retrieves it. He then spontaneously rings the bell with the right hand and the left hand goes through the motions of bell ringing.

(b) The examiner bangs the tin cup on the table. Robbie at first makes no attempt to reach for it. The cup is banged again. He reaches out and retrieves it.

Age: 0:11:2

Robbie's mother reports that Robbie has begun to creep.

Age: 0:11:21

Robbie is on hands and knees during the observational session. The bell is rung by the examiner about three feet away from Robbie's position. Robbie creeps toward the bell in a purposeful movement, retrieves the bell with his left hand, rolls over on his back, bell held in hands, and kicks his feet joyfully.

One month later we see Robbie pursuing objects through creeping, using minimal sound cues. His mother is proud and mildly exasperated. She cannot hide things from him, she says. When she tries to get her sewing basket out of his reach, he discovers it in each new place. Both parents wonder if Robbie can see, after all. (We know he cannot, but arrange for another ophthalmological examination at their request. The original diagnosis is confirmed.)

To test Robbie's pursuit on sound cue we improvise a test that parallels mother's sewing basket "experiment."

Age: 1:0:19

(a) Robbie is playing with a large cardboard box on the rug. He is fingering it and exploring it. We then slide it across the rug to a new position. Robbie immediately locates it and creeps to it.

(b) The examiner then picks up the box and moves it carefully to another position, giving barely audible cues. This time Robbie does not search and we realize that the camera motor, which has just been started, is masking sound for him. We turn off the camera and record his behavior in note form.

(c) The examiner lifts up the box carefully, sets it down a few feet from the place where Robbie last had contact with it. The only sound heard by the investigators was the faint scratching of the lid of the cardboard box as it abraded another surface of the box in coming to rest on the rug. Robbie immediately crawled to the box and retrieved it.

(d) The experiment is repeated with two other locations. Robbie retrieves the box each time, using minimal sound cues as the box makes contact with the rug.

From the parents' reports we learn at this visit that Robbie creeps to the television set, turns it off and on. When the heater comes on (there are floor grills) he is attracted to the sound of air moving, goes in search of the radiator and puts his hand over the grill to feel the heat. When his mother is cooking, Robbie is attracted by the kitchen sounds and smells, and creeps into the kitchen. During 5 weeks of creeping he has learned the map of his small home, can easily find his way about.

Summary

The stage-specific characteristics of prehension in Robbie's study can be generalized to our group of 10.

1. Search for the tactile object is initiated beginning at seven months in Robbie's case. On sound cue alone there is no behavior of search or reaching, until eleven months of age. Confronted with the sound of familiar toys the child behaves as if there were "nothing there," from which we can conclude that sound alone does not confer substantiality upon the object at earlier stages.

2. Search on sound cue alone is finally linked to the achievement of a stage in the development of the object concept. When Robbie at eleven months makes a sure reach for objects on sound cue alone, he also demonstrates that he attributes the *beginnings* of permanence to objects, that he can believe that the object is "out there," external to himself, has properties of its own.

These findings, we believe, are significant for the study of ego formation in the blind infant and promise some insight into the role of vision in facilitating and insuring the autonomous functions of the ego. Apart from the unique problems of the blind infant in establishing human relationships, the adaptive problems of the first year are made infinitely complex by the difficulties in utilizing sound and tactile experiences in constructing an object world. We can demonstrate, in the case of Robbie and in other cases known to us, that sound is not an equivalent of vision in search, in reaching, and in attaining an object. Where vision unites the sound and tactile qualities of objects in early experience, the tactile and auditory properties of the same object remain discrete experiences for the blind child well into the third quarter of the first year. The experience of "something out there" must occur before a child can endow a thing with objective qualities. Vision insures that the thing presented as a picture, the thing grasped, and the thing heard will together bring about identity of an object. Vision facilitates the encounter of the hands with the thing "out there," and, with practice, produces the sure reach for the object that will later lead to the construction of an object concept. Vision enables the child to construct the invisible displacements of an object between the ages of eight and twenty months, and to believe in the permanence of objects independent of his perceptual experience.

But for the blind child "something out there" is a chance encounter for most of his first year. An accidental swipe of the hand may bring him into contact with an object. But an object lost is an object swallowed up in a void. Even the human object, when attachment is demonstrable, is ephemeral for most of the first year and remains at the disposal of need and magic far beyond the time that sighted children have achieved object permanence.

And because tactile experience alone cannot serve the construction of an object concept, the blind child is dependent upon acoustical tracking and his own mobility to augment tactile experience in the discovery of the object world. But sound may not inform him until late in the first year. And mobility, ironically, is dependent upon the incentive of a sound stimulus for reaching. In all these ways the early ego development of the blind child is imperiled. We are beginning to understand the clinical picture of the deviant blind child who remains arrested at the level of mouth centeredness and nondifferentiation. The blind child who finds the adaptive solutions—and Robbie is one of them—must take a long and treacherous detour to the discovery of the object world.

Chapter IX

EDNA ADELSON AND SELMA FRAIBERG

Gross Motor Development*

IN THIS CHAPTER we will describe the characteristics of gross motor development in the 10 blind infants who were the subjects of this study.

Among children in the general population designated as blind there are marked delays in locomotor achievements by sighted standards. In one metropolitan sample studied by Norris, Spaulding, and Brodie (1957), in a group of 66 children blind from birth and neurologically intact, only 50% were walking independently at twenty-four months.

Preliminary gross motor findings on a smaller number of infants were reported in earlier publications (Fraiberg and Freedman 1964, Fraiberg, Siegel, and Gibson 1966, and Fraiberg 1968). In those papers we described the patterns which emerged consistently for each of the children: (1) Postural items testifying to neuromuscular maturation in control of head and trunk appeared within the range for sighted children; (2) The mobility items which normally follow each postural achievement were considerably delayed; (3) The onset of self-initiated mobility was related to the demonstration of each child's ability to reach out and attain an object presented by sound cue alone.

* This chapter, in slightly different form, was originally published and copyrighted by The Society for Research in Child Development, Inc.

Gross Motor Development

Our prehension study provided the first clues to the delayed mobility of blind children. As described in Chapter VII the blind child does not reach for and attain a sound object until the last trimester of the first year, and proficiency in "reach on sound" may not be attained until the next trimester. When sound provides the lure for reach, the blind child begins his mobility.

In this chapter we will bring together our central findings on the characteristics of gross motor development in our blind research sample. To support our early hypothesis that there is a unique pattern for normal gross motor development in the healthy blind child we will use motor items from standard developmental scales to compare the achievements of children in our group with those of sighted children. To demonstrate the effect of our intervention program we will compare our group with the larger blind sample studied by Norris, Spaulding, and Brodie in 1957. In a concluding section we will examine in some detail the impediments to locomotion which appeared in longitudinal profile and the implications of these findings for the study of the role of vision in motor development of intact sighted infants.

Data Sources and Scoring Methods

As described in Chapter III, our observations on gross motor development were derived from twice-monthly observations of the infant in his home. Postural and locomotor observations were recorded in descriptive detail in the narrative record and in film samples taken monthly.

In analyzing the gross motor material, we used the filmed demonstration of achievements wherever possible. A second choice was the observer's detailed description in the notes. There were very few instances when we relied upon a parent's report.

We rounded the ages to the nearest half month before obtaining the age range and median age range for an item. Three babies in

the group were 3 months premature. We corrected those ages for
all comparisons with sighted children. However, for comparison with one other blind research group (Norris, Spaulding, and
Brodie 1957), uncorrected ages were used to correspond with
Norris's procedure.

Intervention

Severe maternal and sensory deprivation are often added to a
blind infant's primary handicap. The profound effects of these
deprivations can outweigh and obscure the effects of blindness itself Freedman and Cannady (1971), in a study of delayed mobility, found significantly greater delays in infants who had suffered
severe environmental deprivation than in infants who were blind
from birth. All of the children in our sample received educational
guidance from our Project from the time of entry into the program. The first babies provided many of the essential clues to the
impediments of blindness in the areas of mother-child interaction, adaptive hand behavior, gross motor development and the
construction of an object world. As our knowledge progressed we
were able to translate our research findings into a developmental
guidance program (Fraiberg, Smith, and Adelson 1969, Fraiberg 1971).

In the area of gross motor development we inferred from the
lag between postural readiness and the "mobility" item which
should normally follow each postural achievement, that an external stimulus normally provided by vision creates the incentive for
reaching and extension of the trunk which initiates the locomotor
sequence. From our blind prehension study we learned that
sound does not provide a stimulus for intentional reach and attainment of an object until late in the first year. The first demonstrations of "reach on sound" in our sample appear in the last
trimester of the first year and do not become proficient for an-

other 3 to 6 months. No child in our sample demonstrated a form of prone progression or upright progression before he had first demonstrated, in our prehension study, "reach on sound cue alone," i.e., the coordination of ear and hand which enabled pursuit by hand and extension of the trunk toward an external lure. (See Chapter VII, also Fraiberg and Freedman 1964, Fraiberg, Siegel, and Gibson 1966, and Fraiberg 1968.)

In the developmental guidance program we encouraged and promoted all those experiences in which sound and touch could bring meaning and reward. And, because the baby's human partners give the most salient meaning to all sense experience, our program was centered in the parent-child relationship. Physical closeness united with the sound of the parent's voice to provide the first union of tactile-auditory experience for the children. Parents were encouraged to talk to their blind baby when approaching and while holding him for feeding, dressing, cuddling or comfort. In this way the familiar voice from afar could eventually become related to remembered and anticipated events. It was important to link words with concrete experience and objects. At the same time, we created settings, in the crib or playpen or at the table, where interesting playthings remained within easy reach, to encourage coordinated two-hand activity and to offer opportunities for spontaneous exploration and mastery with objects that made sounds as they were touched and manipulated. In these and other ways we aimed at building into earliest experience a sound-touch identity for people and for things.

We reasoned that everything we did to promote sound-touch experience for the hands would facilitate the coordination of ear and hand in directional reach and attainment of an object. We reasoned further that everything we did to facilitate "reach on sound" would have an effect in initiating locomotor sequences. Wherever vision would normally facilitate a baby's experiments in a new posture, we built in sound-touch experience which would make the new posture "interesting" for a blind child and lure him into postural shifts and mobility. We also suggested to parents that they play infant games with the baby to encourage him to use his body in many different positions, so that all postures became comfortable and familiar to him. Our interventions, in a sense, provided the experimental conditions for examining certain hypotheses which appeared early in our work, and undoubtedly affected each child's development.

Comparison Groups

Initially, in order to compare the gross motor achievement of our 10 blind infants with the normal sighted population, we chose the gross motor items and criteria described by Gesell and Amatruda (1947). These cover a broad scope, giving the major mobility milestones of creeping and walking as well as a wide variety of precursor postural achievements. Norms for the age of each achievement are also provided.

In 1969, the Bayley Scales of Infant Development were published. These were based on a more representative sample of the sighted population and provide the researcher with a normal age range as well as median age of achievement. This gain, however, is somewhat offset for our purposes by the loss of several items that are of particular interest to us. Therefore Table 5 and Figures 1 and 2 in the Results section of this chapter which compare our blind group with the sighted population do not include all the items of the gross motor sequence that we wished to examine. "Bridging on hands and knees" and "Creeping" do not appear in the tables and figures; these items are treated separately. For one item, "Walks well across room," which is not in the Bayley scales, we have, with reservations, used the item from the Denver Developmental Screening Test for roughly comparable sighted age range and median age.

We also wanted to be able to compare our findings for 10 blind infants with a larger blind population. For this we have used the group of 66 blind infants in the study reported by Norris et al. (1957). Norris used locomotor items from the Maxfield-Fjeld Tentative Adaptation (for visually handicapped preschool children) of the Vineland Social Maturity Scale. As with the Bayley scales comparison, all gross motor items that we consider pertinent to the blind child's motor development do not appear in Figures 1 and 2 and Table 5 in the Results section. It should be noted that several items on the Maxfield-Fjeld are credited by parent report.

Certain differences between the Child Development Project blind infants and the blind infants in the Norris study should be kept in mind. Both groups excluded children with additional handicaps. The children in the Norris group probably had some advantage over the total or near total blindness of the children in the Child Development Project group since the Norris criteria included varying degrees of "educational blindness." Any child in that group could be "expected to require the use of Braille for his education," but need not be totally blind. The Norris children, however, may have been disadvantaged by the greater number of premature births (87% compared to 30%) and multiple premature births (21% compared to none). In addition, some Norris subjects did not enter that study until half a year later than the oldest subject in our group (up to fifteen months old compared to eleven

TABLE 4
Sample Criteria for the Two Blind Studies

CHILD DEVELOPMENT PROJECT (N = 10)	NORRIS (N = 66)
1. No other handicap.	1. No other handicap.
2. Total blindness or only minimal light perception.	2. Total blindness or varying degrees of "educational blindness."
3. Premature births = 30% of group.	3. Premature births = 87% of group.
4. Entered study group by 11 months.	4. Entered study group by 15 months.
5. Visited every 2 weeks.	5. Visited every 3 months.

TABLE 5

Gross Motor Items and Age Achieved by Blind
(Child Development Project) and Sighted (Bayley)

ITEM	AGE RANGE †		MEDIAN AGE		DIFFERENCE IN
	SIGHTED	BLIND *	SIGHTED	BLIND	MEDIAN AGES
Elevates self by arms, prone [a]	0.7– 5.0	4.5– 9.5	2.1	8.75	6.65
Sits alone momentarily	4.0– 8.0	5.0– 8.5	5.3	6.75	1.45
Rolls from back to stomach [a]	4.0–10.0	4.5– 9.5	6.4	7.25	.85
Sits alone steadily	5.0– 9.0	6.5– 9.5	6.6	8.00	1.40
Raises self to sitting position [a]	6.0–11.0	9.5–15.5	8.3	11.00	2.70
Stands up by furniture [a] (Pulls up to stand)	6.0–12.0	9.5–15.0	8.6	13.00	4.40
Stepping movements [ab] (Walks hands held)	6.0–12.0	8.0–11.5	8.8	10.75	1.95
Stands alone [a]	9.0–16.0	9.0–15.5	11.0	13.00	2.00
Walks alone, 3 steps [a]	9.0–17.0	11.5–19.0	11.7	15.25	3.55
[Walks alone, across room] [a]	[11.3–14.3]	12.0–20.5	[12.1]	19.25	7.15

NOTE: All ages given in months.

* Ages rounded to nearest half month,
3 cases corrected for 3 months prematurity.
a: 1 child had not achieved by 2 years.
b: Not observed for 1 child prior to walk alone.
[]: Item from Denver Developmental Screening Test.
† Age range includes: 5–95% of Bayley sample
25–90% of Denver sample
10–90% of Child Development Project sample

months). They were also seen less frequently (usually at 3-month intervals compared to 2-week intervals).

Results

THE BLIND AND THE SIGHTED—A COMPARISON

We were interested in determining whether our earlier hypothesis held up in the completed sample, i.e., that postural achievement for the blind child tends to be on schedule, whereas self-initiated mobility is usually delayed. Figure 1 compares the age range and median ages for the Child Development Project blind group with the ranges and median ages for sighted children as given by Bayley. The sequence of motor items is essentially simi-

FIGURE 1

Blind* and Sighted Median Ages (using Child Development Project blind group)

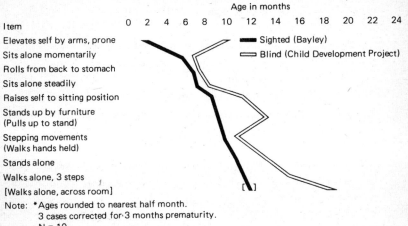

Note: *Ages rounded to nearest half month.
3 cases corrected for 3 months prematurity.
N = 10.
[ ] from Denver Developmental Screening Test.

lar for both the blind and the sighted children. Age, sex, light perception, and prematurity are not systematically related to gross motor development within this group of 10 blind children.

The achievements for which our blind infants closely approximated the sighted age range are: "Sits alone momentarily," "Rolls from back to stomach," "Sits alone steadily," "Takes stepping movements when hands are held," and "Stands alone." The sitting, standing, and stepping items would seem to indicate a normal sequence and rate of maturation for control of the trunk, the ability to bear weight on the legs, and the ability to make alternating leg movements with support. "Bridging on hands and knees" is another postural item close to sighted norms. For our blind group the age range for bridging was six and a half to fourteen months, the median age 9.25. Gesell places the sighted norm at 40 weeks (about nine months). Adequate head control was also demonstrated by each of the children in the group. However, it does not appear as a separate item in the table or figures since we have direct observations for only three of the children who were seen before four months. The other children were first seen at four to eleven months (with age correction: four to eight months). According to the parents' reports they held their heads erect and steady within the sighted range. "Rolls from back to stomach" is the only mobility item to fall within the sighted range and remains an enigma at present.

The achievements for which our blind infants are delayed beyond the sighted age range are: "Elevates self by arms, in prone," "Raises self to sitting position," "Stands up by furniture (pulls to stand)," "Walks alone, three steps," and "Walks alone across the room." These all involve some form of what we shall call self-initiated mobility. Creeping is an additional mobility item that is delayed. For our blind group the age range was ten and a half to twenty-four months, median age 13.25. Gesell places the sighted norm very close to the age of bridging, i.e., 40 weeks. For our group there is a 4-month delay between these two items, one postural, the other involving mobility related to that posture.

Gross Motor Development

In Figure 2 below it can be seen that for the 5 items shown with a striped bar (4 of them postural) very few of the blind infants (10–20%) are delayed past the upper limits of the sighted age range. However, for the 5 items shown with solid bars (self-initiated mobility) a larger proportion of the group (40–90%) are delayed beyond the age range for sighted infants.

In Figure 1 the median ages for blind and sighted are plotted beside each other and the connecting curves drawn for each. There is a repeated pattern of convergence for postural items, and a marked divergence (indicating delay) for items requiring self-initiated mobility or shifts of posture in response to external stimuli at a distance.

These findings would seem to support our earlier suggestion that blindness does not affect gross motor development in some uniform fashion. Blindness has relatively little impact upon postural achievements in the otherwise normal and well-stimulated blind infant. However, blindness is associated with a marked delay in the achievement of mobility skills. We would argue from

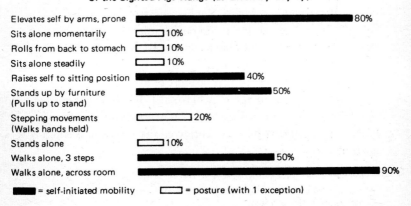

FIGURE 2

Percentage of Our Blind Sample Who Were Delayed Past the Upper Limits of the Sighted Age Range (as Given by Bayley)

Elevates self by arms, prone	80%
Sits alone momentarily	10%
Rolls from back to stomach	10%
Sits alone steadily	10%
Raises self to sitting position	40%
Stands up by furniture (Pulls up to stand)	50%
Stepping movements (Walks hands held)	20%
Stands alone	10%
Walks alone, 3 steps	50%
Walks alone, across room	90%

■ = self-initiated mobility   ▭ = posture (with 1 exception)

this that vision must play a more central role in the achievement of mobility and locomotion than it does in the establishment of stable postures. Our prehension study indicates that for the blind child there will have to be some adaptive substitution of distant auditory stimuli for distant visual stimuli to prompt the beginnings of self-initiated mobility. This substitution, in our experience, does not occur until the end of the first year.

Comparison of Two Blind Groups

Since the number in our group was small we wanted to compare our findings with a larger similar group yielding comparable data for gross motor items. We also wanted to see whether our intervention program, which focused on human relationships and the construction of an object world, had affected gross motor achievements. Accordingly, we have used the largest group reported in the literature, that of Norris et al., with an N of 66.

A simple direct comparison, as could be done with Bayley's data for sighted children, was not possible with the Norris data for the blind; Norris does not provide percentiles or median ages.* There are 7 items for which both studies used comparable criteria and for which Norris reported the age by which 50–74% (>50%) of her group received credit. We have compared this with the age of achievement of the sixtieth percentile of our group (see Figure 3). There are 9 items for which Norris reported the age of achievement for 75% or more of her group (>75%). We have compared it with age of achievement for the eightieth percentile of our group (see Figure 4). To match Norris's procedure for calculating age we have not corrected the 3 cases of premature birth in our group.

* The Norris data are reported as <25%, >25%, >50%, or >75% of the sample having achieved an item during a particular 3-month interval. Not all these breakdowns are given for each item.

Gross Motor Development

FIGURE 3
Two Blind Groups Compared: Norris > 50%, with Child Development Project Sixtieth Percentile. (No Age Correction for Prematurity)

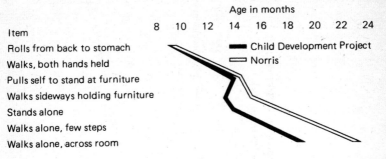

Age in months

Item	8	10	12	14	16	18	20	22	24

Rolls from back to stomach

Walks, both hands held

Pulls self to stand at furniture

Walks sideways holding furniture

Stands alone

Walks alone, few steps

Walks alone, across room

━━ Child Development Project

▭ Norris

In both figures the similar shapes of the curves would indicate that our group of 10 did resemble the Norris group of 66. The items have been arranged to correspond to the actual order of achievement of the blind children, which is slightly different from the order for sighted children. The similar regular pattern of gross motor development shown by both groups probably represents the normal developmental sequence for the child who is blind from birth and who has no other handicap.

Further examination of Figures 3 and 4 shows an age advantage for the Child Development Project blind group, an advantage that increases over time. In Figure 4 the groups are only 2 months apart initially, but 7–13 months apart for the last 3 items in the sequence. We believe that the earlier ages for gross motor achievements of the children in our blind group represent the cumulative effects of the intervention program. Delays in mobility and locomotion were lessened when we were successful in providing early auditory-tactile experiences that sustained interest in the external world, encouraged physical activity, and ultimately permitted sound to serve as a lure for forward progression.

209

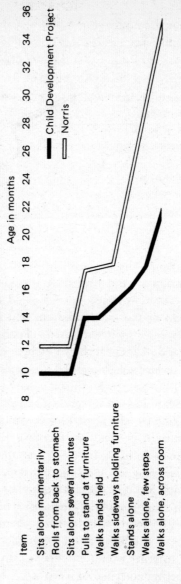

FIGURE 4

Two Blind Groups Compared: Norris 75%, with Child Development Project Eightieth Percentile. (No Age Correction for Prematurity)

Item

Sits alone momentarily
Rolls from back to stomach
Sits alone several minutes
Pulls to stand at furniture
Walks hands held
Walks sideways holding furniture
Stands alone
Walks alone, few steps
Walks alone, across room

Age in months

8   10   12   14   16   18   20   22   24   26   28   30   32   34   36

━━━ Child Development Project
▭▭▭ Norris

Gross Motor Development

Discussion

There is a start-and-stop character to the normal pattern of gross motor development in blind children that is confusing to the researcher and distressing to the anxious parent. In early infancy the blind baby supports his head well when he is held upright or in a supported sit. Placed on his stomach, however, at any age up to five months he is unlikely to bring his arms forward in order to raise his head high and clear his chest from the surface. There is nothing in his other behavior to indicate a lack of strength or coordination of his arms or neck or back, but suddenly he seems inadequate. A few months later the blind babies are sitting, briefly at first and then well, and doing so within the normal range for sighted infants. But they do not advance to the next set of accomplishments, which would involve moving themselves from supine to sit or from sit to stand, at anything like the rate of progress for the sighted child. Creeping is markedly delayed. Development seems to have come to a halt. Toward the end of the first year, blind children take steps with hands held and can stand alone within the sighted range although the medians are about two months later. Once again, however, there is a disquieting pause before the next steps (quite literally) are taken. The sighted child can walk independently about 3 months after he walks with his hands held. The blind child may not do so for 8 or 9 months.

We are not concerned with the simple performance of any motor item for its own sake. There are children with severe motor handicaps who develop adequately in most other areas. For the young blind child, however, anything that further restricts his already limited access to external stimulation is of great moment because it may prevent his acquisition of objective information about events and objects around him, and it may encourage a dangerous passivity and subjectivity, thus threatening all of early ego development. Gesell and Amatruda (1947), Norris, Spaulding, and Brodie (1957), and Parmalee, Fiske, and Wright (1959) have found that blindness from birth need not by itself cause serious developmental delays. Yet we know that a large number of congenitally blind children do meet with grave difficulties that result finally in deviant personalities with pessimistic prognoses. The blind child's special pattern of gross motor development claims our attention because the periods of delay that are "normal" for the blind child probably represent periods of serious developmental hazard.

Undoubtedly equilibrium and fluent motor coordination are affected by lack of visual feedback, and there certainly are fewer possibilities for imitation. Nevertheless, control of the head and trunk in sitting and standing positions and the alternating leg movements taken with hands held are achieved entirely within the sighted range. When there is still a delay in mobility even with well-mothered, well-stimulated blind infants, it is probably related to a lack of external incentive during most of the first year when sound by itself cannot substitute for sight as a distance sense.

In infant testing we use visual lures to entice the sighted child to pull himself up to a stand or to move forward in prone. We know he is likely to reach for whatever he sees from four and a half months on. Less often noted is the fact that the sighted infant does not reach for what he only hears but cannot see until late in the first year. (See Piaget 1952, Fraiberg, Siegel, and Gibson 1966, Freedman, Margileth, Fox-Kolenda, and Miller 1970, and Chapter VIII.) This has special significance when we wish to lure the blind infant into motion, to get him to pull up to a stand, or to move ahead to get a toy beyond his immediate reach. Until he has demonstrated a response of hand movement to seek an object at a distance by sound alone, we cannot lure him from one place to another; he remains immobile in spite of demonstrated motor competence. This point has been examined in detail in Fraiberg, Siegel, and Gibson (1966). It has been borne out in the cases we have seen since then.

Perhaps the best way to appreciate the blind child's dilemma would be to look closely at gross motor development from the very beginning of the first year. We will do this by dividing the first year into 4-month intervals, comparing normal sighted development with normal development for the blind child for each period.

0–4 months: The early developmental pace is a rapid one. If we observe a sighted infant when he is picked up and held against the shoulder of his mother, we note his increasing ability to adjust to her posture and to control the position of his head. From as early as 1.3 months median age, he turns his head spontaneously from side to side and "inspects" the surroundings (Bayley). When wide awake and active he seems to seek stimulation with his eyes and by the turning of his head multiplies the visual possibilities. At about one and a half months he turns his eyes toward a light source. If at two months we place this baby on his stomach, he responds by bracing himself with his arms to lift his head high and to raise his chest off the flat surface. This puts him in the best possible position to continue to look around, which he will do until his arms and back tire. This mobility of the head in the service of the eyes continues. At three months the sighted baby tracks a rolling ball or follows a moving hoop or a falling object. At nearly four months he turns his head to the sound of a rattle or bell.

Now let us turn to an alert, wide-awake blind infant. He, too, will mold comfortably to his mother's chest and shoulder. He, too, will soon be able to carry his head high and steady. We would have guessed that erect head posture depended upon fixation of the eyes on some reference point in the visual field. Yet this seemed not to be so in the blind infants we followed. But even at this early age there were two important differences between the blind and sighted infants. First, whether the blind baby was held upright against his mother's shoulder, or settled comfortably upon her lap, he did not move his head from side to side; he tended to keep it centered. He could turn his head (2 of the 3 children we saw before four months did turn to the sound of a test bell), but he seldom did so. Sound did not seem to have the same exciting and attracting qualities for the blind infant of this age that sight provided for the sighted infant.

Second, the parents reported that their blind infants did not like the prone position. Each mother placed her baby on his stomach on the floor to show us what she meant. We saw all too clearly. The babies struggled to clear their heads and noses from the surface by arching the back or stretching the neck. They protested and looked uncomfortable and unhappy or else gave up and simply rested with cheek upon the floor. There was no sustained lifting of the head and no bracing with the arms to aid them in maintaining a more comfortable, more interesting posture. The sound of favorite toys or mother's voice, the touch of gentle patting on head or back made no difference. Just as the blind baby did not scan the world about him by moving his head when he was held by his mother, so in the prone position, he did not raise his head to take in more of the external world around him. For him there was no adaptive advantage in head mobility, no enticement, no reward that could equal what was usually offered by visual stimulation.

Elevating the head and chest by use of the arms when prone was one of the items that was delayed by more than 6 months in comparison to the sighted median age. For almost all the blind infants in our group it did not occur until after they were able to roll over from back to stomach, which they did within the sighted age range, four to ten months. This, then, represents a different order of achievement from that of the sighted infant, but it seems to be normal for the infant who is born blind.

4–8 months: This is a period when the sighted child gains full mastery over the sitting position. By six and a half months he can sit independently and steadily. Placed on the floor in the supine position at the same age, he can roll over and get onto his stomach. At an earlier stage he reached out into the visual environment with his eyes and his head followed, moving from side to side or up and down. Now he reaches out with his arms. His eyes and hands have been coordinated since four and a half months. On his stomach he looks about, reaches out with his hand, and in so doing pivots out of his original position. By seven months he will move ahead to get an attractive toy that is held in front of him out of his reach. One way or another the sighted child can begin to get from here, where he is, to there, where the toy is. He sees it, he wants to hold it, he moves toward it by crawling or creeping or hitching in sit.

What of the blind child? He has no trouble maintaining a good sitting posture, at first briefly, and then for a longer period. He may not find it interesting if he does not have something to play with but he can sit independently well within the sighted age range. He can also roll from his back to his stomach within the sighted age range. Of course this puts him in a position he has never favored and so he is likely to roll over once again into supine. The blind baby can sit and can get onto his stomach. What he cannot do, or rather, what no child we observed would do before ten and a half months, is use his own mobility in attempts to get closer to a toy that he likes when it is held in front of him but out of his reach. If a toy he is playing with is removed from his grasp so that he cannot touch it, the blind infant can search with both arms across the table top or through the space that lies within arm's reach in front of and to the side of him. If the toy is not there, he is at a total loss to know what to do. He has no clues about its location or even its continued existence. One way to offer him additional cues is to use a sounding toy, such as a bell, or a favorite musical stuffed animal. For some of the children this made no difference whatsoever during this period. There was protest over removal of the toy, quiet listening, and then blank-faced passive waiting without reaching, even though we sounded the toy very close by. Other children, however, did react with their hands even though they did not make attempts at a directed reach or locomotion. It was through those hand responses that we were able to watch the blind child gradually unite tactile and auditory experience. The eventual coordination of ear and hand in reaching out for the distant object (which occurs much later than the eye-hand coordination of the sighted child) would finally motivate him to creep * toward an interesting object that he heard and wanted to grasp. But the median age of 13.25 months for that mobility item was 6 months later than the sighted child's crawl or creep or hitch (Bayley: 7.1 months).

It should be added that this delay cannot be accounted for by any equivalent delay in fine motor coordination. The blind children were using their hands well. They demonstrated mutual fingering and transferring of an object from hand to hand, bringing toys to the mouth and banging toys on the table in an age range that overlaps the sighted age range. And they were in most cases given good experience in hand play with toys that combined interesting tactile and auditory qualities (Chapter VII).

8–12 months: In this last period of the first year the sighted child is quick to take advantage of the possibilities for combining his old skills with his new maturation. Once he discovers how to get up into a sitting position he sets his sights higher and soon can pull himself up to a stand. With the support of a helpful adult or a piece of furniture he begins to take steps. He experiments with letting go and standing alone, and near his first birthday can take several steps as he hurls himself toward his waiting mother's arms. It will not be long before he gains sufficient control of an unsupported stand and alternating leg movements to be able to make his way across an entire room.

In supine or in prone positions the infant is in touch with the floor from head to foot. When he sits up, only half of his body, his buttocks and legs, rests on the floor. When he finally stands and lets go of the supporting rail he feels the floor with only the bottoms of his very small feet. With each postural advance he gives up a major portion of his actual physical contact with the real world.

* For "creep" we are using Gesell's definition in which the baby is locomoting on hands and knees. At this stage of data analysis we have not found examples of other forms of forward progression corresponding to the Bayley item "Prewalking progression."

Gross Motor Development

There is a definite pleasure in new motor mastery. There is an urge to motor activity at this age that is unmistakable. But we may overlook, in observing the sighted child, the contribution of vision to his eager self-confident adventuring. Each change in position from sit to stand, or from stand to sit, each step he takes whether supported or not, produces an endlessly varied and fascinating series of visual spectacles. Wherever he casts his eyes, the space is furnished with a mixture of shadows and textures and patterns and contrasts and 3-dimensional objects, including the people he knows. One glance brings him the entire scene and informs him about his relationship to each element.

While the sighted infant is advancing from crawling to creeping and to independent walking, the blind child has yet to make his first attempt at independent mobility. He sat independently within the sighted age range and he will stand independently within the sighted age range. He will also support himself upon hands and knees at pretty close to the sighted age range. But he does not move into, or out of, or forward from these postures on the same timetable as the sighted child.

This delay is not for a lack of motor impetus. Many of the children rocked vigorously and perhaps impatiently in sit, on hands and knees, and in stand. Peter Wolff (1968) has described these patterns at transition points in sighted children as well. The rhythmic activity diminishes and disappears as mobility is mastered in relation to each posture. In the blind infant it may be more prolonged because at each point along the gross motor sequence the self-initiated mobility that should follow upon the new posture is delayed. The blind infants' median ages for getting up into a sit and for pulling up to a stand at furniture lie at or beyond the upper limits of the sighted age range, and while Gesell describes the 40-week-old infant as bridging on hands and knees and almost immediately creeping thereafter, the median ages of bridging and creeping in our blind group were 4 months apart.

Each instance of marked delay in motor progress for the blind suggests strongly the effects of the missing sense, vision. When the normally fluid transition from "independent sit" to "shifts into and out of sit" does not occur, we infer that motivational factors provided by vision are present in the sequence for sighted children but are absent for the blind children. We can trace the development of a motivational force in our observations of hand behavior in the blind child. When the blind infant does not persist in his efforts to retrieve a toy we have taken from him, when he does not reach out to take hold of an attractive toy that we sound within arm's reach we speculate that for him there are as yet no furnishings and objects surrounding him except those that exist when he is in immediate contact with them. He acts as if the fallen toy has totally disappeared, as if the sounds of familiar objects were disembodied and had no connection with the same objects that he himself held and manipulated to produce sounds. (See Chapter VII and Fraiberg, Siegel, and Gibson 1966). If we can fairly describe the sighted infant's larger environment as fully furnished and tempting, for the blind infant the appropriate adjectives might be featureless, unattractive, possibly frightening.

In the last trimester of the first year most of the blind children in our group had reached out into space with their hands for something they heard and wished to hold. Thus they indicated an awareness of a solid, graspable object "out there." Once this reach on sound was achieved mobility soon followed. And as each child began to raise himself into a sit and up to a stand and to creep across the floor he mapped the space around him as he went and began to furnish the void, slowly. When he stood up he came upon things from a new angle and needed to remap his entire space once again. He could not do this with one sweeping glance as the sighted child can. He had to do it painstakingly at first, one step at a time so to speak, feeling his way repeatedly as he gained familiarity with his old world in a new position.

If we were to stop our observations at the end of the first year, less than half of the blind infants would have begun to creep, and only one child would have taken first steps and begun to walk well. The others would take considerably longer. The median age for creeping was 13.25 months, probably 6 months late by sighted standards (Gesell). The median age for independent walking across the room was 19.25 months, a 7-month delay.

In gross motor development lack of vision presents the blind child with a double handicap: he has only one instead of two distance senses and the one he has is the lesser one, at that, since sound does not begin to function as a clue to the presence of an out-of-reach object until late in the first year. Evidently a child who is born totally blind cannot make use of distant sound cues from an invisible object any earlier than a sighted child. He remains in a void until he can seek his own direct contacts with the external surroundings; ironically, until he has an incentive to move into those surroundings he cannot discover their existence. Once "reach on sound" has been achieved he can soon be lured into motion and can begin to cope with the relatively less difficult problems of balance, coordination, speed, and safety.

If the blind child is provided with good mothering and the chance to become familiar with many body positions, and if his hands and ears are given months of varied play experience with toys that unite tactile and auditory qualities, he will have found interest and taken pleasure in the space immediately around him. He will then be ready to move forth into a larger space when he becomes aware of the interesting possibilities just beyond his reach.

Summary

The gross motor development of 10 infants blind from birth was observed from birth to two years. There was a regular pattern of development for the blind infant, but it differed from that of the sighted infant. Adequate neuromuscular maturation was demonstrated throughout the first year in the postural items which all occurred within the sighted age range. But there was a considerable delay in self-initiated mobility. We infer from this delay that vision must play a more central role in the achievement of mobility than it does in the establishment of stable postures.

Vision provides the sighted child with a lure, an incentive at a distance. Early eye-hand coordination enables him to reach out for what he sees and wants. Eventually shifts of arm and body extend the reach of the hand and the child moves from one place to another in pursuit of what he sees.

Ear-hand coordination, i.e., reach for an invisible distant object on sound cue only, normally occurs late in the first year for the blind child as well as for the sighted child. Until sound at a distance can provide a lure, until the blind child is reaching out for and seeking what he hears, he remains immobile in sit or in stand. Only after he has become practiced in reaching on sound will he begin to creep and walk, slowly mapping the concrete world around him.

The prolonged period of immobility during the first year of life represents a serious threat to the ego development of the blind child. It lessens his ability to explore independently, to discover by himself the objective rules that govern things and events in the external world. In an intervention program based upon uniting sound and touch, first centered in the child-parent pair and later in the play experiences given the child, we were able to decrease the interval between postural achievements and mobility in comparison with another group of blind infants. At present, however, it seems unlikely that the delay can be completely eliminated since sound does not provide the same adaptive advantages as sight.

Chapter X

SELMA FRAIBERG

The Acquisition
of Language

LANGUAGE ACQUISITION in the blind infant was one of the major areas of our study. In a world without pictures how does the blind baby name objects, make his wants known, combine words in the progression toward syntactical complexity and invention in language?

In the larger population designated as blind, gross delays in language acquisition are commonly reported and constitute a major problem in the education of the young school age child. Since this is a mixed population, with a large incidence of multiple handicaps and neurological impairment, we cannot make fair inferences from these findings. As far as we know, no language study exists which is based upon a group of blind children strictly comparable to ours and employs the data collection and scoring procedures that we have followed.

In our own group of infants, blind but otherwise intact, we can more fairly assess the effects of blindness per se in the language acquisition period. Moreover, since all of our children were probably advantaged through our educational program, in which we maximized the experience of the blind infant, we can assess those limitations or impediments in language development that can be fairly attributed to blindness itself.

Intervention

We did not provide "speech training" for our blind infants in our guidance program. We did not provide an "infant curriculum" in this or any other aspect of our intervention program. As clinicians and developmental psychologists we chose another route.

We saw language as a component of sensorimotor organization which was inextricably linked with the development of human attachments, prehension, gross motor development and representational intelligence. It was our hypothesis that the reported delays in language development among children blind from birth reflected the experiential poverty of the blind infant. We saw the impediments of blindness in the human "dialogue" of signs and signals between the blind baby and his partners. We saw the unique problems for the blind infant in adaptive hand behavior, which deprived him of the experiences of a richly furnished world of persons and things essential for naming and the attribution of qualities in language development. We saw how the delays in locomotion further reduced the blind child's experience in discoveries of persons and things and in representing this world through language.

We reasoned that everything we did to facilitate the blind child's development in the areas of human attachments, in tactile and auditory experience with persons and things and in locomotor experience would affect the progress of language. We also reasoned that everything we did to maximize the language environment in the home would affect the acquisition of language in blind children as it does with sighted children.

In earlier chapters we have seen that our intervention had positive effects in facilitating the blind baby's attachment to his mother, with close correspondence in milestones to those of sighted children. We saw in our report on prehension that expanding the blind infant's tactile-auditory experience with persons and things was essential to the coordination of ear and hand and for attributing substantiality to things and persons "out there"—a crucial first step in naming. In our report on gross motor development we saw that our interventions facilitated locomotion in our group of blind children (and brought them closer to sighted-child ranges than to blind-child ranges). We reasoned that locomotor experience had effects upon language development through enlarging the blind infants' experience.

In our work we maximized the language environment for the blind child through encouraging vocal dialogues between parents and child and through naming (even in the preverbal period) the persons and objects and actions which the blind baby experienced.

Some of our blind babies would have been disadvantaged in language experience even if they had been sighted. In the range of families represented in our families we had three families for whom "talking to a baby" was alien to their styles of child rearing. For a sighted child in these environments perhaps the worst thing that might have happened would have been a baby who was "slow in talking." (And in each of these families with other siblings, the sighted siblings were in fact retarded in speech development.) But a blind child is doubly imperiled in a world in which his partners "don't talk to babies"; he would be deprived of a primary mode in "knowing" his mother and other persons and in being introduced to a world of objects. We were able in each instance to help these parents understand the meaning of "talking to the baby," with demonstrably good results.

Limitations of this Study

The most interesting questions for us and for the developmental linguist cannot be answered in this chapter. Developmental linguistics is a comparatively new field, and those questions which have to do with the acquisition of grammatical form and syntactical complexity are in the earliest stages of investigation. No scales exist which permit comparison between a sighted child population and our blind group in these crucial areas.

The language items on standard infant scales are not necessarily the "sensitive" items from a linguistic point of view. But in a territory that has not yet been mapped, these language milestones represent the only fixed points, the known territory where earlier explorers set up their flags. Among the earlier scales (Gesell, Cattell) the median ages for attainment of these milestones differed from scale to scale because of differences in sample and scoring. By 1969 Nancy Bayley published her *Scales of Infant Development* which meets the requirements for adequate standardization in sample and rigor of administration, and we have selected this instrument for comparison of our blind group with a sighted population in those areas of language development where comparisons can be fairly made.

Observations and Scoring

Our data on language acquisition are derived from verbatim records by the observers. All notations on the baby's early vocalizations, examples of receptive language, use of words as referents, simple sentences, and later, complex discourse were recorded in context in a descriptive narrative. This gave us a large bank of data on every child, which was later coded and analyzed.

In this report I have selected a group of items in which the language capacities of our blind children can be fairly compared with those of sighted children, using criteria from the Bayley Scales (1969). It should be noted that at the time our study was designed the Bayley Scales had not yet been published. However, our own verbatim records required no on-the-spot judgments or scoring by the observers, and we were able to return to the data bank during the evaluation period, search the records for the descriptive items, and make post-facto judgments using stringent Bayley criteria. Following is a summary of our procedures for data analysis and scoring:

(1) A first sorting of language items was made using *observer reports* only.

FIGURE 5

Language Milestones: Child Development Project Blind Study

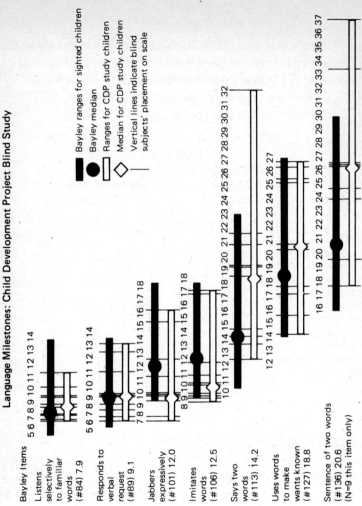

(2) Using Bayley criteria, a second sorting of items was made for each child, and the items were examined without scoring.

(3) All ambiguous items were discarded.

(4) Team meetings were instituted for scoring.

(5) Credit was given on the basis of team consensus.

TABLE 6

Language Items: Median Ages
Blind (Child Development Project) and Sighted (Bayley)

| | AGE RANGE | | MEDIAN AGE | |
ITEM	SIGHTED	BLIND	SIGHTED	BLIND
Listens selectively to familiar words	5.0–14.0	6.6–11.5	7.9	8.6
Responds to verbal requests	6.0–14.0	6.6–13.5	9.1	9.8
Jabbers expressively.	9.0–18.0	6.9–16.0	12.0	9.4
Imitates words	9.0–18.0	8.9–17.5	12.5	10.3
Says two words	10.0–23.0	12.7–32.0	14.2	18.5
Uses words to make wants known	14.0–27.0	13.2–26.9	18.8	20.6
Sentence of two words (N = 9 this item only)	16.0–30.0	17.9–37.3	20.6	26.3

Selection of Items for Comparison

A number of the language items on the Bayley scale cannot be employed for testing the blind child, either because vision is required for the task or because the manual instructions explicitly require a visual stimulus in the test procedures. Thus all items in the early smile sequence in the Bayley are tested by means of visual stimuli—the presentation of E's or mother's face. And, although all of our blind infants can demonstrate smiling in response to mother's or father's voice within the same age range as the sighted child's smile to the human face gestalt, we cannot substitute "voice only" for the visual presentation without violating the test. Then, since there is no Bayley item which specifically tests smiling response to *voice only*, we have chosen to eliminate the social smile from our inventory of comparison items.

Similarly, for items such as Bayley #80, which combines both verbal instructions from E and an imitation of a task demonstrated by E with the baby's visual attention, we cannot substitute another form of the task for the blind baby. The task itself, however, which requires the baby to place a cube in the cup upon E's demonstration and verbal request can be achieved by a blind baby if he has been given motor guidance by E in learning the task, followed by verbal instructions to reproduce the act. However, we cannot assume the privilege of substitution and have therefore chosen to eliminate this item from our comparison inventory.

Again, in Bayley picture-identification items of the second year we would violate the integrity of the test if we substituted tactile-recognition items for visual-recognition ones. Other tasks in the second year, which test both comprehension of language and comprehension of visually perceived relationships between the parts and the whole ("mend the doll"), cannot be administered. It is of considerable interest, however, that blind children can demonstrate tactile recognition of objects and name them within sighted-child ranges, and this can be fairly demonstrated through a strict administration and scoring of Bayley #113 ("says two words"), #127 ("uses words to make wants known"), and Bayley #136 ("sentence of two words").

Finally, then, the language items which have been selected for comparison represent only those Bayley tasks which can be administered fairly to a group of blind children without modifying manual procedures. In this selection we cannot, of course, see the full range of a blind child's language capacities. The blind child's differentiated repertoire in smiling and in tactile exchange is not represented in this facet of the language study because, of course, we have no comparative data for sighted children. The eliciting stimuli for these language behaviors must be restricted to sound and touch, a circumstance which affords no fair comparison with sighted children. These language behaviors which are uniquely constituted for the blind child are examined in Chapters V and VI.

Following these requirements for comparison we found 7 language items on the Bayley which could be fairly applied to our blind sample.

In Figure 5 the language achievements of our blind infants are recorded for 7 items. The Bayley ranges for each of these items are represented by the black bar. Ages for three premature infants are corrected for prematurity in the figure and in protocols.

Selected Items: Data Summary

In the following pages we shall examine the items selected for comparison with norms for sighted children. For some items, particularly the advanced language items, I will include excerpts from our protocols.

THE EARLY VOCALIZATIONS

We have not included in our tables a group of Bayley items in the zero- to seven-month range attesting to the quality and range of early vocalizations. These are: *"Vocalizes once or twice"* (0.9), *"Vocalizes at least four times"* (1.6), *"Vocalizes two different sounds"* (2.3), *"Vocalizes attitudes"* (4.6), *"Vocalizes four different syllables"* (7.0), *"Says dada or equivalent"* (7.0).

All children available to us for study in the zero- to seven-month range produced a range of vocalizations which distinguished them in no way from sighted children. Since the later language items testify for both the physiological capacity to produce a full range of vocalizations and the higher-level achievements of imitation of syllables, words, and speech cadences, an item analysis of the early vocalizations adds little of interest to this study.

As Lenneberg (1967) demonstrates through a range of empirical studies, the capacity to produce speech sounds of increasing complexity of articulation has specific neurophysiological correlates in maturation. In those instances where maturation itself is impeded by defects in the child's physiology (e.g., mongolism) the timetable for the sequence of differentiated sounds shows variance with that of intact children but consistency with the child's own rate of neuromuscular development. Lenneberg also adduces from the differentiated articulations of congenitally deaf children in the period under six months of age that these early utterances can be produced even under those conditions in which the child cannot hear these sounds from the speech of partners or as echoes of his own productions. Typically, these spontaneous utterances of congenitally deaf children do not become further differentiated after six months of age and may in fact drop out of the repertoire as inutile, having no sign function.

In examining the biological foundations of language, Lenneberg in no way diminishes the importance of the language environment in the period of language acquisition. An impoverished language environment will be reflected in the poverty of the child's own language and will appear as measurable deficiencies through testing in the second year. But if I read Lenneberg correctly, he is saying that the capacity of the human infant to produce certain sounds that are uniquely within the repertoire of our species is given in human biology. Whether or not these differentiated sounds will evolve into new combinations learned, new combinations invented, and ultimately into the complexities of discourse will depend upon both progression in physiological maturation and the furnishing of the materials of language normally provided in the environment.

We are not surprised, then, that our group of otherwise intact blind infants cannot be differentiated from sighted children in the measurement of their attainment of these vocal milestones on the Bayley scale. Certain differences which we can report impressionistically cannot be measured on existing scales. There is a consensus among our staff and independent observers that there may be quantitative differences, that the amount of spontaneous vocalization during a single observational session is less than we are accustomed to hear among sighted babies, even among the "high vocalizers" among our children under one year of age, and even when the amount of vocal stimulation and reinforcement in the environment is very high. As suggested in Fraiberg (1974) and in Chapter V, these differences in quantity (assuming our impressions are fair) may reflect the absence of visual stimuli which are potent elicitors of vocalization in normal sighted children. (The sight of the human face—even when the partner is not speaking— may elicit vocal "greeting" sounds from the baby. A colorful hanging in the crib, or a mobile without sound, can elicit a volley of utterances from a sighted baby.)

But the discrete utterances which are uniquely human appear in a normal progression in the first months of life for our blind infants. This inventory from the records of Ronnie may suffice to document the point.

"Vocalizes 2 different sounds" (#30) (1–5, median 2.3)
0:2:11 Ronnie's vocalizations now include a recently acquired *'gagagaga'* . . . as well as such expressive vocalizations as a laugh, a cry, a groan and a grunt.

As Ronnie is lying in the crib, banging the toys of the cradle gym, we hear *'ememem'* sounds.

"Vocalizes attitudes" (#35) (3–8, median 4.6)
0:5:3 Ronnie was vocalizing a great deal during this session. . . . He listens and responds with *enthusiastic 'ahahaha'* sounds . . . . During the interruption of the pat-a-cake sequence with mother, there is a surprised look on Ronnie's face and then a *melancholy 'ahahaha'* chant.

"Vocalizes 4 different syllables" (#79) (5–12, median 7.0)
0:4:20 Ronnie doesn't like to have his bib tied on. He made some harsh, complaining *"uh"* sounds. In the course of this session we hear the syllables *"ha"* and *"huh"* and *"aw aw aw"* and *"mamamama."*

"Says *'dada'* or equivalent" (#85) (5–14, median 7.9)
0:4:20 says *'mamamama'* (cited in preceding example).

The Acquisition of Language

The items selected and recorded in Table 6 and Figure 5 permit a close comparison between sighted and blind infant achievements during the language acquisition period. These items, which emerge in the six- to thirty-month range, test the child's capacity to understand verbal requests, imitate words, to employ words as referents, to express wants, and to combine words in simple sentences. Here we are no longer testing the child's innate capacity to produce discrete utterances in the vocal repertoire of his species but his capacity to make meaningful utterances, to classify and label, and finally to employ his vocabulary to generate new combinations—to invent with language.

In the following pages we can examine five of these items with excerpts from the protocols. In all instances we have credited only those performances which were in accord with Bayley's procedures and criteria for scoring.

"Responds to verbal requests" (#89) (7–17, median 9.1)
Determine whether the child has learned to perform any act in response to a spoken request. (It is often necessary to suggest something the child has learned.) Common early responses include waving in response to *Bye-Bye*, clapping hands in response to *Pat-a-cake*, or responding to such questions as *Where is the light?* or *Where is the clock?* or *Where is daddy?* If you cannot elicit a response, ask the mother to try, but make sure she uses words only and no gestures.

Credit if the child responds in any appropriate manner to any verbal request unaccompanied by a gesture.

Blind Group: This item was passed by 100% of our sample within the Bayley ranges, with 50% above the median. It is of considerable interest that nearly all of the items which we credited for our blind children were in the context of interpersonal games. *Pat-a-cake* was a great favorite among our blind children and we have numerous examples of *pat-a-cake* on spoken request by mother or observer. Other games included a version of *peek-a-boo* for a blind baby (which is described below), a game "show

231

me your tongue," "come to mommy and get a kiss," and "give mommy a kiss."

In all cases we ascertained that no tactile or motor cues were given. At least 2 demonstrations of the game were required for credit. This is beyond the requirement of Bayley procedures but essential to rule out chance in the case of a blind child. To further strengthen the case for the blind child's demonstration, we tallied all instances of "response to spoken requests" for each child. Following the first credited demonstrations for each child, we begin to get a proliferation of instances of "games on request," and an expanded repertoire of games on request. This means, of course, that the blind child's response to the spoken request as credited in the first instances was a fair measure of the child's emerging ability to understand key words.

Pat-a-cake

Six of the credited responses (first examples in each protocol) in Figure 5 were for pat-a-cake on request. One example follows:

Jamie, 0:9:12 (recorded on film with transcript of verbal cues)
Mother asks Jamie to "pat-a-cake" (no motor cues given). Jamie claps his hands together. . . . After an interval, observer repeats the request. As she says the words 'pat-a-cake' Jamie claps his hands.

Peek-a-boo

Several of our parents found a way to adapt 'peek-a-boo' for their blind infants.

Paul, 0:7:23
Paul is on the floor and father covers his face with a light comforter. Father says, "Paul, where are you?" Through the quilt one could see Paul's arms come up and begin to pull the light cloth from his face. The game was repeated several times. Each time, waiting for the spoken words, "Paul where are you?", Paul uncovered his head.

Within a few months this game becomes a great favorite of Paul's and he begins to initiate the game with his parents.

Come to mama; and get a kiss
Toni, 0:11:15

The Acquisition of Language

Toni is in her walker, propelling herself around the room. Mother demonstrates a game for us. Mother says, "Toni, come to mama and get a kiss." Toni, with a big smile, orients her walker and scoots across the room to mama. She is rewarded with a kiss. This is repeated several times in this visit and subsequent visits.

Pat Mommy's face
Kathie, 0:6:17
A favorite game. Supine, facing mother. Mother says, "Pat mommy's face." Kathie reaches up and touches mother's face. Other examples in this session and later sessions. (Pat-a-cake added to repertoire within two months.)

Where is your tongue?
Jackie, 0:8:26
A favorite game. When mama says, "Where is your tongue?" Jackie sticks out his tongue. (Pat-a-cake on request added to repertoire within a month.)

"Imitates words" (#106) (9–18, median 12.5)
In a playful way, say to the child several words such as *mama*, *dada*, and *baby*. Also, while presenting other test items, note the child's attempts to imitate the examiner's or the mother's words. Record what the child says, and indicate the accuracy of his imitation.

Credit a recognizable imitation of any word, even if it consists of vowels only.

Blind Group: This item was passed by 100% of our blind children within the Bayley ranges with 70% above the median. This good achievement among our blind children may have been facilitated by the unique dilemma of the blind infant and his parents. Vocal exchanges and reciprocal imitation are among the few avenues of parent-baby discourse that are not disrupted by the visual deficit, and one that parents and baby tended to exploit as a social medium.

Our inventory of word *imitations* does not discriminate the blind baby from the sighted baby. "Ma-Ma" "Da-Da" "bye-bye" "good" "caca" (cookie).

"Says two words" (#113) (10–23, median 14.2)
Note any words the child applies appropriately to a specific object or situation. Observe whether the words are spoken spontaneously or

imitatively. Ask the mother what words the child uses, and attempt to elicit them from him, in meaningful use or in verbal imitation.

Credit if the child says two different words during the period of observation. Credit 'mama' and 'daddy,' if used meaningfully. Approximations are acceptable as long as their intent is clear.

Blind Group: Scoring: Our criteria may be more demanding than Bayley's. In all instances we credited the child with two words "in meaningful use." (The Bayley instructions which also include credit for verbal imitation appear ambiguous to us, since verbal imitation is on a lower level of cognition and actually is credited in Bayley #106 ("imitates words") at 12.5, 2 months earlier.)

All items employed in data analysis were retrieved from the descriptive protocols. Our design from the start of the study had separated observer reports from mother's report and, since our own interest in "first words" centered in "word as referent," recording procedures called for explicit descriptions of context so that usage could be judged by independent scorers. Several levels of data sorting described earlier preceded the actual scoring sessions, and items which passed the final screening represented the staff consensus and were credited.

For correspondence with Bayley procedures, we chose the *first instances* recorded in a single observational session in which *two words* were employed by the child in a context which established its meaning both to the observer and independent judges. (We have instances in our records of *one* word, e.g., mama, bopple, under one year of age.)

In Figure 5 we see that 90% of our blind sample was credited for two words within the Bayley ranges, with 20% above the median.

The credited selections follow:

Paul, 1:0:21
At one point, when he pulled himself up on his mother's knee, he clearly said *"mama"*. . . . As his father was leaving and speaking to Paul and mother, I (observer) heard Paul say *"dada."*

The Acquisition of Language

Karen, 1:1:23
Karen reaches and touches the camera equipment and says *"whatsit?"* ("What is it?")
Karen is sitting on the couch. J. (student assistant) comes over and plays the musical toy and talks to Karen. *"Whosit?"* ("Who is it?") she says to J.

Jamie, 1:2:4
Jamie, sitting on the edge of his rocking chair, kicking the runner.
Having tired of kicking the runner of the rocker, Jamie said *"down,"* and scooted down so that he was able to touch the floor. He then stood erect, holding onto the rocker to steady himself. His mother stooped down immediately, about one foot from him, and said, *"one-two."* In response to her cue, he took two steps forward and she caught him as he pitched forward. He smiled with delight. He then said, *"ock!"* (his name for rocker) and mother put him back into the rocker.
Note: *"ock"* for rock and rocker appear correctly used in several contexts in this session and earlier observations.

Kathie, 1:2:25
Mother puts Kathie's bib on her. She sits patiently, asking for *"cookie."* Mother gives her a seashell (which she knows and likes). Mother says, "What is this?" Kathie says, *"sell," "sell."*

Toni, 1:6:16
(Toni lives in a double house, and her Aunt Nan lives next door with a separate entrance.)
Several times we saw Toni creep to the door of Aunt Nan's house and call *"Nan! Nan!"*
We heard her call *"Jane! Jane!"* to her sister.

Robbie, 1:7:3
Uses *"mama"* and *"dada"* in this session with clear reference to mother and father.

Ronnie, 1:7:3
Ronnie, supine on floor, drinking his bottle. He puts the bottle down against his chest and begins to say, *"ba-ba-boo,"* which is his name for bottle.
In his rocking chair, twisting his torso, elevating his legs. Observer asks him if he is going to stand up. At first he says *"no"* and continues his rocking. But finally says, *"yeah!"* He then moves forward, places his feet firmly on the floor and begins to elevate himself.

Sitting in rocker, says "*ca-ca*" (cookie).
Says "*how do!*" in greeting.

Carol, 1:8:27
Observer held a watch up to Carol's ear. Carol, smiling, said, "*tick-a-tick-a*" (her word for watch).

Carol has played peek-a-boo with the observer, using the observer's silk scarf. A favorite game. Today, without prompting from the observer, and in the midst of a social exchange between observer and baby, Carol says "*peek-a-boo*" (to invite a game, as O heard it). The observer plays the game with her. At one point, as the observer picked up Carol, Carol said "*up.*"

Joan, 1:9:19
Feeding sequence. . . . She was particularly vocal during this period. Said "*hi*" to the observer and said "*all gone*" after Irene fed her a second bite.

Jackie, 2:8:0
(Jackie, who has not produced more than one meaningful word in any session prior to this one [and could not be credited for two words] surprises the observers by producing several on this occasion.)
Mother hands him his plastic cup; he says "*milk*". . . . Plays with the telephone, says "*hello*" into it. . . . Says "*Hi!*" to his brother when he came in from kindergarten.

(Other words and phrases listed by the observer may be echo forms and are therefore not credited.)

"Uses words to make wants known" (#127) (14–27, median 18.8)
Notice whether the child uses words to make his wants known. At first, this is usually a single word such as "*up,*" "*down,*" "*bottle,*" etc. spoken in a commanding tone or accompanied by gestures.

Credit if the child uses one or more words in an effort to make his wants known.

Blind Group: This item was passed by 100% of our blind group within the Bayley ranges, with 40% above the median. Credit was given for the first recorded item in the child's protocols.

Karen, 1:2:7
To invite a tickling game, says to mother: "*Tickle, tickle, tickle,*" and mother ran her fingers up and down Karen's tummy.

The Acquisition of Language

At one point mother said, "Karen do you want to go bye-bye?" Karen thought for a moment and then answered with a question, *"car?"*

Kathie, 1:3:22
(Kathie loves to sing. *"Sing"* is one of her favorite words.)
Kathie to mother: *"Sing! Sing!"* Mother: "No, Kathie, I'm too tired to sing right now. You sing." Kathie did indeed start singing on her own with "dadadada" sound.

Ronnie, 1:5:2
Ronnie was pulling on the bars of the playpen, trying to stand up. Says *"Up! Up!"* and when mother didn't pick him up he began to fret and cry, still pulling on the bars.

Jamie, 1:5:27
As observer speaks to mother about Jamie taking a bath Jamie responds *"No ba!"* (No bath!)

Toni, 1:8:9
When mother removed the pacifier from her mouth, Toni cried *"Mama?"* in a questioning voice. . . . On several occasions when an object was taken away from her or could not be recovered, she uttered a plaintive *"Mama."*

Carol, 1:8:27
Says *"peek-a-boo"* to invite O to play game.
(Cited also in # 113)

Paul, 2:1:13
Trying to turn on the TV Paul says *"Pull! Pull!"* as he has his hands on the button.

Jackie, 2:1:13
Says *"Cookie?"* while mother is washing his face (anticipates dessert).

Joan, 2:2:15
In pediatrician's office, observers present. Walks to her mother. Begins to pull mother to door and pleads *"mama"* while crying.
As Dr. R. places stethoscope on her chest, she cries *"no! no!"* and struggles and reaches toward her mother.

Robbie, 2:2:29
Robbie was lying on the couch with his bottle, when his mother took it away. He protested, saying *"bottle! bottle!"* but made no attempt to actively retrieve it.

"Sentence of two words" (#136) (16–30, median 20.6)
Observe whether the child can put two words signifying two concepts together, such as *"shut door," "daddy gone,"* etc. Two words denoting only one concept, such as *"bye-bye"* or *"all gone,"* are not credited. *"Good girl"* when spoken often refers to a specific art, in which case it is not credited as combining two words, but should it be used to mean approved behavior in several situations, as distinguished from unapproved behavior, it should be given credit.

Credit if the child can put two words denoting two concepts into one sentence or phrase.

Blind Group: This item was passed by 70% of our blind group within the Bayley ranges with 20% above the median. (One child, Toni, had no two-word combinations when last seen at twenty-seven months.)

Jamie, 1:5:27
. . . Now Jamie says to his grandmother, *"Nana, what?"* This is followed by, *"Daddy go."*
As O speaks to Mrs. B. about Jamie taking a bath, Jamie says, *"No ba"* (no bath).

Kathie, 1:7:21
As she comes upon mother at the side of the rug, Kathie asks her *"sing baby-bye,"* which is one of their songs.

Robbie, 2:0:1
(During object concept testing sequence.) Robbie was sitting on the floor with two tin cups directly in front of him, placed one behind the other. He made manual contact with the cups and knew their placement. I took the bell from him, ringing it so that he could follow its trajectory, bypassed cup # 1 and placed the bell in cup # 2. Then I said "Where is the bell, Robbie?" Robbie went directly to cup #2, by-passing cup #1, picked the bell out of cup #2, and said, *"In dah!"*

Carol, 2:1:30
Mother stood Carol on the floor near her. Carol said, *"Sit down"* and sat on the floor near her mother.
Later: Carol had a bowel movement in her diaper. (Mother has begun toilet training and Carol is really not ready for it.) Carol began to cry

as mother began to change her. Mother, seeing Carol's distress, waited a few moments. Later, when mother returns to change the diaper, Carol says plaintively, *"Good girl?"* and mother says, "Yes, you are a good girl."

(Clearly, in the second credited example Carol was seeking approval, following the disapproved act of soiling her diaper.)

Paul, 2:2:7
Observer with a flashlight, flashed the light on and off and put Paul's fingers on the button as she did so, saying "push." Paul wasn't able to do it himself and said, *"You do it."*
Paul walked to the kitchen and said, *"Go away, go away."*

Ronnie, 2:2:13
Ronnie just waking up. Mother asks if he wants to get up. Ronnie: *"No, do' wanna."*
Later says, *"Wan pop,"* meaning he wanted pop to drink.

Karen, 2:2:13
After a drink of milk at her feeding table: Karen put down the glass. Mother asked her if she were full. Karen: *"I'm just full!"* . . . Her mother asked her to have some milk and toast, whereupon Karen pushed the milk and toast away with her left hand. After these movements she said, *"Me's done."*

Joan, 2:9:15
She is afraid of the Beatle doll. Sister goes to get the doll to demonstrate to O. Joan says, *"I won't, beatle bite, bite beyull."* And later, to mother, *"Kill beyull."*

Jackie, 3:1:10
To mother: *"Want cookie. Jackie want cookie!"*

Toni
(No report. Last seen at age twenty-seven months. No two-word combinations in repertoire.)

DISCOURSE AT TWENTY MONTHS

Below is an illustration from our protocols of the highest ranking blind child in our study group.

Jamie, who ranks highest in our group of 10 in language achievements, has been totally blind from birth. He is the child of working-class parents, he has been largely advantaged through parental devotion, much tactile intimacy, and vocal exchanges and games from the earliest months of life.

Jamie, 1:8:12

. . . A little while later he said, "*Mama*" and mama said, "What?" He said, "*I wanna babbo-bah-pop*" (his phrase for bottle of pop). . . . As he was going around the kitchen, he periodically made remarks in the context of a conversational exchange with his mother:

"*Igo chair*" (I go to the chair), "*Igo Ibox*" (icebox). Mother said, "Go to the washing machine." He goes over to the machine and says, "*Washing machine*," approximately. . . . He does the same with stove. Then he went over and touched the playpen and said, "*Pay-pen*," leaving the *l* out.

Somewhere during the course of the morning he also mentioned his wagon, his bike, the tube. He said at one time, "*I got bells*," when he had the toy bell that he owns himself. At one time when "wagon" was mentioned, Jamie said, "*Let's go wagon.*"

This sample of Jamie's discourse at twenty months compares favorably with an above-average sighted child. (At twenty months, we recall, the reasonable expectation for a sighted child is that he demonstrate at least one example of a two-word sentence in a single observational session.)

Jamie's vocabulary includes nominals and action words; his syntax does not distinguish him from a sighted child. He has a syncretic form of "I" ("*Iwanna*," "*Igo*") which he employs for self-reference and, in this respect, he shows some precocity since, typically, this syncretic form of "I" does not emerge in the sighted child's discourse until the end of the second year.

Discussion

The picture that emerges for our blind infants as they move upward on the Bayley scale can be summarized thus:

The early language items, the production of differentiated vocalizations and imitation of sounds and words, show a balanced distribution of achievements within the Bayley ranges. These items speak for neurophysiological maturation and performance which is demonstrably not impeded by blindness in this otherwise intact group of blind infants.

As we move up the scale to higher-level tests of language comprehension and usage, the blind babies match sighted babies in the comprehension item "Responds to verbal requests" with all children in the sample within the Bayley ranges and 50% above the Bayley median. They match sighted babies on the item "imitates words" with 70% of our blind infants *above* the Bayley median. These achievements show good and appropriate language capacities in these blind infants and, as suggested earlier, may in fact be facilitated by the unique dilemma of the blind infant, for whom vocal exchanges and games are among the few channels available for reciprocity with his human partners. (We saw vocal exchanges richly exploited by our parents who were as hungry in their own way as their babies for discourse in a common language.)

Then, as we move toward meaningful use of words and two-word combinations, the distribution of credited achievements begins to shift. The item "Says two words" is passed by 90% of our blind group, with 20% above the median. On a slightly more advanced level, "Uses words to make wants known," our blind babies hold their own again, with 100% within the Bayley ranges and 40% above the median. The last item "Sentence of two words" is passed by 70% of the sample within Bayley ranges, and only 20% of the group is above the Bayley median.

Before drawing inferences from these patterns we should note that the shift in distribution of the sample on items which test cognitive capabilities is *not* a morbid downward trend. In those instances in which we were able to follow the later development of children in our sample, language abilities in the three-to-five-year range compared favorably with those of sighted children, and in only 2 cases did we see serious lags in later language achievements.

The eccentric patterns observed in the second-year distribution of the blind children on sighted tests can be fairly examined as an impediment of blindness but one which need not have permanent effects.

What is being tested in these three items is representational intelligence. The sighted child in naming objects has a bank of pictures in his head which can be elicited when one of the pictures "out there" matches or approximates an item in his picture bank. Recognition memory is largely a picture memory for the sighted child; and the picture, as the synthesizer of all sensory data, becomes an economical form in which the memory and the name tag can be retrieved for use. The picture lends itself easily to generalization and classification at higher and higher levels of organization. And, last, the pictures "out there"—an inexhaustible gallery of pictures is available to the sighted child from the moment he opens his eyes. The sighted child spends his days in a state of perpetual intoxication with his picture world, and the pictures lure him on into exercises in recognition, classification, naming, and ultimately to the retrieval of pictures in memory without a presenting stimulus, which Piaget calls "evocative memory."

For the blind child there is no true equivalence in experience. In a world without pictures, his experience with persons and things is both quantitatively and qualitatively meager. The sound-touch experiences provided by persons and things do, miraculously, lead to recognition behaviors for those persons and things which are highly cathected, but the sound-touch experiences depend upon proximal contact, while the sighted child's picture gallery gives him distance contact and multiplies, to the point of saturation (and even sensory fatigue), the number of things and events which are available to him for elementary exercises in sorting, classification, and storage. In quantity of stimuli, we can see that the sighted child's exteroceptive experience is crowded, maximally loaded for learning, while the blind child's world has large empty spaces, and learning and language must exploit near space, chance encounters, and need-related experiences.

But shouldn't mobility enlarge this space, increase the blind child's encounters and the exploitation of the surround? Here we meet another irony and another hurdle for the blind child. As we reported in Chapter IX mobility is delayed for the child who is totally blind from birth. In our highly advantaged group of blind babies (advantaged because our research had given us the educational means to lure the blind baby into mobility) the median age for creeping was 13.25 months; the median age for independent walking across the room was 19.25 months.

Therefore, at fourteen months, when able to produce "two words" for the examiner, the sighted child not only draws upon his saturated visual experience of persons, things, and events, but he has been creeping for nearly 7 months and walking independently for 2 months. He has long ago ceased to be the watcher of spectacles; he has been a traveler for those 7 months, an actor upon things, and he has learned through his own mobility and experimentation the properties of those objects and the identity and class of a large number of them. He has also learned that the objects have names, and how to respond appropriately when fluent speakers of English employ those names, and, finally, that he himself can produce two such names (thus passing the test).

When we now turn to the blind child at fourteen months we find that 2 of our blind children have produced "two words" at ages above the Bayley median and that 8 children pass the test at or below the Bayley median. But 9 of the 10 are within the Bayley ranges for this achievement! When we consider the poverty of experience for the blind child as compared to the sighted child this achievement is impressive. It means that the blind child, through exploiting near space, with no mobility or limited mobility, has a language capability that falls within sighted-child ranges, and that the impediment is reflected only in the clustering of the blind group in the lower ranges of the Bayley. The delay is reflected in the difference in *median* age for the sighted and the blind, which is 6.3 months.

In the next item, "Uses words to make wants known," the blind babies nearly match sighted babies, with 100% within the Bayley ranges and 40% above the Bayley median which is 18.8. The median age for our blind group is 20.75, or a 1.9 month difference between the Bayley median and the median for our group.

For this achievement, blindness appears not to be an impediment, and we are confronted with an interesting puzzle. *To name a need or a want is not more difficult for a blind child than a sighted child.*

This brings me to reflections along these lines: Needs and wants are first experienced in response to endogenous stimuli. These stimuli which register as appetites or motor impulses are, of course, the same for the blind child as for the sighted child. The pathways that lead to registration of a need or want and differentiation and naming of a specific need or want, appear to be undistorted for the blind child. At the threshold of naming a want we can postulate a form of mental representation for the desired thing or action or event. For the sighted child the excitation of need or want may evoke a picture as in the analogy of dreaming where "need gives rise to the image of its satisfaction," and giving a name to the picture of need can follow if the name is available in the child's vocabulary. For the blind child, who has no pictures, we must postulate a form of mental representation in which the characteristics of the desired object or event are derived from non-visual data, and this form of representation is clearly capable of leading the blind child to the threshold of naming and to naming "the want."

Since, on this item, our blind children compared favorably with sighted children in "naming wants," we must conclude that the picture is not indispensable for the representation of needs and wants and for their expression in language. More than this: Where internal need states are the stimuli for expression in language, the blind child's need states are physiologically identical with those of a sighted child. Given the same biological capability for expression in language we should not be surprised, after all, that our blind babies score as well as sighted babies in the task. "Uses words to make wants known" is on a higher level of difficulty on the Bayley scale than the previous item, "two words." The Bayley median age for "two words" is 14.2; for "uses words to make wants known" it is 18.8. Our blind babies passed the higher-level test fairly matching sighted babies in median age of attainment. On the lower-level test there was a 6-month lag expressed in the difference between the sighted and blind medians. The clue must lie in the nature of the task.

The item "two words" (I nearly slipped, significantly, and wrote "two worlds") may be more closely related to exteroceptive experience, "naming objects." Where the stimuli for "making wants known" are endogenous and give the blind child physiological parity with the sighted child, the stimuli for the first words as referents are, in large measure, exogenous, i.e., persons and things. And while the blind child's actual world is furnished with a large number of persons and things, his experience of them is significantly reduced by the condition of blindness and his delayed mobility. The identity of objects which is built into the sighted child's experience through visual pictures and picture sorting, is laboriously achieved by a blind child who must go through manual-tactile-acoustical exercises in synthesis to establish the identity of mother, father, and his favorite sound-making toy before he can confer names upon persons and things.

First words for the sighted infant are, predominantly, nominals, as Kathryn Nelson (1973) found in her analysis of the first 10-word vocabularies and 50-word vocabularies of infants. In her middle-class sample, over 65% of the first 50 words were nominals, specific and general, for persons, animals, objects. Because of differences in sample and methods of recording (Nelson employed parent inventories), we cannot fairly compare the early vocabularies of our blind infants with Nelson's sample. However, a cursory review of the credited words for our blind children on the Bayley "two words" item shows that nominals predominate. It may be the difficulty in naming, in a world without pictures, that we see in the blind child's lower median age for the achievement of this item.

In the item "Sentence of two words" we again find a distribution of scores among our blind group which suggests the impediment of blindness. Our blind median of twenty-six months is nearly 6 months lower than the Bayley median of 20.6. Two children are far below the Bayley ranges at thirty-three and a half months and thirty-seven and a half months respectively. The task is to "put two words signifying two concepts together." The 6-month difference between the 2 medians is the same for this item as the earlier item "two words," which suggests that the same conceptual problems which impeded the blind child in the acquisition of first words are present in the combining of two concepts, and the 6-month lag in both items may be consistent.

Is it experiential poverty which accounts for the blind child's delay in uniting two concepts? Are the linkages of nominals and action words, for example, normally facilitated by vision, in which the person or thing observed and his or its actions are united in a picture or a picture sequence (e.g. "Mama-bye-bye," "car go")? Or, in the case of a nominal and modifier ("big truck"), is blindness an impediment in these constructions because of the unique problem for the blind child in the attribution of actions and qualities to objects which cannot be derived or inferred from his own experience in the second year?

Since, demonstrably, the blind child does "get there," does combine, does move toward syntactical structures of higher and higher complexity, and does speak a respectable English at four to five years of age, the impediment can be largely overcome. What we see, then, in the second year, in the comparison of our blind median age of achievement and that of the sighted, may be an impediment in concept formation which affects naming in the "two words" item and combining two words in the "sentence" item. Without vision, the child must take a long and circuitous route to the construction of a world of objects (and naming them) and to the attribution of actions and qualities to things and persons (two-word sentence).

And as we bring these speculations to a close we are left with the remarkable facts that 2 of our children, totally blind, produced their first two-word sentence at ages above the Bayley median, that 7 of the children in all were within Bayley ranges, and that 2 were below the Bayley ranges for an N of 9 available to us for study in the second and third years.

Chapter XI

SELMA FRAIBERG AND EDNA ADELSON

Self-Representation in Language and Play*

THE ORDERLY progression in the achievement of early language milestones did not prepare us for a detour in the course of language development which appeared in the third and fourth years. The discovery came by chance. Our research commitment to NICHD covered the developmental characteristics of blind infants in the age range 0–2½. But 4 of our older blind children remained in our education program through age five, and, following our usual practice, we maintained our observational and recording procedures during all visits.

It was in this way that we discovered that self-representation in both language and play were impeded for even the 2 highest ranking subjects of our original group. A syncretic "I" ("Iwanna") which had emerged well within sighted-child ranges was slow to evolve into stable and flexible "I," "you" usage, and reversals were recorded well into the fourth and fifth years. A parallel development was seen in the blind child's incapacity to represent

* Earlier versions of this chapter appeared in *The Psychoanalytic Quarterly*, Vol. XLII, No. 4 (1973) and Lenneberg, Eric and Lenneberg, Elizabeth, eds. *The Foundations of Language Development: Multidisciplinary Approach*, vol. 2, New York: Academic Press, © 1975 by UNESCO.

himself in play during the same period. We understood this to indicate the extraordinary problem posed by blindness in constituting a self and an object world and in representing the self as an "I" in a universe of "I's." This protracted delay in the acquisition of a stable "I" usage was seen among our children in a context of advancing language abilities with steadily expanding vocabularies and syntactical structures!

In this chapter we propose to examine the relationship between the blind child's acquisition of "I" as a correct grammatical form and the correlates of "I" in representation of the self in play.

I/Me Usage in Four Blind Children

Jackie, who consistently ranked in the lower half of our group, had not achieved "I" when last seen at five years. At two and a half years his language achievements placed him in the lowest rank in our group of 10. The failure to achieve "I" was also a measure of his impaired ego development. Jackie presented a picture of a disordered personality with frequent regression to echolalic speech. We include this brief description of Jackie who had no "I" at age five, because he fairly represents the large number of blind children who do not achieve "I" or "me" even at school age or later. In Jackie's case, and others known to us, there was no evidence of neurological impairment, and one can fairly consider an alternative explanation for this form of deviant ego development: that blindness imposes extraordinary impediments to the development of a self-image and the construction of a coherent sense of self.

The remaining three children in the older group all achieved "I." Kathie, Paul, and Karen ranked in the upper half of our group on nearly all measures. Their language achievements at two years to two and a half years (judged by vocabulary, two-word combinations and the use of words to make needs known) fell within the sighted age range. A syncretic "I" ("Iwanna") appeared in their language records in the age range two to two and a half years, which again does not distinguish them from sighted children.

From this developmental picture in the language area we would have predicted an unremarkable course, leading within a few months to a stable concept of "I" and versatility in its use. We were not prepared for our findings. The ages for the achievement of the non-syncretic "I" for these 3 children were as follows: Karen, two years, eleven months; Paul, three years, five months; Kathie, four years, ten months.*

The differentiation of a *syncretic* "I" from a *non-syncretic* "I" follows Zazzo's (1949) usage. The syncretic "I" typically appears in the two-year-old's vocabulary imbedded in verb forms of need or want. In the course of weeks or months, "I" is gradually disengaged from this early set and is used inventively in new combinations. The two levels of "I" represent two levels of self-representation. The achievement of the non-syncretic "I" requires a high level of inference on the part of the child in which he demonstrates his capacity to represent himself as an "I" in a universe of "I's." ("I am an 'I' to me; you are an 'I' to you; he is an 'I' to him"; etc.)

We credited the children with the achievement of a non-syncretic "I" when these criteria were met: (1) "I" used inventively in new combinations (disengaged from set phrases); (2) "I" employed with versatility in discourse (management of "I" and "you" with rare or no confusion or reversals). It is of some interest that although these criteria were met by the three children at the ages given above, both Paul and Kathie had occasional lapses in "I-you" usage for many months afterward.

While the achievement of stable "I" usage impresses us as

---

* Since the preparation of this essay we can now add one more report. Carol, the youngest child in our series, was followed by Louis Fraiberg for linguistic study. When last seen, at age four, Carol had not yet achieved "I" as a stable non-syncretic form.

markedly delayed in these blind children, comparisons with sighted children cannot be fairly made through the use of any existing measures. There are no normative data for the achievement of the non-syncretic "I" in sighted children. Gesell and Amatruda (1947), who offer the only developmental scale which includes personal pronoun usage, do not discriminate between the syncretic and the non-syncretic "I." They score pronoun usage on two levels: at twenty-four months they credit the child with the pronouns "I, me, and you, not necessarily correctly"; at thirty months the child receives credit when he "refers to self by pronoun rather than name. May confuse 'I' and 'me'." Gesell and Amatruda accepted parent reports for their langage items, and their scoring, as cited, does not discriminate for our purposes the cognitive values of "I." *

In the absence of comparative measures in standard developmental tests for sighted children, we cannot pursue some of the problems of apparent difference between the range for achievement of a stable "I" in 3 otherwise healthy and adequate blind children and that of sighted children. Yet the differences, on any level of comparison we can borrow, impose themselves upon us. If 3 blind children demonstrate language competence at the age of two to two and a half years, which can be objectively rated as normal for sighted children, if the syncretic "I" appears as a grammatical form in the range for sighted children, how can we explain a developmental course which detours in the middle of the third year and comes back onto the sighted child's route in the fourth or fifth years? Were the apparently "very late" achievers of "I" (Kathie and Paul) cognitively impaired? Was Karen, the earliest achiever of "I," the smartest in the group? Here again, all expectations and reasonable predictions come undone as strangely as the blind child's pronoun usage. At age two and a half years

* The primary source of data for our research group was naturalistic observation in the home, recorded as objective narrative description and documented on film or video tape. Parent report was a secondary source and will be indicated when used.

Kathie and Paul were among 3 of the highest ranking children in the group of 10 in language achievements and in overall developmental achievements. Kathie's good intelligence will speak for itself in the history we present later. Paul, at five years, had a command of language and a capacity for abstract thinking which impresses us as superior even by sighted-child standards. Karen, the first achiever of "I," was a very adequate blind child, whose good language and cognitive capacities at five years did not equal those of Kathie and Paul. We are not able to explain this puzzle.

While we watched the protracted struggle with pronoun usage, another piece of the puzzle was emerging from the patterns of play which we had observed and recorded.

At the age when sighted children begin to *imitate* domestic life in doll play (approximately two years), we find no such examples for the blind children in our group. If we tried to elicit such play, "Let's give the dolly her bottle," "Let's put her to bed," we got no response, not even mechanical compliance. In some instances there were other infants in the house being mothered, or other children in the family playing with dolls. Models were available but were not used.

Again, at age two and a half years, when sighted children begin to *represent* themselves and their world in play, endowing the doll with a personality and an imaginary life, our blind children could not represent themselves or other personalities in play and could not invent in play.

Between the ages of three years and four and a half years we began to see imaginative play emerge in the records of Karen, Paul, and Kathie. In each case the emergence of representational play had correspondence with the emergence of self-reference pronouns "me" and "I." The data invited close scrutiny. They suggested that the acquisition of personal pronouns was closely united with the capacity for symbolic representation of the self and that vision normally plays a central facilitating role in each of these achievements.

After we worked our way through this thicket, we discovered

that René Zazzo (1949) had arrived there by another route in his study of a sighted child. His observations on Jean-Fabien, which will be summarized in the last section of this chapter, were most welcome and provide another framework in which to place our detailed observations of Kathie as she pursued an elusive "I" between the ages of two and five years.

Kathie

In order to examine in some detail the blind child's extraordinary problems of self-representation in language and play, we have chosen one of these children, Kathie, for illustration.

Kathie * has been followed by us since six months of age and is now six years old. She is totally blind. She was 3 months premature. The diagnosis, retrolental fibroplasia, was made at five months of age. She is a healthy, very bright child with no other sensory defects and is neurologically intact.

Kathie is the youngest of 5 siblings. Her parents have shown extraordinary ability to intuit a blind child's experience, and every help that they and our staff specialists could give has been available to promote the fullest use of her good capacities.

Now, at six years of age, she has excellent command of language; she is inventive in imaginative play; she is well behaved but also mischievous and fun-loving. She is in the first grade in a classroom for sighted children and holds her own. She has considerable appetite for new experience. She enjoys cooperative play. She is independent in dressing and feeding. She is fully responsible for her own safety in outdoor play.

The story of Kathie's language and representational intelligence followed a different route from that of the sighted

* For the story of Kathie see Sharon Ulrich, *Elizabeth*, Introduction by S. Fraiberg, Commentary by E. Adelson (Ann Arbor: University of Michigan Press, 1972).

child. In the absence of pictorial memory, there were delays in the evolving forms of mental representation, the concepts of time and causality, and in self-representation and the construction of a world of permanent objects. A simple vocabulary count and identification of word and thing or an analysis of phrase and sentence patterns would not have distinguished her speech at the age of two years from that of sighted children. It was between the ages of two and four that the study of Kathie's speech and play gave us a slow motion picture of the relationship of language to other cognitive processes and thus provided the means for identifying those elements in self-object representation which are dependent upon a coherent and intact sensorimotor organization.

OBSERVATIONS AT TWO YEARS OF AGE

When Kathie was two years, one month old, she became the subject of a linguistic study conducted by Eric Lenneberg with our staff. Speech samples were obtained in home visits and Dr. Lenneberg and Nancy Stein of our staff worked out a dictionary: "What does Kathie *mean* when she *says* . . . ?" Following a 3-month study, Dr. Lenneberg felt that Kathie's language competence compared favorably with that of a sighted child of the same age. Her vocabulary at that time was well within the range for sighted children. She correctly identified members of her family and a number of people outside of the family. She identified by touch or sound and named all the objects in her home with which she had contact. She quickly learned the names of novel objects brought by us. She had 4- or 5-word phrases in which present tense verb forms were imbedded, but not yet used inventively in new combinations.

She could express her wishes in phrases. Here are a few samples: "Wanna hear a record," "Wanna go walkie," "Wanna go lie down," "Wanna hear music," "Want to feel, . . . What's that?" (when confronted with a novel object).

She had a range of useful words for the expression of affective experience: "Feels good!" "Tastes good." And the dictionary records that she used the words "damn" and "shit" when she was angry.

She employed parental admonitions to inhibit forbidden actions. "Don't put your finger in your eye," she said to herself, imitating her mother's voice when she pressed her eye, and sometimes she succeeded in inhibiting the act. "Hot!" she said, to warn herself when near the stove.

There were examples of generalization in our records. At Christmas time, when we brought her a toy-sized Christmas tree, she explored its plastic bristles thoughtfully and said, "Feels like a brush!" She could identify a chair and name it, and generalize from chair to chair.

We heard pronoun reversal and pronoun confusion in nearly all the speech samples we have during this period. When she touched the hair of one of the observers, she said, "My hair," using the wrong pronoun. "Want me carry you?" she said to her mother when she meant that she wanted her mother to carry her. The pronoun "I" was rarely used and, typically, appeared as a syncretic form "ahwanna" or as an "I-you" reversal. However, the pronoun reversals and the unstable use of "I" do not distinguish Kathie at two years from *sighted* children.

In Dr. Lenneberg's unpublished notes he records one item that puzzled him. "All attempts to make her listen to short stories (while sitting on laps and being quiet) have failed." In a summary statement he draws attention to the lack of interest in stories as being one factor that points to "a somewhat different language beginning from that found in sighted children." As it turns out (in retrospect), this puzzle was already one of the clues to certain incapacities in symbolic representation which were later to be of considerable interest in our study of blind children.

Dr. Lenneberg moved to Cornell University and had no opportunity to follow Kathie's language development beyond the age of two years, three months. When we now report further developments in Kathie's language history, we will find much that interests us from a developmental point of view but we will also miss much that Dr. Lenneberg would have brought us from linguistics.

OBSERVATIONS AT THREE YEARS OF AGE

We became aware that, between the ages of two and a half and three years, Kathie's language and her capacity to represent showed marked deviations from that of the sighted child. In both our detailed home observations and in the reports of the mother, it was very clear that Kathie could not represent herself through a doll or a toy. She could not recreate or invent a situation in play. She could not attend to a story or answer questions regarding a story or tell a story herself. She could not spontaneously report an experience. Between the ages of three and four, she still continued to confuse and reverse pronouns, and the concept of "I" had not emerged as a stable grammatical form.

To illustrate the problem, we now present some of our own observations of Kathie at the age of three. In a later section, we will bring in observations of her at four years of age.

When Kathie was three years, twenty-three days, we arranged for her to visit us in our nursery. The nursery visits had been a special treat for her in preceding months. Since we already knew from home observations that Kathie could not invent in play or represent herself in play, we sketched an observational plan and procedures which would tell us more precisely where her incapacities lay and what her limits might be.

We worked out a group of experimental play situations which would permit us to compare a blind child's capacity to represent herself in play with that of a sighted child. We were satisfied that the "pretend" games we had in mind could be played with any sighted child between the ages of eighteen months and two years, giving much leeway for three-year-old Kathie.

In order not to strain Kathie's tolerance, we moved freely between structured play periods and unstructured "free play intervals." In the one-hour observational period which was recorded verbatim and documented on 16mm film, the structured portions

Self-Representation in Language and Play

of the observation totaled 20 minutes. This gave us a balance between the two modes of observation which favored the spontaneous productions and would permit us to fairly assess Kathie's play capacities and language. Kathie's mother was present throughout.

When we now present material from this play session at three years of age, it is important to keep in mind that we already knew Kathie's play incapacities from naturalistic observations in her home, and that the purpose of the structured play observations was to get more precise information regarding the level of symbolic representation available to this bright, three-year-old blind child. When S.F. pursued certain elements in play, though it was clear that Kathie could not follow her, it was because we needed the negative demonstration as much as the positive demonstration both for this period of observation and for our projected retest at four years.

S.F. was not a familiar person to Kathie and therefore gave her a good deal of time to greet old friends at the Project, to get accustomed to a new voice and to begin some verbal exchanges. When Kathie seemed at ease and came close to her at the work table, S.F. hinted that there was something on it. Kathie came over, sniffed, and said, pleasantly surprised, "Play dough." S.F. waited to see what Kathie would do. She squeezed it, handled it, put it down. When it was evident that she would not invent with the play dough, S.F. suggested that they make a cookie and guided her hands with the cookie cutter. Kathie was interested but did not extend the possibilities. Later, to test her notions of "pretend," S.F. asked, "Can I have a bite of the cookie, Kathie?" Kathie, clearly confused but amiable, said, "You have a bite!" and put it in *her own* mouth. Kathie said, reflectively, "This cookie different."

Because of the confusion of "me" and "you" elicited in this sequence, we used a later occasion to test facial analogies. S.F. asked, "Where is my mouth, Kathie?" There was no response, but Kathie's hand moved to *her own* mouth. S.F.: "Where is my nose?" She made no effort to respond. (Neither E.A. not Kathie's

257

mother had been able to get her to correctly name parts on their faces if they used the pronoun "my," as in the question, "Where is my nose?" However, if Kathie's mother asked, "Where is Mommy's nose?" she could respond correctly.)

Knowing how much Kathie loved her own bath at home, we had sketched out a sequence for doll play. There was a basin of water, a doll, and a towel. S.F. brought over one of our dolls and suggested giving the dolly a bath. (We knew, however, that Kathie had no interest in her dolls at home.) S.F. introduced the doll to Kathie, who gave it a few cursory touches and was clearly not interested. S.F. tried to elicit interest. "Where is the dolly's mouth?"—no answer. "Where is the dolly's nose?—no answer. We were unable to get a demonstration when we played this game with other blind children of Kathie's age. Clearly, Kathie could not endow the doll with human characteristics either.

Kathie made it clear she did not want to give that baby a bath but we were not prepared for the bath that took place within a few moments. As soon as Kathie touched the water, she herself stepped into the tiny tub, giving S.F. only a second to remove Kathie's new red shoes. She curled up in the tiny tub, legs folded up, and made joyful screeches. Then followed a series of little chants and songs, her own bathtub songs at home.

After several minutes of splashing and singing, S.F. decided to take a chance on reintroducing the doll. She suggested washing the dolly's hair (guiding Kathie's hands to the doll's hair). S.F. went through a performance in which, representing the doll, she squealed protests and said, "No, no, I don't want a shampoo." Kathie did not pick up the game, but now she did something else.

As she squatted in the tub, pushing herself up and down in the water, she began to carry on a dialogue in two voices: "Swimming in the water." "Mama look at that!" "Whee, whee!" "Can you feel it?" "Okay, you stay in the water." "Okay, you sit down in the water." Very clearly, one voice in this speech belonged to Kathie and one voice to her mother, bathing Kathie.

Before drawing inferences from this last anecdote, let us give a second set of observations which are very similar.

Self-Representation in Language and Play

Later in the session, Kathie was walking around the room when she discovered the sink in the nursery. We did not tell her what it was. She climbed in and examined the sides and faucets with her fingers. One of us said, "What is it?" and, after a moment, she said, firmly, "It's a sink!" Kathie then curled up inside it. She was unmistakably pretending that the sink was a bed and said, in a mother's intonation, "Night-night, have a good sleep, night-night." "Go sleep in the sink." She closed her eyes, then opened them mischievously, and went through the whole routine again, with some variation. "Right here." "You be a good girl!" Once S.F. tried to extend the game by saying, "Good morning, Kathie!" Kathie, not to be distracted, said, "See you in the morning, good night. Then go in pool." (Echo phrases—apparently her schedule for summer.)

Obviously, then, Kathie could "pretend" when she herself was the subject. Could she pretend now with a doll? It was doubtful, but S.F. brought over the doll for an experimental demonstration. She said, "The dolly wants to go to sleep. Let's put the dolly to bed." She then gave the doll to Kathie. Without any ceremony Kathie dropped the doll over the side of the sink and pursued her own game.

In these last two examples (and others which we have in this and other sessions), it is very clear that Kathie had a form of "pretend" in which she could take herself as object and play "subject and object" in a game. But she could not yet move beyond to the further objectivation (actually *projection*) which would permit the doll to represent Kathie, while Kathie herself represented her mother to that doll.

Note, too, how important it is for her to get *into* the basin, to put herself *into* the sink for "pretend." Where a sighted child would be able to *imagine* her doll as herself in the basin or the sink, Kathie is still obliged to "go through the motions," to transpose through action that which would be transposed through vision. We must remember, of course, that sighted children in nursery school also enjoy fitting themselves into the doll bed or the doll carriage, but by this age they can move flexibly between such egocentric play and representational play, sometimes placing the doll, sometimes themselves, in the bed or carriage.

Along with these failures in self-representation, we see throughout this session, even in this condensed form, that "I" and "you" are not yet used correctly, which ties in with observations in which subject and object pronouns are confused in comprehension, as in following the directions for the game "Where's my nose? Where's your nose?" The pronouns do not yet define subject and object, which may indicate the level of her conceptual development; she cannot yet see herself as an object to others. She is indisputably "Kathie" to herself and to others, and her mother is "Mommy," but she cannot assimilate the semantic ambiguity in which she is a "you" to others and they are a "you" to her. The same ambiguity bedevils her in comprehending "me" and "my" usage in the game, "Where's my nose?," etc. Yet she could correctly identify facial parts by pointing if the questioner used the form "Where is Mommy's nose? Where is Mrs. Adelson's nose? Where is Kathie's nose?"

From the protocols of this session and home visits during this period we do not yet have an example of "me" usage in self-reference. Typically, when Kathie wanted something she would say, "Give it to her!" in the echo form.

The first example of "me" in self-reference (not echo or reversal) occurs at three years, six months and the context happens exactly to catch a transition point. Kathie's mother called her in the midst of play. Kathie was clearly annoyed at the interruption. She roared at her mother, "You leave her alone!" Then, shortly afterwards, "Leave *me* alone!"

The question should be raised: "Would Kathie's performance in the nursery have been more fairly tested if the play sequences had been undertaken by one of her old friends on the staff, or her mother?" To test this possibility, we invited Kathie and her parents to another play session 4 months later and recorded the visit on video tape. This time E.A., a familiar person, took over some of the play sequences and we also involved the mother

Self-Representation in Language and Play

in a "Where's my nose? Where's your nose?" game. Even under these most favorable circumstances the limits of Kathie's performance remained the same.

Now we would like to suggest that the observations on subject-object in play and the problem of expressing subject and object in language have a unified core in the capacity for a certain level of mental representation. The capacity to represent oneself in play is a measure of the level of conceptual development in which the self can be taken as an object and other objects can be used for symbolic representation of the self (Piaget 1952). Kathie's play incapacities at three years are exactly mirrored in speech, in her pronoun reversals, and in her difficulties in achieving "I" as a stable concept and a stable grammatical form. Yet this child at the age of three years has a rich vocabulary, if we make allowances for the restricted experience of a blind child, and her syntax does not jar the ear until we examine the sentences in which pronoun usage governs order and coherence. She is not retarded or in danger of autistic development.

OBSERVATIONS AT FOUR AND FIVE YEARS OF AGE

Let us observe Kathie between the ages of four years and five years, as Evelyn B. Atreya and Edna Adelson continued to follow her progress.

Between the ages of four and five, Kathie began to represent herself in doll play and, in a parallel development, we also began to see new complexities in syntax, a stabilization of pronoun usage and, finally, the emergence of "I" both as a concept and a grammatical form.

At four years, six months, we got observations in doll play that paralleled in all significant ways the doll-play of sighted children at ages two to three. Kathie was a solicitous mother to Drowsy and Pierre, her two dolls. She fed Drowsy from a toy nursing bottle (filling it herself and capping it with the nipple). She murmured endearments. To Drowsy: "Want to give me a kiss?" "Bye

bye, Drowsy." "Did you bump your head?" (Rubs it to make it feel better). "She's crying. She wants her bottle." She also spanked her dolls in anger and scolded them for misdemeanors. She toilet trained both dolls by placing them on her old potty chair.

Around the same time, Kathie acquired an imaginary companion she called "Zeen." Kathie carried on conversations with Zeen in two voices. When addressed by a friendly adult, Zeen was willing to extend the conversation. At lunch, when the observers were having coffee, E.A. asked what Zeen would like. Kathie, in an animated voice, said, "Here he comes. He's driving up the driveway driving a car. He has got to go home to make a cup of tea."

It was Zeen who spilled the macaroni all over the kitchen floor, Kathie told her mother righteously when she herself was caught in the act.

After tracking Zeen for several months in our study, E.A. one day asked the direct question: "Where is Zeen's house?" Kathie said, "You gotta walk outside," and then, "Wanna go for a walk?" E.A. accepted the invitation and Kathie took her for a walk to Zeen's house. Kathie told her that she would show her Zeen's sandbox and Zeen's house which had a door that you could open and close. It was a long walk to Zeen's house. And it was a cold day. E.A. complained of the sniffles and her need for a Kleenex. Kathie said, "Here's a Kleenex" and produced an imaginary tissue which she used to wipe E.A.'s nose. They walked for a long time and had many interesting encounters on the way. Finally, it dawned on E.A. that since Zeen was an imaginary person with an imaginary house, they were probably never going to get there. And they never did.

Around the same period we received the first report of a dream. Kathie wakened one night very much upset and told her mother: "I stuck my foot in it and it turned on." In the morning Kathie reported her dream again but changed the detail to, "She bumped her foot." Mother could give us no clues regarding this dream.

Self-Representation in Language and Play

While this may not have been Kathie's first dream, it was the first dream reported to mother.

Verbatim speech records from visits at this time showed an increase in the number of sentences which include a grammatically correct use of "I" but there were still instances in which pronoun reversals appeared.

At four years, eight months, mother reported that Kathie began to ask, "Today is what day?" And then, in a very rapid progress, it was reported to us that she began to learn the days of the week and the time concepts of "tomorrow" and "yesterday." As we were sorting data for this period, we made a discovery. The first record of use of the past tense appeared at the same time. Kathie had taken a walk to the outer limits of her home property. She reported when she came back, "I found Robinsons' house!"

One month later, at four years, nine months, we have the first report in our records of Kathie's ability to reconstruct from memory an event of the previous day. Kathie was playing with her mother's cigarette lighter. The next day Kathie's mother could not find the lighter and asked where it was. Kathie thought for a moment and said, "It's on the floor by the rocking chair." (It was.)

As late as Kathie's fifth birthday there were still occasional lapses in her use of "I." On the day of her birthday there was a routine visit to the doctor's office. Mother reported that Kathie told the doctor that it was her birthday. He asked her how old she was. Kathie: "She's four. No, *I'm* five years old."

Here are a few samples of Kathie's conversations at the age of five, as reported by mother:

Kathie bumped into a little girl in the doctor's office.
Kathie: "Who is this?"
The little girl: "Karen."

Kathie: "Where does your daddy work?"
Little Girl: "At Marshall's."
Kathie: "Does he work on a farm?"
  (Kathie's father did.)

Kathie overheard a mother spanking her baby during a visit to Kathie's home. Kathie said: "*Don't* spank the baby." The mother, embarrassed, said she wasn't hurting the baby.
Kathie: "Oh, did you do it gently and softly?"

Kathie, at five years, one month of age, overheard the bus driver of her school bus say, "Darn!"
Kathie: "Are you swearing?"
"No," said the bus driver, embarrassed.
Kathie, persisting: "Do you swear?"

At five years, three months, we have the following observations which tie together concepts in language and in play.

E.B.A. was doing a video tape at Kathie's house to document play and language. At one point Kathie was feeding Drowsy, the doll, with the toy nursing bottle. She stopped for a moment and addressed the photographer: "Joy, what are you doing?" Joy said that she was taking pictures. Kathie said, "Oh, are you going to take my picture while I feed the baby?"

At another point, Kathie said that Drowsy was taking a nap. She whispered, "Don't wake him up!" Kathie began to make snoring noises as if pretending that Drowsy was asleep. "That's Drowsy," she explained.

Later, everyone reviewed the tape in the kitchen. As Kathie heard the voices on the tape, she asked, "Evelyn, who is talking?" E.B.A. told her that it was Kathie talking to her mother. Kathie seemed to listen intently to the voices on the tape and to respond to them. She began to identify her own words on tape and when she heard herself snoring for Drowsy on tape, she laughed out loud.

In these fragments from five years, three months of age, we see versatility in syntax, good pronoun usage, stable forms of "me" and "I," and an objective concept of self which permits her to identify her own voice on tape and to laugh at her own clowning on tape.

Self-Representation in Language and Play

Comparisons of a Blind Child with a Sighted Child

In summary, Kathie's capacity for self-representation in play and acquisition of the concept "I" finally did emerge in a coherent cognitive structure. Yet both were late acquisitions by sighted child expectations which probably can be placed in the range two and a half to three years of age.

The relationship between self-representation and personal pronoun usage has not been rigorously examined in the sighted child literature. Zazzo, whose longitudinal study of one child (1948) is unique in the literature of developmental aspects of pronoun usage, has produced promising hypotheses which he had hoped would lead to controlled experimental research. His work has not yet been extended. While our own work was designed without knowledge of Zazzo's study and his hypotheses, there is close correspondence between his findings and ours on self-representation and the pronoun "I."

In his study *Image du Corps et Conscience de Soi*, Zazzo follows the grammatical transformations of self-reference pronouns in relation to the child's behavior toward his mirror image. The child was his son, Jean-Fabien, and the mirror observations were recorded between the ages of three months and two years, nine months. (Photographs and home movies were also employed for picture identification, but our summary will confine itself to mirror image.)

At two years, three months, Jean-Fabien made his first (and untutored) identification of the baby in the mirror. After a moment's hesitation, he said, "Dadin," the name which he used for himself. (From Jean-Fabien's behavior during this period, it appears to us that the response "Dadin" is an identification of his image, but the "Dadin" in the mirror is uncertainly himself —perhaps in the nature of "another Dadin!")

From two years, four months to two years, five months Jean-Fabien uses a syncretic form of "*je*" ("*ch'sais pas*"). At two years, five months Zazzo reports he has the pronouns *"elle," "i" ("je"* [syncretic]), *"ca."* At two years, six months, he begins to use *"moi-tu."*

At two years, eight months, Jean-Fabien responds to his mirror image for the first time with the phrase, "C'est moi." At a later point in the essay, Zazzo adds that the phrase *"C'est moi"* was accompanied by a gesture in which Jean-Fabien pointed to his own chest. In all later variations in responding to his mirror image, the child used the phrase *"moi, Jean-Fabien."*

At two years, eight months, the pronoun *"je"* is disengaged from syncretic forms, and the author cites examples of discourse in which *"je"* is used inventively and in free combination. During the same period, Zazzo reports in his later text, the momentary confusion before the mirror which preceded each self-identification had disappeared.

Zazzo's findings corroborate our own in essential aspects. The grammatical transformations in self-reference pronouns follow a progression that is linked with stages in the evolution of the self-image; the non-syncretic "I" closes the sequence and signifies the child's capacity to represent himself as an object in a universe of objects. For the sighted child, and more so for the blind child, the achievement of the concept "I" is a cognitive feat. The consistent, correct, and versatile employment of the pronoun "I" tells us that the child has attained a level of conceptual development in which he not only endows himself with "I," but recognizes that every "you" for the child is an "I" for the other, and that he is a "you" to all other "I's." This is a leap out of his own skin, so to speak, and one that is normally facilitated and organized by vision. Even when there are no mirrors and no pictures to consult, self-image evolves through increasingly complex forms of mental representation in which the body self is given objective form, a "double" as Zazzo suggests, an image of the self.

For the blind child, the constitution of a self-image and its representation through "I" can appear in a protracted development. We have used self-representation in play as the only means available to us to examine parallel representation of the self in pronoun usage. If we can grant some equivalence between Kathie's self-representation in play and imagination and Jean-Fabien's response to his mirror representation, we can compare the characteristics of self-representation and pronoun usage in the two children.

Following is a short summary:

Kathie, at two years, two months and Jean-Fabien at two years, four months both employ a *syncretic* "I" and, more commonly, their own first names for self-reference. Jean-Fabien can name himself in the mirror. Kathie has no form of self-representation in her play.

At two years, eight months, Jean-Fabien has "*moi*" and "*tu*" in his vocabulary. In the mirror, he identifies himself with the words, "*C'est moi.*" Kathie's "me" and "you" appear in echo responses which inevitably lead to reversals. She cannot represent herself in play.

At two years, ten months, Jean-Fabien's "*je*" has completed the course of disengagement from syncretic usage, and is used freely and inventively in discourse. The momentary confusion which had preceded mirror identification of himself has now disappeared, which indicates that he now feels at one with his mirror image. It is assimilated to "I." Kathie's "I" is still employed in syncretic forms. "Me" and "you" are still embedded in set phrases as echo responses and appear as reversals. She cannot yet represent herself in play.

At three years, six months, Kathie employs "me" for the first time in our records.

At four years, six months, Kathie becomes a solicitous mother to her dolls and invents an imaginary companion.

At four years, ten months, her "I" is now demonstrably a stable form which is used inventively in discourse, but there are still occasional lapses.

From this concise summary, we can see that the two children whose "I" first emerged in syncretic form at two years, two months—two years, four months followed divergent paths in the acquisition of the non-syncretic "I." The sighted child traveled a route which brought him to a stable concept of "I" at two years, ten months. The blind child's route brought her to the same point at the age of four years, ten months. Jean Fabien's travels took him six months. Kathie's took her two years and eight months.

The parallel developments in self-representation and pronoun usage from these two independent studies speak strongly in favor of Zazzo's view, which is also our own: that the acquisition of personal pronouns goes beyond practice with grammatical tools. It goes beyond the influence of the language environment, which we can demonstrate through the incapacities of Kathie in self-reference pronouns while living in a home with six highly verbal family members. The hypothesis in these two independent studies links self-reference pronouns to self-image.

The blind child's delay in the acquisition of "I" as a concept and a stable form appears to be related to the extraordinary problems in constructing a self-image in the absence of vision. The blind child must find a path to self-representation without the single sensory organ that is uniquely adapted for synthesis of all perceptions and the data of self.

In infancy, most of the data of self are integrated into a body schema by submitting experience to visual tests. We need only reflect on the hands as a model. Through countless experiments before six months of age, the infant makes the discovery that "the hand" that crosses his visual field, "the hand" that he brings to his mouth, "the hand" that grasps an object is part of himself, an instrument that he controls. The games which he plays with his hands before his eyes are experiments in self-discovery. It is vision that gives unity to the disparate forms and aspects of hands and brings about an elementary sense of "me-ness" for hands. Body image is constructed by means of the discovery of parts and a progressive organization of these parts into coherent pictures. In constructing a body image, vision offers a unique advantage that no other sensory mode can duplicate; the picture replicates exactly, and the picture by its nature can unite in one percept or a memory flash all the attributes and parts into a whole. Once the picture is there, it does not need to be reconstituted from its parts.

The blind child has no sensory mode available to him which will replicate his own body or body parts. The blind child is obliged to constitute a body image from the components of non-visual experience available to him, not one of which will give him, through objective reference, the sum of the parts. His tactile, auditory, vocal, kinesthetic, and locomotor experience will give him a sense of the substantiality and autonomy of his own body, but these sensory modes bind him to egocentric body and self-experience and cannot lead him easily to the concept of self in which the self can be taken as an object, the indispensable condition for the non-syncretic "I." Self-image, which Zazzo suggests is a double, a replicate, a kind of mirror image of one's own person, is literally a picture of oneself, however distorted that picture may be. "I" is the externalization of that picture into a community of pictures each of which is an "I."

For the blind child there is no single sense that can take over the function of vision in replicating body image. When Kathie, at five years, three months, identifies her own words and her voice on tape, she has demonstrated a form of self-recognition which still offers imperfect comparisons with Jean-Fabien's identification of himself in the mirror at two years, eight months.* The voice on tape is an aspect of self, one of the components of self-image that can now be identified in objective form. But the voice does not replicate body image; the mirror image replicates it exactly and instantly.

For the blind child, the level of inference required for the construction of the non-syncretic "I" goes beyond that of the sighted

---

* Even as Jean-Fabien had had the mirror available to him for many months before he identified himself, Kathie had had experience with tape recorders in her home for some time before this occurrence. This need not have been her first identification of herself on tape, but it was our first observation.

child. The blind child must infer from his own consciousness of himself as an entity a commonality with the consciousness of others who are "I's." He must construct a world of human objects, each of whom is an "I" to himself, by granting forms of substantiality and "I-ness" to these human objects whom he has identified as having attributes similar to his. He must do this without the one sensory mode that would describe, through the visual picture, the commonalities and the generalizations that lead to the concept "I." Yet, when he does achieve "I" as a stable form and when he represents himself in play by means of a doll or an imaginary companion, he has indisputably externalized a form of self, reconstituted the self as an object. Our scientific imagination is strained to reconstruct the process.

The blind child's route to "I" and self-representation is a perilous one. Many blind children do not make it. In the blind child population a very large number of children at school age or later do not have "I" or any other self-reference pronouns in their vocabularies. From the study of Kathie and other healthy and adequate blind children, we can understand without difficulty why the pronoun "I" and forms of self-representation in play are delayed in comparison with sighted children. The more difficult problem is to understand how the blind child achieves this prodigious feat.

Chapter XII

SELMA FRAIBERG

Conclusions

AS THIS FINAL CHAPTER is written, it is 15 years since a group of blind young children in a New Orleans social agency brought our attention to the extraordinary adaptive problems presented by blindness in the sensorimotor period of development. The central questions which emerged from the clinic led to the longitudinal developmental studies which we have reported in this volume. As the story emerged we were able to translate our findings into a guidance program on behalf of blind young infants. The research, which began with unsolved clinical problems, found solutions, and the gift from science was returned, as it should be, to the clinic.

In this chapter we shall summarize the major findings and their implications for developmental theory in the sensorimotor period and for the evaluation of blind infants.

Central Findings

Our findings cannot be generalized to the larger population known as "blind," for reasons which we have emphasized at various points in this volume. In the general population designated as blind there are children who have varying amounts of useful vision, and there is a high incidence of brain damage and multiple handicaps. Many children in the larger population lost their vision *after* the crucial period of sensorimotor organization and were advantaged in early personality development through the establishment of primary visual-motor schemas.

Total blindness from birth is, fortunately, a rare occurrence. Our criteria for the primary research group—blind from birth, (minimal light perception admissible), neurologically intact, no other sensory or motor handicaps—were met by only a small number of the children referred to us despite the fact that during the decade of the University of Michigan study we had all the resources of a major medical center in case finding. (See Chapter IV for sample and selection criteria.)

Our criteria, then, provided optimal conditions for the study of the effects of a single sensory deficit, blindness, upon the organization of personality in the sensorimotor period. Our concurrent intervention program maximized the potentials for adaptation in the areas of human attachments, prehension, locomotion and language development.

We are, then, able to say, "Our findings are derived from longitudinal studies of 10 children blind from birth but intact in all other systems, whose development was facilitated by a home-based education and guidance program." Under these optimal conditions for study, the effects of blindness per se could be examined, and inferences regarding the function of vision in sensorimotor organization could be made through the study of the effects of the deficit. Blindness as an impediment to adaptation was clearly discerned in each of the areas of development in this study, even when we employed our knowledge to facilitate development and helped the child and his parents find adaptive solutions.

In relation to the larger population designated as "blind" our babies, then, were *advantaged* through intactness of other systems and *disadvantaged* by their total blindness from birth.

Our central findings are summarized in the following pages:

Conclusions

HUMAN ATTACHMENTS

At the point that each child entered the study (ages one to eleven months) and without prior intervention, we were able to identify the extraordinary problems for the blind baby and his parents in making the vital human connections. Blindness had robbed the baby of a large part of the vocabulary of signs and signals which are read by his partners as "recognition," "knowing," and "preference and valuation." In Chapters V and VI we described the unique course of smiling, the absence of differentiated and modulated facial expressions, and the reactions of the baby's parents to a child who "spoke an alien language."

We described our educational work, in which we became the interpreters to the parents of the blind baby's language of preference and valuation (often read through motor signs and vocalizations) and succeeded in bringing about the conditions under which the baby achieved focused human partnerships, and the parents found rewards in their babies. Even grief and depression at the birth of a blind baby could be overcome to some measure when the baby brought his own gifts of love and valuation to his parents.

Our findings, as reported in Chapter VI, reflect our interventions on behalf of the baby and speak for the potential of blind infants in attaining qualitatively good human attachments. For comparison with sighted children, we employed specific indicators of human attachment and age of onset which were emerging from a large number of studies of sighted children during the sixties.

In our blind group we saw that discrimination of mother and stranger and negative reactions to the stranger, appeared within the ranges for sighted children. When mobility emerged in the second year there were patterns of following the mother, returning to the mother as a secure base, and distress when mother could not be located. The onset of separation distress was delayed by sighted-child norms, and the delay was linked in our thinking to the blind child's concomitant delay in achieving the concept of the mother as object (stage 4 on a Piagetian scale). Thus, with the "mother not present," the affective sense of "loss" appears to be linked, as it is in the sighted child, with the emergence of the concept of mother as "object," external to the self. Without an elementary sense of mother as object there can be no sense of "loss."

Qualitative differences between the attachment behaviors of our blind children and sighted children were seen chiefly in the high level of distress when the mother left the child's perceptual field and could not be found, or when the child was separated from the mother for a few hours or longer. This speaks for the helplessness of the blind child when his mother is not present, and it also relates to a conceptual problem for the blind child in the second year, who does not yet have a mental representation of the mother which can sustain him in her absence.

In short, where the capacity for focused affectionate attachment could be assessed and compared with that of sighted children, our blind babies compared favorably with sighted babies. (This tells us, of course, that the tactile-auditory vocabulary of discrimination and love available to the blind child could serve him well in human attachments; vision is not indispensable for the formation of human bonds.) Differences between our blind babies and sighted babies appear only in the delay in the constitution of mother as object, and here the visual deficit is reflected in the unique problems of the blind child in conferring objectivity upon persons and things in the second half of the first year.

PREHENSION

Seven of our 10 babies entered the study between the ages of four to eleven months, or, with correction for prematurity, four to eight months. These children, who had received no prior intervention, gave eloquent testimony at the point of initial observation for the impediment of blindness in the area of prehension. During a period of development when the sighted child is achieving, or has achieved, proficiency in the coordination of reaching and attaining an object within his reach (three to seven months),

Conclusions

these blind babies made not a gesture of reach for persons or toys at tactile remove even when voice or sound provided cues. Sound did not yet connote substantiality for the blind baby.

The characteristic posture of these babies seen in initial observation was one in which the hands were maintained at shoulder height with inutile fingering. A biological sequence, normally facilitated by vision, had been derailed by blindness. Where vision would have brought the hands together at midline, for mutual fingering, transfer, and coordinate use, the hands of the blind baby remained at their station at the shoulders, a posture seen typically in sighted children only during the neonatal period. When toys were offered and placed within the blind baby's grasp we did not observe interest or investment in exploring the toy in our first observations. We did, however, see interest in and exploration of the faces of parents and familiar persons during the same period.

The blind baby's hands, which must serve as primary sensory organs (not "intended" in the biological program) were mainly inutile hands as we saw them in these initial observations.

We could now understand why a very large number of children blind from birth have "blind hands," too. A very large number of blind children of school age, among them children who have no neurological impairment, have hands which do not make sensitive discriminations, do not seek or explore objects, and are, of course, incapable of braille reading. It is impossible to estimate how many of the uneducable blind children in special classes today are the children who reached an impasse in adaptive hand behavior during the sensorimotor period. Those of us who have seen blind infants without intervention and blind school-age children who could not find the adaptive solution in infancy, can recognize, with pain, the hand stereotypies of the school-age blind child and those of blind infants who have not yet found the adaptive solutions. The stereotyped fingering, and the stereotyped posture at shoulder height speak for the failure of those hands to find meaning in experience. What we see in these hands

275

are simple reflex movements, exercised in the near void of personal experience—empty, inutile, vestigial patterns.

Our prehension findings, reported in Chapters VII and VIII, represent the attainments of our blind group as facilitated by our intervention program. We employed game strategies to bring about midline organization of the hands and reciprocity between the hands, the essential conditions for all later stages in adaptive hand behavior. With the collaboration of our parents we provided both interpersonal exchanges and experiences with toys to create a maximally engaging and interesting surround in which the hands, now organized at midline, could reach out and make contact with persons and things within range and obtain rich, polysensory experience in exploring the qualities of persons and things. Where vision normally lures the child to discoveries of his surround, we created the conditions under which persons and things could provide tactile-auditory lures. There is reason to believe that our interventions facilitated the coordination of ear and hand in reaching for and attaining objects in the last trimester of the first year (median age 8:27, ranges 6.5 to 11 months).

It is of special interest, then, that even with intervention our blind infants did not achieve the coordination of ear and hand within age ranges that correspond to the coordination of eye and hand in sighted children. In Chapter VIII we offered our evidence that the coordination of ear and hand for the blind child is a conceptual problem. In the absence of vision the blind infant must infer the substantiality of persons and things "out there" when only one of the attributes (voice or sound) is given him. Thus the tactile-auditory unity of a person or thing experienced manually, for example, is broken up when the same person or thing manifests itself through "sound only" at tactile remove. The blind baby must reconstitute that unity in space before he will reach for a person or toy with the "expectation" that sound connotes substantiality. In support of the evidence from our blind studies we cited the observations of Piaget (1954) and the study of Freedman et al. (1970) which show that a sighted child will not

Conclusions

uncover a screened toy which is experimentally sounded under the screen until the last trimester of the first year.

GROSS MOTOR DEVELOPMENT

As early as the period of the New Orleans studies, our observations of Toni and the larger group of blind children in the Family Service Society program had provided us with both a picture of typical delays in the achievement of locomotor milestones and a useful hypothesis for the examination of these delays. Typically, we saw that the *postural* attainments of these blind children appeared within the ranges for sighted children, but that the *mobility* items which normally followed each postural attainment were delayed markedly and fell outside of sighted ranges. We reasoned that if the postural attainments spoke for neuromuscular adequacy, the locomotor delays were related to the impediments of blindness. Our hypothesis was that mobility for the sighted child was initiated through visual lures "out there" and that the blind child was impeded in his locomotor development through the absence of a lure that substituted for the visual incentive. We had already seen that sound for Toni did not constitute a lure for either reaching or locomotor progression until ten months of age.

As we described in Chapter IX, the clues to the blind baby's locomotor delays came from the prehension study. Until the blind baby could demonstrate "reach on sound cue only," he had no incentive, no stimulus "out there" to lure him into creeping, cruising, or walking. In fact, no child in our group learned to creep or to find any mode of forward progression until he had first demonstrated "reach on sound cue only." We saw, then, that mobility in sit, in bridging, and in stand was, in fact, a form of reach, the extended "reach" of the torso toward a lure in space. We also saw—but only for a brief interval with most of our babies—motor stereotypies in the blind baby during these periods of "postural readiness" and "no mobility." Thus, a child with good control of his trunk in a bridging posture, with "readiness," we would say, for creeping, might be observed on all fours, rocking steadily, "ready to go" with "no place to go." The motor impetus, which normally leads to mobility, was exercised in a vacuum. Again typically, when mobility was achieved, the stereotyped rocking was extinguished. This becomes an important clue to the origins of motor stereotypies commonly seen in the blind population. If there is a long delay in the achievement of mobility—and this is characteristic of the general blind population—the patterns become stereotyped and later employed as an all–purpose, undifferentiated form of discharge.

Our intervention, as described in Chapter IX, demonstrably facilitated the locomotor development of the children in our group. We were able to compare their locomotor achievements with those of sighted children and with a comparable blind infant population (Norris). Our blind group came closer to sighted-child norms than to blind-child norms. Thus, free walking was achieved by our blind group within the ranges twelve to twenty months. The ranges for sighted children are eleven to fourteen months. In Norris's study 50% of her sample had achieved free walking at two years of age.

Yet it is important to note that we did not employ "mobility training" in our intervention program. These good achievements in our blind group actually reflect our educational work in the areas of human attachments and prehension. Through the enhancement of the blind baby's surround, through providing the lures of persons and things "out there," the child who had postural (maturational) readiness for mobility and an elementary concept of the object in space had the incentives for creeping and for walking. Under these circumstances sound could now substitute for sight in providing a distant lure for initiation of the mobility pattern.

We could test this experimentally. If a blind child had attained "midline reach for the person or toy on sound cue only" and had also attained a stable bridging posture (maturational readiness for creeping) he typically began to creep within a few days after the demonstration of "reach on sound." If he did not find mobility

Conclusions

spontaneously, we could lure him into creeping by choosing a propitious moment when he was up on all fours and sounding a toy within a few inches of his hands. He would then attempt a reach which propelled him forward a few inches. We might need to sound the toy again. The baby, predictably, advanced a few inches more and finally attained the toy. Within a few days this mobility pattern—which is characterized in its practice phase as a reach and a collapse, a reach and a collapse—became a fluid and coordinated pattern of creeping. The practice phase and the attainment will strike the reader as identical to that which is seen in sighted babies lured by the distant object.

This, then, is not "training," a method commonly employed by educators of the blind, but a form of guidance which derives from the developmental principles we had uncovered in our research. If the developmental principles are not available to the parents or the educator there is great peril for the baby in finding the route toward mobility. Clearly, if a baby has not yet demonstrated "reach on sound," all efforts to entice him to creep with a distant voice or sound will fail. Many blind babies have been wrongly labeled as "retarded" or "neurologically impaired" on the basis of motor performance alone. Many parents and educators may attempt to "teach" a blind baby to creep by putting him through the exercise of creeping, manipulating his legs and arms. It is a method doomed to failure and typically results in a resistant and outraged baby who flips over on his back and has a monumental tantrum.

An educational program that is attuned to developmental principles needs to take into account the impediment of blindness to "reach on sound" and to provide the blind infant with the incentives for initiating mobility. Then it can confidently wait for the baby to "invent" mobility for himself. Except in the cases of severe brain damage (seen in our consultation group) the blind child will then become mobile without a protracted delay. In the case of the brain-damaged blind child it is, of course, not blindness alone that is the impediment to mobility but the second damaged system which affects maturational processes and is further caught up in the constrictions of blindness. In our consultation-education program group we have helped many blind children with neurological impairment to achieve free mobility following the same principles we have described. For these children, of course, the delays in the achievement of mobility are marked. (They would also occur, of course, if the child were brain-damaged and sighted.) In working with these children, we watch for signs of maturational readiness in the attainment of trunk control, and we facilitate, when possible, the conditions for achieving control of the trunk. The brain-damaged blind child, in contrast to our otherwise intact blind babies, will show the effects of neurological impairment in marked delays in achieving *postural* milestones. Even here, however, we must be cautious, in the interpretation of retardation in postural attainments, since if there are no positive indications of neurological impairment it is important to ascertain through home visits whether or not the blind child is being deprived experimentally of the conditions which lead to adequate control of the trunk.

LANGUAGE

Our findings in Chapter X show that the majority of our advantaged group of blind babies attained language milestones during the first two years within ranges for sighted children. The typical delays in language acquisition reported in the general blind population need careful analysis. Our own findings suggest that for those blind children who are neurologically intact, and intact in other systems, the delays in language acquisition may reflect experiential poverty.

Our education and guidance in the area of language learning during the first two years of life was very largely based upon the developmental principles which underlie language acquisition for intact infants. There was no formal "speech training," even as there was no formal "training" in any area of our intervention program. We reasoned that everything we did to promote human

Conclusions

attachments, manual tactile, aural experience, and locomotion would affect the investment of persons and things; and the representation of persons and things would, in turn, lead to naming wants, naming things, and to combining words. In those cases where the home language environment was poor and would have affected language learning even in a sighted child, we provided much help to the parents in understanding how vocal discourse with even a young baby leads him to produce his own sounds, later to imitate sounds and words, and finally to the acquisition of words. Through our own discourse with babies during our home visits we demonstrated to some puzzled, amused, and initially unbelieving parents who never "talked to" babies, that their babies responded to these speeches in very specific ways. Parents who had never done so with their sighted babies began to play the game and were, predictably, rewarded. A ranking of our babies according to "maximally stimulating language environment" and "minimally stimulating language environment" shows a pattern that reflects exactly the quality and quantity of the language environment. The highest-ranking babies on each item of the Bayley scales were the children of the highest-ranking language environments. The two children who appear outside the Bayley ranges for the higher-language items are children who reflect the limitations of their language environment even with our guidance.

Yet the distribution of scores on 2 of the advanced language items shows a clustering below the Bayley median. We suggested that here the scores may reflect the impediment of blindness in concept development.

In Chapter XI we see that blindness demonstrably impedes representational intelligence in the period two and a half to four years for 5 children who were available to us for study beyond the age limits of our original investigation. The acquisition of the non-syncretic "I" is a late achievement even for our two highest-ranking children. The capacity to represent the self as "I" and to represent the self in play are both delayed as compared with estimated sighted norms. Kathie, our highest-ranking

SELMA FRAIBERG

girl in overall development, was employed to illustrate the extraordinary problem for a blind child in representing the self as
"I" in a universe of "I's." Her language profile shows a detour
for a 2½-year period, then comes back upon the main pathways
between the ages of four and five. By age five her discourse can be
barely distinguished from that of sighted children.

When we consider that these delays in the acquisition of stable
"I–you" concepts appeared in a group of blind children who had
no neurological impairment and were educationally advantaged
through our program, the implications for the larger population
of blind preschool children are sobering.

We can now understand that among the large numbers of blind
children who show undifferentiated personalities at school entrance there must be an unknown number who are neurologically
intact but impeded in their development by the extraordinary
problem for the blind child in constituting an "I" and a "you."

For some of these children there may still be hope that an "I"
will be constituted in the further course of development. This is
not, of course, a prescription for speech training. The concept of
"I" will not be attained through lessons in "I" and "you."
Through our own work we are convinced that this conceptual education must concern itself with the strengthening of human attachments, in the home and the school, and with the provision of
an environment in home and school which lures the child into discoveries of himself and the external world.

A CONCISE SUMMARY

As we have examined each sector of development in our group
of blind children we find that we have come full circle to the central finding: We were able to facilitate the blind infant's development in every sphere of development, but the impediment of
blindness could be discerned at every point in development at
which *representational intelligence* would lead the sighted child into
the organization of an object world. We could facilitate the affective ties to human partners, but the constitution of those partners

Conclusions

as objects was delayed by comparison with sighted-child norms. We could facilitate the coordination of hand and ear, but this coordination was still dependent upon the blind child's ability to attribute substantiality to persons and things when only one of their attributes, sound, was given. We facilitated locomotion but we could still discern the impediment to locomotion, the absence of the distant lure usually provided by vision, the reach for "something out there." We saw that blindness was not a major impediment to the acquisition of language in the first two years of life when we were able to maximize the experience of the blind child and his language environment. But the impediment of blindness revealed itself most cruelly in the protracted delay in the constitution of a stable concept of "I."

Finally, the effects of intervention can be summarized: In those areas of development where comparative data are available, our educationally advantaged blind infants came closer to sighted-child ranges than blind-child ranges.

Appendix

Methods: Supplementary Information

Areas of Study

The 5 major areas of the study as described earlier, were human attachment, prehension, gross motor development, language, and object permanence. The present volume is primarily concerned with our findings in the first 4 of these 5 areas.

Since data collection covered virtually all behaviors observed in a single session, other areas of interest to us emerged from the raw data and were given code classifications for later study. These areas were: behavior toward inanimate objects (toys); feeding; sleep; affectivity; conflict and defense; self-stimulating behaviors. Data in these areas are referred to only incidentally in the present volume.

Observational Procedures

Observers.   Following the principles described in Chapter IV, only senior investigators were given the responsibility for observation and recording. In the pairing of teams one or both members were senior investigators.

Setting. Each baby was visited in his home at twice-monthly intervals for sessions ranging from 1 to 1½ hours. Visits were timed to coincide with a morning or afternoon waking period, and observations were fitted into the normal routine of that period. Nearly all of the data required for our study could be obtained through observing a feeding, a bath, a play time with mother, a diapering or clothes change, and a period of self-occupation with or without toys. A small amount of time in each session was employed for testing procedures in the areas of prehension and object concept.

The observation period began with an informal session with the mother in which we obtained her picture of the baby's development in the 2–week interval. The mother's report was recorded in a detailed narrative. The selection of material she reported to us and the qualitative aspects of her mothering were noted. During this time, the second observer was recording the baby's activity when the mother was not interacting with him.

Recording. The 2 observers made continuous notes as they followed the baby in typical routines of his waking period, as described above. To insure coverage of all items which had to be gathered for comparative developmental study, the observers memorized our coding schedule with particular reference to the developmental period appropriate to each baby. We did not use a check list as such, for this would have defeated our objective of observation in natural context. We did not impose any specific order or sequence in data collection except during formal testing procedures.

Film Documentation. At monthly or twice–monthly intervals (depending on the age of the child) we recorded film samples of behavior in the areas of (a) mother–child interaction, (b) feeding or play, (c) prehension, (d) gross motor achievements, and (e) self-occupation. We used an Arriflex movie camera, three floodlights on tripods, and Plus-X film. The photographing did impose a degree of constraint on the observational session, and we tried to keep this within the minimum required for useful documentation and study (approximately 400–600 feet of 16mm film). We did not film continuously throughout the hour but obtained samples in the areas under study.

During filming, one of the observers recorded continuous notes. These notes indicated when the camera was off and on, what demonstration was being attempted, what stimuli not caught by the camera might be causing the infant's response (someone across the room calling the infant, an unexpected loud noise outside), what verbal communication was occurring between the adults or between the infant and mother. These notes enabled us to review the film with an understanding of the context in which it was made. Since the film was silent and not continuous, the notes were essential to supply the complete background.

The film record was reviewed on a variable-speed projector at the scheduled case review of each baby with other senior investigators present. It proved indispensable for certain areas of our study. In prehension, for example, the patterns of adaptive hand behavior in the blind infant were entirely new to the professional student of child development who had been trained in observation of sighted infants. We needed to draw inferences from subtle, fleeting hand and finger movements which could be obtained only through slow-motion study.

The cinema record served data collection in 2 other ways: first, the film itself was available for repeated study and comparison; second, a recorded narrative of each film was transcribed, the written protocol that resulted was entered into the baby's record as a separate document, and was coded. The transcript was obtained as follows: As the film was reviewed at 1/3 speed, with other staff members present, the senior investigator of the baby's research team recorded on a dictaphone a complete narrative of the film sequence in fine detail. Where there was disagreement among the viewers regarding specific detail, the disputed film sequence was run over again. "Consensus" or "no consensus" in observation was recorded for the coders. The transcribed narrative of the film became a flexible document which made possible retrieval of any items of information recorded on film, and served as source material for coding and evaluation.

Our guidance program became a third source of information in following the baby's development. There were typically two or more regularly scheduled guidance visits per month, based upon requirements of the case and varying with the age of the child.

The scheduled guidance visits, or guidance offered in the regular observational session, were recorded in narrative form, following the same method employed in the general research plan. Educational strategies and counsel offered were recorded in explicit detail: "I said . . . ," "I suggested . . . ," "Mother said. . . ." In this way our interventions could be examined in relation to other variables in the study. The guidance protocols became a rich source of qualitative data and gave other dimensions to our study. The recording methods, entirely compatible with those employed in the primary investigation, made it possible for us to employ the general coding schedule for retrieval of data from this source.

Evaluation of Data

Data evaluation was conducted on several levels of complexity:

(1)   The preliminary indexing and tabulation of data were performed by student assistants under the supervision of senior staff members. A rigorous training in the use of our code schedule was a prerequisite for this work. Frequent cross checks were made to insure reliability.

Assistants read the protocol and classified the data into the major categories of our study by means of tabulation symbols in the margins. In the tabulation of data the categories were further broken down into subdivisions following the code schedule. This, then, enabled us to make comparisons within our sample.

The tabulated data gave us a shorthand summary which served certain purposes of the investigation. At the same time, each item which was tabulated in code had a cross-reference by page and line to the original protocol so that the descriptive and qualitative aspects of the behavior studied could be given separate treatment.

(2) The major areas of the study were then divided among senior investigators for intensive mining of content, refined sorting, the construction of individual and group profiles, and comparisons within the group.

(3) Team and group meetings of senior investigators were instituted to discuss (and argue) criteria, to review problems of judgment and scoring, to credit by consensus. The N of 10 provided its own constraints. If there was no consensus in crediting an item, we discarded it and moved up the ladder in our protocol sequence until we found one which was finally credited by consensus.

(4) In final tabulation and write-up, the chief investigators made their own last checks and reviews, consulting the original protocols and films.

Bibliography

Adelson, E. and Fraiberg, S. (1972): "Mouth and Hand in the Early Development of Blind Infants." In J. Bosma, ed., *Third Symposium on Oral Sensation and Perception*. Springfield, Ill.: Charles C Thomas, pp. 420–430.

———— (1974): "Gross Motor Development in Infants Blind from Birth." *Child Development* 45, no. 1:114–126.

Ainsworth, M. D. (1967): *Infancy in Uganda: Infant Care and the Growth of Love*. Baltimore: Johns Hopkins University Press.

———— (1973): "The Development of Infant-Mother Attachment." In B. M. Caldwell and H. N. Ricciuti, eds., *Review of Child Development Research*, vol. 3. Chicago: University of Chicago Press, pp. 1–94.

Ambrose, J. A. (1961): "The Development of the Smiling Response in Early Infancy." In B. M. Foss, ed., *Determinants of Infant Behavior*, vol. 1. London: Methuen, pp. 179–201.

Bayley, N. (1969): *Bayley Scales of Infant Development*. New York: The Psychological Corporation.

Bell, S. J. (1970): "The Development of the Concept of Object as Related to Infant-Mother Attachment." *Child Development* 41, no. 2:291–311.

Bender, M. B. (1952): *Disorders in Perception*. Springfield, Ill.: Charles C Thomas.

Benjamin, J. D. (1963): "Further Comments on Some Developmental Aspects of Anxiety." In H. S. Gaskill, ed., *Counterpoint*. New York: International Universities Press, pp. 121–153.

Blank, H. R. (1957): "Psychoanalysis and Blindness." *Psychoanalytic Quarterly* 26:1–24.

———— (1958): "Dreams of the Blind." *Psychoanalytic Quarterly* 27:158–174.

Burlingham, D. (1961): "Some Notes on the Development of the Blind." *Psychoanalytic Study of the Child* 26:121–145.

———— (1964): "Hearing and Its Role in the Development of the Blind." *Psychoanalytic Study of the Child* 19:95–112.

Cattell, P. (1940): *The Measurement of Intelligence of Infants and Young Children*. New York: Johnson Reprint Corporation.

Chang, H. (1952): "Functional Organization of the Central Visual Pathways." *Association for Research in Nervous and Mental Disease* 30:430–453.

Emde, R. N., and Harmon, R. J. (1972): "Endogenous and Exogenous Smiling Systems in Early Infancy." *Journal of the American Academy of Child Psychiatry* 11, no. 2:177–200.

Emde, R. N., and Koenig, K. L. (1969): "Neonatal Smiling, Frowning, and Rapid Eye Movement States: II, Sleep-Cycle Study." *Journal of American Academy of Child Psychiatry* 8, no. 4:637–656.

Escalona, S. K., and Corman, H. H.: *Albert Einstein Scales of Sensori-Motor Development* (unpublished). From the Child Development Project, Albert Einstein College of Medicine.

Fraiberg, S. (1968): "Parallel and Divergent Patterns in Blind and Sighted Infants." *Psychoanalytic Study of the Child* 23:264–300.

——— (1969): "Libidinal Object Constancy and Mental Representation." *Psychoanalytic Study of the Child* 24:9–47.

——— (1971a): "Intervention in Infancy: A Program for Blind Infants." *Journal of the American Academy of Child Psychiatry* 10, no. 3:381–405.

——— (1971b): "Separation Crisis in Two Blind Children." *Psychoanalytic Study of the Child* 26:355–371.

——— (1971c): "Smiling and Stranger Reaction in Blind Infants." In J. Hellmuth, ed., *Exceptional Infant*, vol. 2. New York: Brunner/Mazel, pp. 110–127.

——— (1974): "Blind Infants and Their Mothers: An Examination of the Sign System." In M. Lewis and L. Rosenblum, eds., *The Effect of the Infant on Its Caregiver*. New York: John Wiley, pp. 215–232.

——— (1975): "The Development of Human Attachments in Infants Blind From Birth." *Merrill-Palmer Quarterly* 21, no. 4:315–334.

Fraiberg, S., and Adelson, E. (1973): "Self-Representation in Language and Play: Observations of Blind Children." *The Psychoanalytic Quarterly* 42, no. 4:539–562.

——— (1975): "Self-Representation in Language and Play: Observations of Blind Children." In E. Lenneberg and E. Lenneberg, eds., *Foundations of Language Development*, vol. 2. New York: Academic Press, pp. 177–192.

Fraiberg, S., and Freedman, D. (1964): "Studies in the Ego Development of the Congenitally Blind Child." *Psychoanalytic Study of the Child* 19:113–169.

Fraiberg, S., Siegel, B., and Gibson, R. (1966): "The Role of Sound in the Search Behavior of a Blind Infant." *Psychoanalytic Study of the Child* 21:327–357.

Fraiberg, S., Smith, M., and Adelson, E. (1969): "An Educational Program for Blind Infants." *Journal of Special Education* 3, no. 2:121–139.

Frankenburg, W. K., and Dodds, J. B. (1967): "Denver Developmental Screening Test." *Journal of Pediatrics* 71, no. 2:181–191.

Freedman, D. A., and Cannady, C. (1971): "Delayed Emergence of Prone Locomotion." *Journal of Nervous and Mental Diseases* 153, no. 2:108–117.

Freedman, D. A., Fox-Kolenda, B. J., Margileth, D. A., and Miller, D. H. (1970): "The Development of the Use of Sound as a Guide to Affective and Cognitive Behavior—A Two-Phase Process." In S. Chess and A. Thomas, eds., *Annual Progress in Child Psychiatry and Child Development*. New York: Brunner/Mazel, pp. 187–194.

Gesell, A., and Amatruda, C. (1947): *Developmental Diagnosis*. New York: Hoeber Division of Medicine, Harper & Row.

Gewirtz, J. L. (1965): "The Course of Infant Smiling in Four Child-Rearing Environments in Israel." In B. M. Foss, ed., *Determinants of Infant Behavior*, vol. 3. New York: Wiley, pp. 205–248.

Gibbs, E. L., Fois, A., and Gibbs, F. A. (1955): "The Electroencephalogram in Retrolental Fibroplasia." *New England Journal of Medicine* 253:1102–1106.

Griffiths, R. (1954): *The Abilities of Babies: A Study in Mental Measurement*. London: University of London Press.

Hartmann, H. (1952): "The Mutual Influences in the Development of Ego and Id." *Psychoanalytic Study of the Child*, 7:9–30.

Hoffer, W. (1949): "Mouth, Hand and Ego-Integration." *Psychoanalytic Study of the Child* 3/4:49–56.

Keeler, W. R. (1958): "Autistic Patterns and Defective Communication in Blind Children with Retrolental Fibroplasia." In P. H. Hoch and J. Zubin, eds., *Psychopathology of Communication*. New York: Grune and Stratton, pp. 64–83.

Klein, G. S. (1962): "Blindness and Isolation." *Psychoanalytic Study of the Child* 17:82–93.

Lenneberg, E. H. (1967): *Biological Foundations of Language*. New York: Wiley.

Lenneberg, Eric, and Lenneberg, Elizabeth (1975): *Foundations of Language Development*, vol. 2. New York: Academic Press.

Levinson, J. E. (1951): "EEG and Eye Disorders, Clinical Correlations." *Pediatrics* 7:422–427.

Linn, L. (1953): "Psychological Implications of the Activating System." *American Journal of Psychiatry* 2:61–65.

Maxfield, K. E., and Fjeld, H. A. (1942): "Social Maturity of Visually Handicapped Preschool Children." *Child Development* 13:1–27.

Morgan, G. A., and Ricciuti, H. N. (1969): "Infants' Responses to Strangers During the First Year." In B. M. Foss, ed., *Determinants of Infant Behavior*, vol. 4. London: Methuen, pp. 253–272.

Nelson, K. (1973): "Structure and Strategy in Learning to Talk." *Monographs of the Society for Research in Child Development*, no. 149. Chicago: Child Development Publications.

Norris, M., Spaulding, P., and Brodie, F. (1957): *Blindness in Children*. Chicago: University of Chicago Press.

Omwake, E. B., and Solnit, A. J. (1961): " 'It Isn't Fair': The Treatment of a Blind Child." *Psychoanalytic Study of the Child* 16:352–404.

Parmelee, A. H., Jr. (1955): "Developmental Evaluation of the Blind Premature Infant." *AMA Journal of Children's Diseases* 90:135–140.

Parmelee, A. H., Cutsforth, M. G., and Jackson, C. L. (1958): "The Mental Development of Children with Blindness Due to Retrolental Fibroplasia." *AMA Journal of Children's Diseases* 96:641–648.

Parmelee, A. H., Fiske, C., and Wright, R. (1959): "The Development of Ten Children with Blindness as a Result of Retrolental Fibroplasia." *AMA Journal of Children's Diseases* 96:198–220.

Piaget, J. (1952): *Origins of Intelligence*. New York: International Universities Press.

——— (1954): *The Construction of Reality in the Child*. New York: Basic Books.

——— (1962): *Play, Dreams and Imitation in Childhood*. New York: Norton.

Polak, P. R., Emde, R. N., and Spitz, R. A. (1964): "The Smiling Response to the Human Face. I. Methodology Quantification and Natural History; II. Neural Discrimination and the Onset of Depth Perception." *Journal of Nervous and Mental Diseases* 139:103–109 and 407–415.

Provence, S., and Lipton, R. C. (1962): *Infants in Institutions*. New York: International Universities Press.

Robson, J. (1968): "The Role of Eye-to-Eye Contact in Maternal-Infant Attachment." In S. Chess and A. Thomas, eds., *Annual Progress in Child Psychiatry and Child Development*. New York: Brunner/Mazel, pp. 92–108.

Roskies, E. (1972): *Abnormality and Normality: The Mothering of Thalidomide Children*. Ithaca: Cornell University Press.

Saint Pierre, J. (1962): "Étude des differences entre la recherche active de la personne humaine et celle de l'objet inanime." Unpublished master's thesis, University of Montreal.

BIBLIOGRAPHY

Sandler, A. M. (1963): "Aspects of Passivity and Ego Development in the Blind Infant." *Psychoanalytic Study of the Child* 18:343–360.

Schaffer, H. R., and Emerson, P. E. (1964): "The Development of Social Attachments in Infancy." *Monograph of the Society for Research in Child Development*, no. 94. Chicago: Child Development Publications.

Segal, A., and Stone, F. H. (1961): "The Six-Year-Old Who Began to See: Emotional Sequelae of Operation for Congenital Bilateral Cataracts." *Psychoanalytic Study of the Child* 16:481–509.

Spitz, R. A. (1945): "Hospitalism: An Inquiry into the Genesis of Psychiatric Conditions in Early Childhood." *Psychoanalytic Study of the Child* 1:53–74.

——— (1955): "The Primal Cavity: A Contribution to the Genesis of Perception and Its Role for Psychoanalytic Theory." *Psychoanalytic Study of the Child* 10:215–240.

——— (1957): *No and Yes: On the Genesis of Human Communication*. New York: International Universities Press.

——— (1959): *A Genetic Field Theory of Ego Formation*. New York: International Universities Press.

——— (1963): "Life and the Dialogue." In H. S. Gaskill, ed., *Counterpoint*. New York: International Universities Press, pp. 154–176.

——— (1965): *The First Year of Life*. New York: International Universities Press.

Spitz, R. A., and Wolf, K. M. (1946): "The Smiling Response: A Contribution to the Ontogenesis of Social Relations." *Genetic Psychology Monographs* 34:57–125.

Stayton, D. J., Ainsworth, M. D., and Main, M. B. (1971): "The Development of Separation Behavior in the First Year of Life: Protest, Following, and Greeting." Paper presented in part at the biennial meeting of the Society for Research in Child Development held in Minneapolis, Minnesota, April 1971.

Tennes, K. H., and Lampl, E. E. (1964): "Stranger and Separation Anxiety." *Journal of Nervous and Mental Diseases* 139:247–254.

Ulrich, S. (1972): *Elizabeth*. Ann Arbor, Mich.: University of Michigan Press.

Villay, P. (1930): *World of the Blind*. New York: Macmillan.

Wolff, P. H. (1960): "The Developmental Psychologies of Jean Piaget and Psychoanalysis." *Psychological Issues Monograph No. 5*, vol. 2, 1. New York: International Universities Press.

——— (1963): "Observations on the Early Development of Smiling." In B. M. Foss, ed., *Determinants of Infant Behavior*, vol. 2, London: Methuen, pp. 113–138.

——— (1968): "The Role of Biological Rhythms in Early Psychological Development." In S. Chess and A. Thomas, eds., *Annual Progress in Child Psychiatry and Child Development*. New York: Brunner/Mazel, pp. 1–21.

Yarrow, L. J. (1967): "The Development of Focused Relationships During Infancy." In J. Hellmuth, ed., *Exceptional Infant*, vol. I. New York: Brunner/Mazel, pp. 427–442.

——— (1972): "Attachment and Dependency: A Development Perspective." In J. L. Gewirtz, ed., *Attachment and Dependency*. Washington, D.C.: Winston and Sons, pp. 81–137.

Zazzo, R. (1948): "Images du corps et conscience de soi." *Enfance: Psychologie, Pedagogie, Neuropsychiatrie, Sociologie* 1: (Janvier, Fevrier) 29–43.

Index

ABOUT THE AUTHOR

Selma Fraiberg is Professor of Child Psycho-
analysis and Director of the Child Development
Project of the Neuropsychiatric Institute of the
University of Michigan Medical Center.